THE FAERIE QUEENE
BOOK I

SPENSER

The Faerie Queene

BOOK I

Edited by

P. C. BAYLEY

Fellow of University College, Oxford

OXFORD UNIVERSITY PRESS

OXFORD
UNIVERSITY PRESS

Great Clarendon Street, Oxford OX2 6DP

Oxford University Press is a department of the University of Oxford.
It furthers the University's objective of excellence in research, scholarship,
and education by publishing worldwide in

Oxford New York

Athens Auckland Bangkok Bogotá Buenos Aires Calcutta
Cape Town Chennai Dar es Salaam Delhi Florence Hong Kong Istanbul
Karachi Kuala Lumpur Madrid Melbourne Mexico City Mumbai
Nairobi Paris São Paulo Singapore Taipei Tokyo Toronto Warsaw

with associated companies in Berlin Ibadan

Oxford is a registered trade mark of Oxford University Press
in the UK and in certain other countries

© *P. C. Bayley 1966*

First published 1966
Reprinted (with corrections) 1970, 1976, 1979, 1988, 1989,
1990, 1991, 1992, 1993, 1995, 1998, 1999

Printed in China

CONTENTS

Introduction	I
The Language of *The Faerie Queene* (by Alan Ward)	29
Table of Dates	34
A Note on the Text	37
Dedication to Queen Elizabeth	38
Prefatory Letter to Sir Walter Raleigh	39
The Faerie Queene, Book I	45
Notes	259
Glossary (by Alan Ward)	321

INTRODUCTION

Although in later life he claimed kinship with the noble family of Spencer, as far as we know Edmund Spenser was of fairly humble parentage. His father was almost certainly in a trade associated with the Merchant Taylors Company, at whose newly-founded school in London the boy Spenser became one of the earliest pupils in 1561. He was one of the many of his time whose intelligence and abilities enabled them to climb high. From that time to this, there has probably been no other period when there have been so few bars to advancement. In the time of Elizabeth I, the poor but able boy could go from his local grammar school or a City school to Oxford or Cambridge and so begin a professional career. Spenser, it seems fairly clear, had at various times aspirations to be a don, to be a cleric, to be a government or court official. He did not in fact become a Cambridge don, like his friend Gabriel Harvey; he did not become a cleric, though he did become a bishop's private secretary for a time; he did become a government official, but that was in virtual exile in Ireland.

He was born in London, probably in 1552. At the Merchant Taylors' School he came to the notice of Alexander Nowell, Dean of St. Paul's, and, more important, under the influence of its first headmaster, Richard Mulcaster, an unusually gifted man and an enlightened headmaster, whose ideas on education were remarkably modern. It is difficult not to believe that his influence on Spenser was profound, especially with his insistence on the potentialities of the English language, on the need to enrich it and to forge it into a literary language that could rival the classical tongues and the vernaculars, rich in new literature, of Italy and France, and help it in its turn enrich and make illustrious the

English nation. He wrote in his *Elementarie* (1582): 'I love *Rome*, but *London* better, I favour *Italie*, but England more, I honour the Latin, but I worship the *English*.' He thought the English language 'a tongue of itself both deep in conceit, and frank in delivery... (it) will strain with the strongest and stretch with the furthest, . . . not any whit behind either the subtle Greek for couching close, or the stately Latin for spreading fair. . . . But you will say it is uncouth. Indeed, being unused . . .' Italy and France both boasted a great vernacular literature. England, the English thought, overlooking Langland, Chaucer and Malory, did not. Mulcaster was among the first to urge English writers to take pride in their own tongue, and to encourage unceasing effort in it, and his pupil Spenser was destined to write the first great English poem of the new post-medieval era.

He was indeed the first great English Renaissance writer, the first great national poet, the writer of the first great English epic. *The Faerie Queene*, however indebted it was to the classics and to the Italian romantic epics, was a poem of patriotic inspiration, in its celebration of the Queen, in its foundation on a national legend (that of Arthur), in its showing, among many other things, the glorious descent of Elizabeth, imaged in the Faerie Queene. There is a further debt to Mulcaster perhaps. To him, education was the helping of 'nature unto her perfection, which is, when all her abilities be perfected . . .'; to have 'every part of the body: and every power of the soul . . . fined (refined) to his best'. As a teacher, he insisted on the development of the complete man; Spenser's aim in *The Faerie Queene*, proclaimed in its Prefatory Letter, was 'to fashion a gentleman or noble person in vertuous and gentle discipline', and what he did in the poem was to present in imaginative narrative, in allegory and in symbolism a series of actions showing human nature being brought to perfection, depicting the forces that aid and those which oppose the process.

Mulcaster probably helped Spenser to his first appearance in print, translations of some sonnets of du Bellay and of parts of a translation by Marot of Petrarch. They appeared, while he was still at school, in 1569 in a collection called *A Theatre*, devised by John van der Noodt, a Dutch adherent of the new ideas about vernacular poetry and a poet with a strong moralizing bent. Here Spenser made his first attempts in allegory (although it is the elementary moralistic allegory of the emblembook), and indulged for the first time that taste for melancholy and nostalgic moralizing which was to have its place in almost everything he wrote.

In 1569 he went up to Pembroke Hall, Cambridge, with financial help from Alexander Nowell, who had already made gifts to him and to other poor scholars of Merchant Taylors' School. Pembroke Hall was a left-wing college in religious matters, inclining distinctly to the new Puritan or purifying ideals, and Spenser's path often lay with people of this outlook. Nowell was one. He had had to take refuge abroad during the religious persecutions of Mary's reign, and there had met Edmund Grindal, a former Master of Pembroke Hall and later Bishop of London when Nowell was Dean of St. Paul's. Another was John Young, Master of the college in Spenser's time, who later became Bishop of Rochester and employed Spenser as his secretary. At that time he wrote the ecclesiastical satires, anti-Rome, anti-High Church, pro-purifying, of *The Shepheardes Calender* (1579). He also became known to the leading aristocratic supporter of the purifying movement, and one of the greatest powers in the land, Robert Dudley Earl of Leicester, and to his nephew Sir Philip Sidney. Perhaps through them he gained in about August 1580 the post of secretary to the Lord Deputy in Ireland, Lord Grey de Wilton, who was also particularly zealous in promoting the reformed religion.

Spenser in Ireland

It has been generally assumed that to be posted to Ireland in Elizabethan times was to be sent into outer darkness. Service in Ireland was remote, arduous and often dangerous employment. Ireland had been and was for decades to be a grave of reputations, and the task of imposing an alien government, an alien religion, and standards (even Elizabethan standards) of probity, justice and good government on a backward, impoverished territory was a thankless one. Reasonable equivalents for our time might be service in Kenya during the Mau-Mau troubles which preceded the granting of independence, in Cyprus during the same period, the late nineteen-fifties, or in the Congo as a United Nations officer in the early nineteen-sixties. But fortunes were to be made in Ireland, however exacting and insecure the career. Whatever Spenser's feelings when he knew he was to make a career in Ireland—and no doubt he would have preferred other service— here was his opportunity, and he had to take it. It was to be of inestimable value to him. The experience it offered immeasurably increased his knowledge of the world and of human behaviour, and so affected the writing of his great work.

Ireland gave him a career, the opportunity of further advancement, varied and important contact with human affairs and matters of political moment; it even gave him leisure to write. He had started *The Faerie Queene* before he went, but it was almost entirely written in Ireland. In a thousand details, and in several more important ways, *The Faerie Queene* reveals it. The quality of Ireland, the fascination and repulsion it held for Spenser, its desolation and its surpassing beauty, its romance and its misery, its nobility and savagery, occupied his consciousness and pressed upon his imagination. For in Ireland the great antitheses in life appeared on the surface, palpably. Juxtaposed with a startling clarity were on the one side the right, the nobility, the justice, the truth, the order, the glory of England (as a patriotic Englishman would see it), and on the other, evil, false religion, hatred, cruelty, rebellion, misery, and chaos: in a beautiful land a violent and disordered people. Spenser could have observed the raw material of his poem—human behaviour, right and wrong, beauty and ugliness—anywhere, but Ireland, savage, beautiful, remote, dangerous, captured his imagination in a way perhaps no other land could have done, and presented to that imagination the basic terms and elements of life with extraordinary force and directness.

His prose work *A Veue of the present state of Irelande* (not published until 1633) presents a vivid account of the conditions he found there. He is concerned to outline the terrible state of the country and the factors which had brought it about, and to present a comprehensive plan for the pacification of that 'wretched Realme'. Ever since England had claimed sovereignty over Ireland in the time of Henry II (although in fact only the territory of the Pale, surrounding Dublin, was ever in complete subjection), she had suffered the legitimate penalty of overlords, constant insurrection. In Elizabeth's time Irish hatred of England reached one of its periodic climaxes of intensity, and the rebellions of the north-east and south-west in the fifteen-sixties, when Spenser was still at school, were followed by another series of rebellions and by attempts by France, Spain, and the Papal power to intervene against the Protestant oppressor. An attempted invasion using Smerwick as the base was halted in September 1580 by the Lord Deputy and the loyal Anglo-Irish Earl of Ormonde: Smerwick was recaptured and its defenders slaughtered. Spenser was there. He gives a detailed account in *A Veue*, 'myself being as near then as any'. No doubt the battles and sieges of *The Faerie Queene* owe something to the poet's actual experience of war and bloodshed, gained first at Smerwick.

It is remarkable that he managed to write so much, while most actively engaged in public affairs. His first job was something between that of an A.D.C. to a Commander-in-Chief and that of a Private Secretary to a Viceroy. But in August 1582 the Queen was finally persuaded that the Lord Deputy's policies were too severe, and Grey was recalled, like Sir Artegall in Book V of *The Faerie Queene*. Spenser remained, in less glorious but probably more lucrative and leisured employment, and gradually became something of a landowner. From 1583 he is described as 'gentleman', and is recognized as a person of some consequence. Ireland, or Dublin rather, he found to be not without its cultivated life, and we have in *A Discourse of Civill Life*, by a friend of his, Lodowick Bryskett, Clerk of the Council in Dublin, an account of a cultured and literary circle there, and references to Spenser and to his work '*in heroical verse* under the title of a *Faerie Queene*'. In 1589, Spenser succeeded Bryskett as Clerk of the Council of Munster, having deputized for him for some years before. Although life in Munster, still not properly settled, despite the 'plantation' of English landowners, farmers, and labourers, was different from life in Dublin, he evidently had time to write. At the end of the year 1589 he came to London, and early the following year published the first three books of *The Faerie Queene*.

In the October eclogue of *The Shepheardes Calender* Piers had urged the poet Cuddie to 'sing of bloody Mars, of wars, of giusts' (jousts). Ireland was indeed a land 'of bloody Mars, of wars, of giusts', and Spenser began singing of it very soon after arriving there. He who was proposing to emulate if not to 'overgo' Ariosto's poem of love and war, *Orlando Furioso*, must have realized how significant that experience was. The rude foresters, the 'salvage' men, the cruel knights, the base churls, the lawless infidels, the cannibals and pirates, the sieges and pursuits, the poor hovels, the castles, the savagery, the rapine, the terror, as well as the beautiful landscape and the noble and courageous

heroes, owe much to medieval romance or to the recent recru-
descence of romance in epic form in Italy, in the work of Boiardo,
Ariosto and (very recently) of Tasso, but assuredly they also are
in debt to the beautiful but wretched realm of Ireland.

Spenser neglected

It is commonly assumed that because Spenser wrote of questing
knights in Faerie Land, his work is slight, and without much
reference or relevance to real life. Many critics of Spenser,
especially in the nineteenth century, praised him above all for his
pictorial power, and some of them advised their readers to go to
Spenser 'as to a gallery of pictures' not worrying about the
meaning. These perhaps are representative of the nineteenth
century's love of anecdotal painting: others, representative of the
preoccupation of that century with high-minded sentiments,
emphasized above all the moralizing, uplifting aspects of the
book. Both emphases have deterred readers. And all new readers
must initially be deterred by the mere size and scale of *The Faerie
Queene*, let alone its complicated narrative. Further, the very
form Romance is one that many readers find off-putting. The
present dislike of the Victorian taste for a pre-Raphaelite kind of
Romance of wishy-washy characterization and elevated moral
purpose, and of the Romantic taste for hectic description,
together with the subsequent decline in the popularity of narrative poetry and the increasing dominance of the novel, have all
contributed to Spenser's signal fall in popularity. *The Faerie
Queene* was in every nursery and schoolroom in Victoria's reign,
often suitably bowdlerized, but very few nurseries or even
schools have a copy of it now.

Another reason for his neglect is almost exactly opposite to
the criticism that he is superficial, unreal, remote from life.
It is that he is so much involved in the life, actual and physical
as well as imaginative, of his time that true appreciation of him

demands a great knowledge of his century, that fascinating
century mid-way between the Middle Ages and the Renaissance.
There is truth in this. There is no more central Elizabethan
figure than Edmund Spenser: the grammar school boy and
university graduate employed by the State and rising in social
rank through public service but even more through the success
of his creative writing; the classically educated boy, deeply versed
in the work of Homer, Plato, Aristotle, Virgil, Ovid; the late
medieval man saturated in Romance, Chaucer, Malory, the
Bible, the homiletic tradition and in popular taste and tradition;
the Renaissance man intimate with the work of Dante, Boccaccio, Boiardo, Ariosto, Tasso, and seeking to write for his
own country a romantic epic like those of Italy; patriot, anti-
Papist, allegorist, sonnetteer, epic poet, satirist, pastoralist, prose
chronicler, public servant. No one else quite blends so many
sources, so many cultural traditions, makes so original if eclectic
a new form, and is so profoundly concerned with man's life on
earth, however remote the world he seems to picture forth.

The idealist poet

Spenser never outgrew the youthful idealism which lay behind
his translations for *A Theatre* and the ecclesiastical eclogues of
The Shepheardes Calender. He was in love with the idea of virtue.
The long sub-title of *A Theatre*, which emphasizes the contrast
between 'the miseries and calamities that follow the voluptuous
Worldlings' and 'the great joyes and plesures which the faithfull
do enjoy' would serve as a synopsis of much of *The Faerie Queene*.
Behind the ecclesiastical satire of *The Shepheardes Calender* is
the love and praise of simple virtue. *Mother Hubberds Tale* (1591)
and *Colin Clouts Come Home Again* (1595) display and satirize the
corruption and privilege which mar England and even Elizabeth's
court and are a part of that falseness which corrupts men's
dealings with men and so with God. *A Veue*, much condemned

for its advocacy of harsh and thorough subjugation of the Irish, has running through it a constant virtuous purpose, that of bringing 'evill people by good ordinaunce and government . . . from theire delighte of licentious barbarisme unto the love of goodness and Civilitye'. The *Complaints* (1591), *Daphnaida* (1591) and the Platonic Hymns in honour of Love and Beauty, and of Heavenly Love and Heavenly Beauty (1596), are all chiefly concerned with virtue. Sometimes he sings of the loveliness of virtue, sometimes of the danger virtue is always in, sometimes he praises the golden age, sometimes he attacks his own because it is not golden, sometimes he writes of the impermanence of human virtue, the fleetingness of beauty, the transitoriness of human achievement, all against the sure background of belief in God and love of God.

The poet of virtue

The Faerie Queene is above all a Christian work. It is founded upon an unquestioning acceptance of the primary relation of creature to Creator, the need for men to live in the light of and by the help of God's grace, and it steadily points towards a time, as he expresses it in the final cantos,

> when no more *Change* shall be,
> But stedfast rest of all things firmely stayd
> Upon the pillours of Eternity....
> . . . .
> But thence-forth all shall rest eternally
> With Him that is the God of Sabbaoth hight.

Of course the Christian emphasis varies from book to book. Book I is the most openly Christian and doctrinal, dealing as it does with man's relations with God, illustrated in a sort of Pilgrim's Progress through the world of error, doubt, sin, temptation, pride, and despair, and culminating in the clear allegory of the Red Cross Knight's fight with and victory over the dragon, representing Satan. It is the book of holiness, about the achieving of Truth. Book II is concerned with man's relations with himself, with his control over his passions and desires. It is the book of the virtue of Temperance. Books III and IV are about Love, Book V about Justice and Order, Book VI about Grace and the true Courtesy by which it is shown in the world of men. You could say that Spenser presents the 'theological' virtues, Faith and Charity in Books I, III and IV and also in Book VI, the 'cardinal' virtues Temperance and Justice in Books II and V. But that would be to codify *The Faerie Queene* too much. Although we are always conscious of the great simplicities of his moral concern, despite the complexity and sometimes the confusion made inevitable by the magnitude of his undertaking and the scope of his material, it is an ever-shifting pattern he presents. The colours are primary colours, but they blur and blend and are in constant movement. So he gives us simplicity in multiplicity, straightforward guidance through an intricate succession of stories, and lucidly Christian moral suasion in an imaginative romantic narrative of extraordinary variety and inspired by an unprecedented range of literary, doctrinal, and popular source-material.

His great achievement, setting aside his imaginative and pictorial skill, metrical ability, and story-telling and world-creating power, is his success in convincing us of the loveliness of virtue. It is this which makes *The Faerie Queene* the greatest of all English imaginative works of high seriousness and moral purpose. We all know the complaint that Milton's Comus is more beguiling and attractive than the Lady, God and Christ pale and cold beside the human warmth of Satan, however fallen. Milton wrote of 'virtue in her shape how lovely' but was unable to convince us of the loveliness of virtue. Spenser leaves us in no doubt, and, as far as any work of literature can influence a man's life, he makes us love virtue and want to be virtuous. He does it by fairly obvious methods, chiefly of emphasis on the radiance, beauty, and gloriousness of the good characters, and by using evocative words and images in describing bad or meretricious characters to alert us, as it were, to their fraudulent appearance of goodness or superficial attractiveness. For he is wise, and usually shows us the attractions of sin, worldliness, and the life of the passions. He does not simply delineate their vileness, although he makes perfectly clear his disapprobation, censure, or disgust.

But the poem is more than a straightforward presentation of good and evil. It is not a naïve and impossible romance set in a romantic never-never-land. It is rooted firmly in life, in real experience and real knowledge of human behaviour and motive, however marvellously imaginative its action and episodes. And the variety of human behaviour shown is immense.

I will only cite a few examples: the humorous account of the sleeping God of Sleep (I.1.41–44); the description of Duessa's false swoon (I.2.44–45); the reconciliation of Duessa and the Red Cross Knight (I.7.3–4); Una's grief and Arthur's consoling of it (I.7.38ff.); the vivid depiction of Ignaro at Orgoglio's castle (I.8.29–34); Trevisan's fear (I.9.21ff.); the specious reasoning of Despair (I.9.38ff.); Una's anguished anger when the Red Cross Knight despairs (I.9.52–53); the Red Cross Knight's grievous sense of his own unworthiness (I.10.62–63); the varied reactions of the people after the Dragon is slain (I.12.9–12); the perplexity of the King after hearing the false messenger (I.12.29–30).

Spenser's models in epic and romance

Spenser is indebted for the form and much of the material of *The Faerie Queene* to two different kinds of romance writing: medieval romance with its simple form of quest or journey ending in combat, and Italian epic romance with its fantastic proliferation of intertwined narratives.

Although medieval romance began with a purely delighting purpose, the fact that its pattern was of quest or journey and much of its material combat or conflict offered obvious possibilities of allegorical interpretation. It is natural to see the course of human life as a journey, and many of its incidents as struggles or battles. The metaphor is well-worn. We journey through the vale of woe, walk confidently in the high places, journey to our everlasting rest, battle with rivals, foes or our worse natures, struggle with temptation or sin. To a poet with a serious moralizing purpose who was also deeply interested in medieval life and literature, and, a typical Elizabethan, fascinated by the legendary past (much of which he thought of as not legendary but historical), medieval romance provided an obvious model. The form was in fact having its last period of great popularity in the middle and late sixteenth century when many romances were republished. Even the playwrights were to take it up into the drama. Furthermore, some of the later romance-writers had been evidently aware of the serious implications which the form could be made easily to carry. Magic events or episodes in the early romances were sometimes given a supernatural cast later: in *Sir Beves of Hamtoun*, for example, in which the hero, fighting with a dragon, is twice restored when at the point of defeat by the waters of a fountain into which he falls. It is not merely a magic fountain, as Spenser realized when he took the episode into Book I of *The Faerie Queene* in Red Cross Knight's fight with the dragon. No one can read the story of the Grail in Malory without being aware of the extent to which romance material has been made to carry a serious spiritual purpose. (The French source of this book was of course even more explicitly doctrinal, and almost certainly of clerical authorship.) Spenser was fortunate in having a popular form hand-tailored, as it were, to fit his purpose. Books I and V, and Book II to a lesser extent, are sturdy offspring of medieval romance. Holiness, Justice, and Temperance are their subjects, and the virtuous states which the three knights, Red Cross Knight, Sir Artegall and Sir Guyon, are questing respectively to achieve. Perhaps at some stage the whole poem was to consist of a series of quests in the medieval romance form. If so, Spenser realized that there would be some danger of monotony if the twelve books (or even twenty-four as he suggested as a possibility in the Prefatory Letter) were all to follow this pattern and he made use of the very latest form in which Romance material had come into a new life, the romantic epics of Italy.

These varied, involved, fantastic and delightful poems were a completely new hybrid, epic in scale and length and in numbers of characters, and epic in their background situations, but romantic in story-matter and in wild imaginativeness of invention. The background situation is the epic 'matter' of the wars of Franks and Saracens, Christians and pagans, descended from the epic material that had dealt with Charlemagne and his peers. Indeed in some of them Charlemagne appears, although it is one or other of his 'douceperes' or twelve peers, Orlando or Rinaldo or Godfrey of Boulogne, who is always most prominent. Boiardo's unfinished *Orlando Innamorato* (*c.* 1480), "Roland in love," was taken over and completed by Ariosto in *Orlando Furioso* (originally published in 1516), "Roland mad for love." The titles do not suggest epic, but rather Romance at its most romantic. I would prefer to call them *epic romances*, to distinguish them from two other works which may more appropriately be called *romantic epics*, Trissino's *L'Italia Liberata dai Gotti* (1547) "Italy freed from the Goths", and Tasso's *Gerusalemme Liberata* (1581), "The freeing of Jerusalem" (from the Turks). The *epic romances* of Boiardo and Ariosto are romances on an epic scale, but predominantly romances. The subject matter, love and chivalry, unrolls within an epic situation, of war between Christian and infidel. Trissino's and Tasso's are *epic* poems, dealing seriously with the military and spiritual struggle of Christian and pagan, but Tasso especially adorns the serious theme with all the fantastic trappings of Romance: magic, the supernatural, enchantresses, magicians, giants, invincible armour and magic spears or swords, disguise, lady-knights, love-pursuit and love-complications (Erminia loves Tancred who loves Clorinda). By a marvellous alchemy, the romantic and the epic strains harmonize, though I think the epic *romance* assimilates epic seriousness more happily than the romantic *epic* does romantic ingredients, which sometimes seem to be romantic diversions. (The long episode of the seduction of some of the Christian knights by Armida in *Gerusalemme Liberata*, a primary source for much in Book II of *The Faerie Queene*, seems if not a truancy from epic purpose at least a diversion too powerful not a little to disturb the balance of Tasso's poem.)

Spenser knew and loved the work of all these Italian writers, and his indebtedness to Ariosto and Tasso is apparent in every book of *The Faerie Queene*. But Ariosto's inspired frivolousness he often made serious, and Tasso's seriousness he lightened with fancy, and made more organically a part of his narrative and intellectual purpose. Where Ariosto employs Allegory, as in the episode of Time throwing names into Lethe in Book 35, or in Rinaldo's encounter with the woman-shaped monster with a thousand eyes and ears, representing his jealousy, in Book 42, it is rather a decorative and ingenious fancy, than integral and profound as in Spenser. Where Ariosto presents the 'arborification' of Astolfo, it is for the fun of the magic and the surprise. But in Spenser the 'arborification' of Fradubio is serious and almost frightening, and the episode also strongly reinforces the moral purpose.

Duessa's repeated tempting of the Red Cross Knight has something in common with Armida's temptings in Tasso, but Tasso's enchantress enchants the reader too, while Spenser has portrayed Duessa so carefully and subtly that the reader can never forget that she is the evil emblem of Deceipt. Spenser's characters and incidents tend to enter our consciousness and to remain there as part of a newly created mythology.

Ariosto wrote a great hurly-burly of a romance, full of invention, fun, and surprise, and full too of convincingly life-like characters. His heroine Bradamante, for example, the original of Spenser's Britomart, is markedly more alive and human. He made a romance convey an impression of the fullness and variety and multiplicity of life, indeed he made a romance on an epic scale. The way in which Spenser was to 'overgo' Ariosto was by greater seriousness. His was not simply a tale of love and war and adventure. His lovers, knights, warriors, giants, monsters, magicians, his pursuits, imprisonings, and battles, symbolize the love and war and adventure and activity of real life, and in the last resort, too, symbolize the unending war of good and evil in life. Tasso sought to deepen, strengthen and spiritualize the epic romance. He made the war of Christendom against heathenism a complete symbol of the perennial struggle of the forces of light against the powers of darkness, where Ariosto had ignored the suggestion that civilization was fighting barbarism and had, as it were, deliberately eschewed the epic possibilities of his story. I would claim that Spenser in *The Faerie Queene* successfully wrote a poem romantic in form and incident yet epic in its implicitly religious and moral purpose and subject, and in its symbolizing (not representing) the epic fullness of life. He avoided (perhaps he could not have achieved) most of the realism and the humour of Ariosto, and he avoided the unresolved tension in Tasso's poem between the romantic, the realistic, the symbolic, and the religious. His poem is less lifelike but more true, less regular but more uniform, less crowded but more complete than *Orlando Furioso*, and more romantic but not less epic than *Gerusalemme Liberata*. Further, the extended allegory of *The*

Faerie Queene, perceptible now more now less clearly through the romantic narrative, is 'general' allegory having reference to all human activity in an imaginary world cognate with the real world. Ariosto's poem is really not allegory at all, and Tasso's is 'particular' allegory, basing a representation of the struggle between true and false, good and evil, on one particular event— the siege of Jerusalem. Spenser does not rest all, like Tasso, on one great action, nor does he content himself, like Ariosto, with an enormous canvas and a marvellous multiplicity of narratives. His story-telling carries as grave a message as Tasso's religious epic, and this purpose is not a confined or particular one, but an un-limited and general one that touches human life at many points. As C. S. Lewis said: 'The things we read about in it are not like life, but the experience of reading it is like living. . . . We feel that his poetry has really tapped sources not easily accessible to discursive thought. He makes imaginable inner realities so vast and simple that they ordinarily escape us. . . . To read him is to grow in mental health.'

Poetic technique

A new reader of *The Faerie Queene* will be struck first by the archaic language and diction. Spenser had already in *The Shepheardes Calender* experimented with archaic language in order to give a feeling of ancient days. In *The Faerie Queene*, too, he wanted to give an initial impression of 'far away and long ago' and he also needed to create the glamour and imaginative force and sense of a reality rather more than human appropriate to his fabled land of 'Faerie'. Although we are meant to feel at the end (and I think we do feel) that the events and characters really relate to the events and persons we encounter in our own lives, Spenser needed to create an entire, different and self-consistent imaginary world, and his chief weapon was his choice of an archaic vocabulary and diction, owing much to Chaucer, Malory and the romance-writers, and something to French and to dialect too.[1] In fact he rather used words that were going out of currency than invented new 'old' ones, although he often invented his own deviant forms of words. Ben Jonson complained that 'in affecting the ancients he writ no language' and it is true that what he did in *The Faerie Queene* was deliberately backward not forward looking. But for its purpose it is difficult to imagine anything more perfectly suited. It is worth observing, too, that he had unimpeachable authority behind him. Aristotle in the *Poetics* thought that in heroic poetry words of all kinds might properly find a place, and that clearness freed from the commonplace could be justifiably attained by the alteration of words, as in lengthening and contraction, and by coinage. Italian Renaissance theorists, such as Vida, recommended (as had Horace) the moderate use of archaic terms, of borrowings from the ancients, and even coining, and Vida had especially commended the use of compound words. Tasso followed in pointing out how Homer, Virgil, and Dante had all enriched their poetry by drawing upon many sources in order to enrich their vocabulary. In France, the writers of the Pléiade, and especially Du Bellay (whose work was well known to Spenser, and some of whose poems he translated or adapted), had prescribed the enriching of the vernacular with archaic, foreign, dialect, and newly-coined words. It should also be mentioned that his was a very 'English' vocabulary, with little use of Latin forms. He who intended to write a great national epic did well to write it in so essentially English a vocabulary and style. The language, like the poem itself, looks difficult and complex, but is basically simple and clear. Coleridge declared that there was 'no poet whose writings would safelier stand the test of Mr. Wordsworth's theory than Spenser'.

It is generally accepted that Spenser also found an admirable verse form for his poem. The Spenserian stanza, his own inven-

[1] See note by A. Ward, p. 29.

tion, is big enough to carry a lot of sense and to advance the narrative without becoming monotonous. Chaucer's *rime royal* (ababbcc) and the *ottava rima* (abababcc) are both a little short for the purposes of so vast a poem, and in both cases the rhyming couplet with which they end might have tolled if not intolerably then trivially on the reader's ear. Spenser clearly was indebted to both for his nine-line stanza; (ababbcbcc). Possibly the uneven number of lines of Chaucer's *rime royal* suggested the unevenness he adopted; but by a stroke of genius Spenser gave further unevenness and variety by making the final line a 12-syllabled alexandrine after the preceding 10-syllabled lines. That alexandrine provides a splendid conclusion to the stanza and Spenser shows how varied in its sound and sense it can be. It can well sum up what has gone before with proverbial or sententious comment:

> God helpe the man so wrapt in *Errours* endlesse traine.[1]
> (I.1.18)

> or

> For bloud can nought but sin, and wars but sorrowes yield.
> (I.10.60)

It can give a splendid variety of onomatopoeic effects:

> The mightie trunck halfe rent, with ragged rift
> Doth roll adowne the rocks, and fall with fearefull drift
> (I.8.22)

> or

> But farre within, as in a hollow glade,
> Those glaring lampes were set, that made a dreadfull shade.
> (I.11.14);

---

[1] I have taken all my examples from Book I, although in some cases better examples could be found elsewhere.

or

> From heaven high to chase the chearelesse darke,
> With merry note her loud salutes the mounting larke.
> (I.11.51)

In all of these examples the effect depends largely on the greater length of the concluding alexandrine. Spenser subtly varies the alexandrine, too, by moving and occasionally indeed removing the caesura. In

> *Hymen iô Hymen*, dancing all around,
> Whilst freshest *Flora* her with Yvie girlond crownd.
> (I.1.48)

and:

> The neighbour woods around with hollow murmur ring.
> (I.8.11)

the alexandrine has no strongly marked caesura and this gives an added length and an increased sense of movement appropriate to the subject-matter. In

> Was swolne with wrath, and poyson, and with bloudy gore.
> (I.11.8)

the alexandrine has two caesurae, and this double checking admirably assists the sense and vividness of the line. Bringing the caesura forward, as in

> and all his vitall powres
> Decayd, and all his flesh shronk up like withered flowres.
> (I.8.41)

emphasizes the significant part of the statement, and the falling cadence of the long rest of the line is aptly expressive of its meaning. Moving the caesura back to the end of the line, as in

> nor *Hebrus* match this well:
> Into the same the knight backe overthrowen, fell.
>
> (I.11.30)

throws the emphasis right to the end, and in this example, is effectively onomatopoeic.

Splendid as many of the alexandrines are, they are more justly to be considered in relation to the whole stanzas in which they appear, and indeed to the whole poem, when the effect of variation and the sense of conclusion they give are clearly seen. To the reader they give a regular defined period of pause and a feeling of control which are necessary but which do not become tedious. The variation which Spenser gives to the rhythm and balance of the alexandrine markedly helps to vary the general rhythm of the succession of stanzas, which might otherwise be too even. It has been well said that its effect is like that of a ninth wave breaking farthest up the beach, and so temporarily disturbing the even rhythm of the tide.

As for the stanza itself, it is infinitely varied and intricate. The variety and intricacy are achieved by constant assonance, both between lines and within lines, by great rhythmical variation, and by masterly use of rhetorical devices. Of rhetorical devices, he especially uses *onomatopoeia* and alliteration: look, for example at the account of Night's horses (I.5.28); of the smoke from artillery fire in the simile in Canto 7, stanza 13; at the description of the Cave of Despair (I.9.33ff.) and the fall of the Dragon (I.11.54); *repetitio* and *hyperbaton* or deliberate changing of the natural order of the words:

> Life from *Sansfoy* thou tookst, *Sansloy* shall from thee take.
>
> Therewith in haste his helmet gan unlace,
>> Till *Una* cride, O hold that heavie hand,
>> Deare Sir, what ever that thou be in place:

> Enough is, that thy foe doth vanquisht stand
> Now at thy mercy: Mercie not withstand:
> For he is one the truest knight alive,
> Though conquered now he lie on lowly land,
> And whilest him fortune favour, faire did thrive,
> In bloudie field: therefore of life him not deprive.
>
> (I.3.36–37)

asyndeton or absense of conjunctions:

> Feare, sicknesse, age, losse, labour, sorrow, strife,
> Paine, hunger, cold, that makes the hart to quake.
>
> (I.9.44)

parenthesis in I.8.40; *reduplicatio*: O too deare love, love bought with death too deare (I.2.31): antithesis or *contentio*, 'a proper coupling together of contraries':

> Henceforth in safe assuraunce may ye rest,
> Having both found a new friend you to aid,
> And lost an old foe, that did you molest.
>
> (I.2.27)

His poetry, which seems to have so natural a flow and variety, is most rigorously constructed on a sure rhetorical basis. The 'linked sweetness long drawn out', the 'mellifluousness' and the 'incantatory effect' which even Dr. Leavis finds, the musicality which most critics recognize in Spenser, do not just come from nature, but are achieved by the poet's exceptional technical skill. As Professor Renwick has observed, their practice in rhetoric gave Elizabethan poets a 'greater control over language than their elders and greater facility and copiousness than their modern descendants'. (*Edmund Spenser*, Arnold, 1925, p. 115).[1]

Because his poem is so vast, it is not easy to select details,[2] but it

[1] H. D. Rix has published in 'Rhetoric in Spenser's Poetry', *Pennsylvania State College Studies*, No. 7, 1940, a valuable paper on the technical aspects of the subject.
[2] I have often drawn attention in the notes to instances of Spenser's poetic methods and of his poetic achievement.

can be said that his technical mastery is especially notable in swift narrative, vivid description and in making the reader 'feel' and be moved by what he reads. A characteristic example of a combination of these three is in the encounter with the fearful Trevisan and later with Despair in Canto 9, stanzas 22ff. He has an unerring eye for telling detail: see especially the account of the House of Pride (Canto 4); Arthur in Orgoglio's castle in Canto 8, stanzas 30–41; and the fight with the Dragon in Canto 11. He is also a superb describer of the natural scene. But he can write effective linking verse—the quiet or informative passages necessary in any long narrative which cannot be expected to keep up full pressure throughout—and excellent dialogue (for example between Una and Arthur in Canto 7, stanzas 39–42, or in Canto 9 between Trevisan and the Red Cross Knight, and then between the latter and Despair.

There will always be some who find his language and diction quaint, and others who cannot respond to narrative verse, or descriptive poetry, or didactic art, or even to the magic melodies of Romance. Dr. Leavis long ago laid it down that Spenser was not in the main line of English poetic development, and therefore, by implication, not to be taken seriously. He found Spenser's language, like Milton's, 'incantatory, remote from speech . . . certain feelings are expressed, but there is no pressure behind the words; what predominates in the handling of them is not the tension of something precise to be defined and fixed, but a concern for mellifluousness' (*Revaluation*, 1936, pp. 56–57). His disciple D. A. Traversi takes the same line, and castigates him for being over-concerned with decoration and moralizing (*Pelican Guide to English Literature*, Vol. 1, 1954). Both exhibit prejudice as well as predilection in judgements that I believe time will not uphold, as it will uphold Spenser; they make the elementary mistake of failing to consider Spenser (and, in the case of Leavis, Milton), historically, and therefore ignore the prime importance to an Elizabethan or a seventeenth-century epic writer of the simple doctrine of decorum, by which an epic theme demands language and versification remote from and richer than the language of ordinary speech or poetry. There are *grotesqueries* and *longueurs* in *The Faerie Queene*, for example the description of the House of Temperance in Book II, Canto 9, and there are passages where the flow of inspiration is temporarily checked. It would be surprising if this were not so. But the high imaginative power, and the fertility of invention and reference, the constant relevance to real life and the remarkably sustained poetic force are to be marvelled at, and will always have their admirers, however few.

Spenser's followers

The style, the language, the stanza form all came together for the first time to make *The Faerie Queene*, and it would be absurd to expect any real successor or imitation. Yet many poets have followed Spenser and so many more have admired him that he has been called the poet's poet. Giles Fletcher in *Christ's Victory and Triumph in Heaven over and after Death* (1610) and his brother Phineas in *The Appolyonists* (1627) and *The Purple Island* (1633) consciously follow him as moral allegorists, as did Joseph Beaumont in *Psyche* (1648). Milton freely acknowledged his indebtedness to 'sage and serious Spenser' and found much in Book II (the Bower of Bliss) and Book III (the House of Busirane) to help him in *Comus* (1637). After this, many writers imitated the Spenserian stanza, but none is in any other sense Spenserian. William Shenstone in *The School-Mistress* (1737) played with Spenser's stanza out of affection and admiration, but ended by writing a *pastiche*. James Thomson in *The Castle of Indolence* (1748), playful also, acclimatized it happily to the eighteenth century. James Beattie in *The Minstrel* (1771–74, unfinished), took it seriously, perhaps too seriously, unlike Pope who in the six stanzas of *The Alley* had given a brilliant hint of surprising

low, satiric, Dunciadish possibilities. The Romantic poets loved
Spenser and wrote in Spenserian stanzas, especially Scott in the
Vision of Don Roderick, Byron in *Childe Harold*, Shelley in *The
Revolt of Islam* and very successfully in *Adonais*, and Keats in *The
Eve of St. Agnes* and in an *Imitation of Spenser*. Scott and Byron
had narrative energy, but in Shelley and Keats most evident are
the qualities for which Spenser is commonly attacked, and of
which he is emphatically not guilty: lushness, overmellifluousness,
vagueness, emotional excess, drowsy metres, a lack of serious
ideas.

Spenser is in fact inimitable. His voice is perhaps the most
individual and easily identifiable of all English poetic voices, but,
more important than that, the peculiarly great multiple vision
and imaginative power were used in a form perfectly selected
for its purpose, a purpose at once instructive and delighting, and
based on immense reading and varied knowledge and a profound
understanding of human nature, and at a time which was ready
and able to receive, understand and respond. His actual influence
was unfruitful, as was Milton's, and as the direct influence of the
greatest must be. There are, as Dryden wrote of Jonson, Fletcher
and Shakespeare as dramatists, 'no bays to be expected in their
walks'.

Book 1

I have printed a summary of the events before the notes on
each canto, but a brief commentary on the book may be helpful.
Book I has the clearest structure and message of all the books of
The Faerie Queene. It follows closely the conventional pattern of
medieval romance, presenting a quest which after many dangers
and adventures for the knight-hero culminates in some great
contest or combat. The quest is that of the Red Cross Knight to
free Una's parents and their land from the oppression of a great
dragon. It should be read primarily as a romantic narrative

imaginatively conceived, and not anxiously as an allegory every detail of which must be teased out. But there are several strands of significance to be descried, and at various points one or other of these strands becomes more important.

First there is a more or less continuous contemporary reference. The Red Cross Knight stands for the newly established Church of England, companioned by Una, Truth, and able with her help to perceive dangers and overcome them (Error, for example), but, when separated from her, in constant peril from false religion, that is from Rome, figured in Archimago (Arch-magician), Duessa ('to be double', i.e. duplicity), and the pagan trinity, Sansloy, Sansjoy, and Sansfoy (lawless, joyless, and faithless). It can be deceived by falseness, as the Knight is in the House of Pride by the machinations of Archimago; laid low by Pride, as the Knight is by Orgoglio; it can fall into Sloth and Despair; but, rescued by grace, as the Knight is by Prince Arthur, and disciplined by Faith, Hope, Charity, Amendment, Penance, and Repentance, it is strengthened to meet its greatest foe. So it can meet the most violent assaults of Satan (the Dragon) and, overcoming it, can be assured that it will be united in the end for ever with Una, Truth.

Secondly, there is an allegory of man's life in the world. The Knight is a newly baptized Christian, wearing for the first time the armour of Christ. He has taken upon himself the quest, which to the medieval mind (and Spenser as an Elizabethan inherited a great deal of medieval mentality and outlook) is the essential duty of all Christian men, to seek out and fight Satan. He is accompanied by Truth (Una), who helps him by warning and counsel, but he is not impervious to the assaults of Falseness and Duplicity (Archimago and Duessa), is separated from Una and readily succumbs, under the power of deception and the subtle and insidious contrivings of Falseness, to a series of temptations: Sloth, which leads in the direction of lechery with Duessa, and which enfeebles him so that he falls an easy victim to Pride (Orgoglio); and then to Despair. But instructed in faith and holiness he is regenerated and comes to the land of Eden to fight the Devil. In the three days' struggle he is twice saved and renewed through the grace of God by the water of life and the balm of the tree of life, and is eventually betrothed to Truth. The Red Cross Knight, is, in short, an Everyman figure shown ultimately to have achieved his knightly quest. He does not 'represent' Holiness, but his journey, quest, and struggle represent the course of life of the ordinary Christian in the fallen world.

But he is also a saint, or destined to become one, not just a Briton or faerie knight: St. George the patron saint of England. He is the only saint in the poem, and this has a double usefulness for Spenser: for St. George's career represents the possibility of mankind's rising from a fallen state to salvation, and in his person he stands patriotically for England's restoration to true faith, that is the triumph of Protestantism in England. There is a sense too, explored by W. Nelson (*The Poetry of Edmund Spenser*, Columbia, 1963, pp. 147ff.), in which the saint's life is 'an imitation of Christ, and his wedding to Una is like the marriage of Christ and his faithful who are His Church . . .'.

The pleasures and riches of the book are many. It has less pure Romance than many of the other books of *The Faerie Queene*, although the relationship between Una and the Red Cross Knight, with its separations and misunderstandings, with the steadfastness of the lady and the waywardness and suceptibility of the Knight, which culminates in the happy harmony of their betrothing, is effectively and convincingly presented. But, as befits the gravity of its subject, which is man's life and purpose in the world, Book I is, essentially, epic rather than romantic. It is a sort of *Aeneid*, its hero bound to a high duty as well as dangerous tasks. The book has a high proportion of great contests, of which the overcoming of Orgoglio by Prince Arthur and the slaying of the Dragon by the Red Cross Knight are the most successful. In the presentation of the grotesque and the macabre, especially in Duessa's journey to the underworld, in the allegorical depictions, particularly of the seven deadly sins, and in emblematic figures like Ignorance and Despair, Spenser's strange imagination has plenty of scope. It is, appropriately, a book much concerned with light and darkness, symbolic as it were of the good and evil in the world. The emphasis on wood and forest, greater I believe than in other books of *The Faerie Queene*, reflects both the idea of forests as wilderness, by which, as Servius wrote of Virgil's forest in the sixth book of the *Aeneid*, Virgil 'signifies that in which beastliness and passion dominate', and Dante's *selva oscura*, the forest of sinfulness and worldliness, the wandering wood of this life. The book moves continually from light to darkness and back again: from the Wandering Wood and Archimago's dark forest-hermitage to Una in the sunny glades with the Lion and then the fauns and satyrs, Duessa in the underworld, the dark dungeons of Orgoglio's castle, the young Arthur brought up in the open air, Despair in his hollow cave, 'Darke, dolefull, drearie, like a greedie grave', the Red Cross Knight rising up freshly at dawn to renew his fight with the dragon; and in this book, more than in the others, we are regularly told of night defacing the sky and bright dawn bringing new hope and joyfulness. So it is a book of greater contrasts than most of the books of the poem, and possibly of greater variety than any except Book V; and all within the tight structure of the quest and conflict pattern.

I have made use of Dean Kitchin's edition (O.U.P. 1867), although the notes are almost completely new. In them I have emphasized Spenser's poetic methods and achievement and the inspiration he got from the classical and Renaissance epics, from

CFQ

medieval romance and from the ordinary life of his time. I am indebted to the Variorum edition of Spenser's works, published by Johns Hopkins University. For further reading I would recommend especially: C. S. Lewis, *The Allegory of Love* (O.U.P., 1936) Chapter VII, the best brief account of the poem; G. Hough, *A Preface to 'The Faerie Queene'* (Duckworth, 1962); W. Nelson, *The Poetry of Edmund Spenser,* (Columbia University Press, 1963); W. L. Renwick, *Edmund Spenser* (Edward Arnold, 1925); and E. de Selincourt, *The Works of Edmund Spenser* (O.U.P., 1912) both for the text and its excellent introduction.

A note for new readers of Spenser

I suggest that anyone reading Spenser for the first time should read first the short passages referred to on pages 11, 20 and 22. They will give a useful first taste of vivid writing and of the human interest of the poem, and will perhaps show how readable Spenser is. In general, read him fast. Don't worry over the allegory, and certainly do not pause to tease out every strand. Spenser is often complex because he is subtle and learned, conscious of the complexity of human nature and tells complicated stories, but his purpose is always simple and clear. Think of him as a narrative poet writing a series of adventures of Romance, rather than as a moral allegorist. If you do so, you will enjoy the story, and the allegory will do its work usually without your realizing it. Re-reading is the time to work at the allegory, and then go for the large and simple significance, not for minute detail. The purpose of allegory is to reveal, not to hide. Spenser knew this well enough, though his most determined commentators sometimes seem to think the opposite.

THE LANGUAGE OF *THE FAERIE QUEENE*
by Alan Ward

SPENSER'S need in *The Faerie Queene* was for an appropriate diction, suited to lofty themes and at the same time suggestive of times past. Archaic elements had to blend with epic ones, and both in turn needed a suitable metrical form. Spenser must have given the most careful thought to his diction, helped in varying degrees by the example of Virgil, and by the theory and practice of the Pléiade in France and the Italian Renaissance poets.

Certain features of the versification need mention. It is interesting that Spenser chose to write his poem in stanzas at all; more so that he rejected existing stanza-forms for one of his own invention. At least three features of this stanza are important with regard to diction: its length (longer than *rime royal* or *ottava rima*), its exacting rhyme requirements (which include a triple and a quadruple rhyme), and its final alexandrine. The length of this stanza, the marked rhythmical regularity of its lines, and the long final line contribute much to the overall sound and movement of the verse.

This concern for the rhythm and sound of the verse is evident also in the extensive use of alliteration and assonance. Alliteration is employed partly for emphasis, partly perhaps to help towards an archaic effect (since poems like *Piers Plowman* had been written in alliterative metre), and sometimes, like assonance, to contribute a pattern of sound to the structure of the stanza. Some alliteration, perhaps assonance too, is onomatopoeic, but here we must remember that English in Spenser's day sounded different from our own, and that there was much variety even in 'accepted' speech. As for Spenser's rhymes, it is fairly clear that some at least are unlikely to have been true ones at the time; e.g. *ame*, 'am,' rhyming with *Dame* and *same* (I.12.30).

As this example suggests, Spenser had the look as well as the sound of his poetry in mind. He seems often to have gone to some trouble to spell rhyme-words so as to rhyme to the eye as well as to the ear, and did not use spelling simply as a means of covering up a 'bad' rhyme. For example, in *straict, pourtraict* (II.1.39) the rhyme is good, but the spelling of *straict* seems to have been specially chosen for its looks. Some of the alliteration, too, seems to be designed more for the eye than the ear; e.g. *malitious mind* (I.6.18). And it is quite likely that one function of the alexandrine was as a kind of visual rhythmical feature in the poem. Spenser also makes some use of archaic spellings, usually indicating archaic pronunciations, and of exotic ones, like *mirrhour*, and *whot* (for *hot*).

Archaism, which we may define as 'any linguistic feature with a distinctly old-fashioned flavour at the time' extends to most aspects of Spenser's language. Not all those features which strike us today as archaic were so then of course, and we have to remember that some archaisms, chiefly from Chaucer, had some literary vogue at the time. But the archaic element must not be underestimated, though there are varying degrees of archaism, and much depends also on the frequency of a given feature. Probably the most successful, because noticeable without being too obtrusive, are the *y-* prefix on verbs, and the *-en* ending on the infinitive and pres. pls. Archaic vocabulary ranges from poetic words like *sheen* (adj.), to the more archaic *lenger*, 'longer', *faitour*, etc. Many archaisms of vocabulary seem to be taken from Chaucer, and the question arises how far some at least of these functioned in fact as archaisms. Chaucer was much read at the time, and some words may have seemed simply 'poetic' ones rich in association because of their original Chaucerian contexts.

Dialectalisms, working in a similar way to archaism, should

be mentioned here as helping to give the language a slight, not too great, a strangeness. But it is probably significant that nearly all dialectalisms in *The Faerie Queene* could also be considered as archaisms. Likely examples are the northern *mickle* and *warke*, 'work', which would not have seemed too outlandish. Too much rusticity would have been as much out of place here as it was appropriate in *The Shepheardes Calender*.

Spenser enriched his vocabulary in a variety of other ways. He borrowed and adapted words from other languages, notably from French, such as *amenage*, *portaunce*; from Italian, such as *belgard*, *sdeign*; and from Latin, e.g. *indignant*, *pallid*. He also coined words, chiefly by adding prefixes and suffixes to existing ones; e.g. *aggrace*, *embrave*; *gronefull*, *jolliment*, etc. Most of these new words have a marked literary air; some an exotic, some an archaic one. Spenser used these coinages particularly freely: less common, though frequent enough, are words where, apparently, beginnings and ends have been omitted; e.g. *bout* for *about*; *aband* for *abandon*. But in these latter, as in many other cases, it is difficult to know whether we have to do with archaic survivals (or revivals), or off-the-cuff Spenserian invention. The question is fortunately only of academic importance.

Other types of Spenserian coinage are: the compound adjective, e.g. *sea-shouldring*; words seemingly a blend of two, e.g. *treachetour*, from *treachour* and Middle English (e.g. Chaucerian) *tregetour*. Also unusual uses of existing words, such as *throb* as a noun (from the verb), and such cases as *revoke*, where the sense of 'to calm, subdue' involves a sufficiently marked shift of meaning to qualify here. Particularly interesting in this group are archaic words used in new ('unhistoric') senses; e.g. *chevisaunce*, *dearnly*, etc. Some of these may represent misunderstandings of ME usage, but Spenser's knowledge of the later medieval language was considerable, and in the case of *chevisaunce* at least we have an almost certain example of a conscious—and inspired—shift of meaning from various unexciting senses to 'heroic enterprise'. And in *The Shepheardes Calender* the word is used as a flower name!

A word should be said about adjectives in general in *The Faerie Queene*. Not only is the poem thick-strewn with them, but to a remarkable degree they are divisible into two closely related categories: what we may call the 'pleonastic' adjective, as in *piteous mone* (I.8.36), *waste wildernesse* (II.1.22), which adds little or nothing to the meaning of the noun; and the 'unremarkable' or 'expected' adjective, which includes conventional and general adjectives, such as *beautie bright* (I.6.9), *golden lockes* (I.11.51), *pleasant dale* (II.1.24). Out of context both kinds are apt to seem redundant, flat, trite. But in operation they are transformed, the pleonastic functioning as a kind of firm but unstrident emphasis (and cf. similar effects achieved by other types of repetition, e.g. *secret meanes unseene*, II.1.1); and the others being particularly appropriate to the generalized world of allegory.

As for Spenser's syntax, it was predominantly the syntax of his day. But three features are especially noteworthy: change of normal word-order, sometimes, as in *Him therefore now . . .* (II.1.3) with strongly Latinate effect; sometimes strangely bizarre, as *On which when gazing him the Palmer saw* (II.12.69). Secondly, ellipsis, usually of articles and pronouns, probably not for compression, as in Milton, but to create a strange, and sometimes an archaic effect; e.g. *With holy father sits not with such things to mell* (I.1.30). Thirdly there is imitation of Latin constructions, as in *Found never help, who never would his hurts impart* (I.7.40); *For when the cause of that outrageous deede Demaunded, . . .* (II.4.29); *Which when none yeelded, . . .* (I.3.13). In these and other cases Spenser's contemporaries, like ourselves, would probably have noticed the imitation, and heard like us the noble overtones of classical style.

The eclectic origin of Spenser's diction will now, perhaps, be clear, even from so brief a sketch; and his success in fusing the diverse elements is seen most clearly when we observe how the most complex stanzas can stand close to the most simple and straightforward ones without incongruity.

TABLE OF DATES

(The dates are given in the New Style)

1552?   Birth of Edmund Spenser.
(1558   Accession of Queen Elizabeth.)
1561–1569 At Merchant Taylors' School.
1569   Contributed verse translations to *A Theatre*, J. van der Noodt.
May 1569 Matriculated as sizar of Pembroke Hall, Cambridge.
1573   B.A.
1576   M.A.
1578   Secretary to John Young, Bishop of Rochester.
1579   *The Faerie Queene* probably begun.
         The Shepheardes Calender entered in Stationer's Register.
1580   *The Shepheardes Calender* published.
         Appointed a secretary to the Lord Deputy of Ireland.
         Spenser–Harvey letters published.
         August. Spenser probably goes to Ireland.
         November. Present at the siege and massacre at Smerwick.
(1581   Publication of Tasso's *Gerusalemme Liberata*.)
1583   Appointed one of the Commissioners of Musters in County Kildare.
1586   Takes over the Kilcolman estate, 3,000 acres, in Munster.
(1588   The Armada.)
1589   November. Spenser returns to England temporarily.
1590   *The Faerie Queene*, Books I–III published.
1591   *Complaints, Daphnaida*, published.
         Granted pension of £50 a year for life.

1594   Married Elizabeth Boyle.
1595   *Colin Clouts Come Home Again, Amoretti, Epitha-lamium* published.
1596   *The Faerie Queene*, 2nd edition, adding Books IV–VI, published. *Fowre Hymns* and *Prothalamion* published.
1598   Appointed Sheriff of Cork. Tyrone's rebellion in Munster.
        December. Spenser back in London.
1599   January. Death of Spenser.
1609   Publication of *Two Cantos of Mutabilitie* in the 3rd edition of *F.Q.*
1633   Publication of prose work *A Vewe of the Present State of Ireland* (written about 1596.)

A NOTE ON THE TEXT

THE first three books of *The Faerie Queene* were originally published in quarto in 1590. In 1596 appeared a second edition, with Books IV–VI added. The fragmentary Book VII did not appear until the Folio edition of 1609. The 1590 edition included a list of *Faults Escaped*. The first three books of 1596 were printed from a copy of 1590; some of the *Faults Escaped* were corrected, but a number of new printer's errors were made.

I have followed J. C. Smith, who edited *The Faerie Queene* for O.U.P. in 1909, and based his text, a collation of 1590 and 1596 with a few corrections also from 1609, on 1596 on the grounds that it 'was produced under Spenser's eye and by his authority'. Smith did not hesitate to depart from 1596 wherever he believed it to be in error, and the error the printer's. But the differences between 1590 and 1596 are almost never important: they very rarely convey a different meaning. I also prefer, with him, the 1596 punctuation, which is much less heavy. Smith did not reproduce long s, &, ô, and superscribed m and n (e.g. frõ, whẽ). I have, in addition, given 'v' for 'u' and 'j' for 'i'. The same text was also used in the Oxford Standard Authors edition of Spenser, by J. C. Smith and E. de Selincourt, 1912, etc.

For speed and ease in reading difficult words are glossed at the foot of each page of the text, but also included in the glossary. Where difficult words appear often, they are glossed the first two or three times they appear.

TO
THE MOST HIGH,
MIGHTIE
And
MAGNIFICENT
EMPRESSE RENOVV-
MED FOR PIETIE, VER-
TVE, AND ALL GRATIOVS
GOVERNMENT ELIZABETH BY
THE GRACE OF GOD QVEENE
OF ENGLAND FRAVNCE AND
IRELAND AND OF VIRGI-
NIA, DEFENDOVR OF THE
FAITH, &c. HER MOST
HVMBLE SERVAVNT
EDMVND SPENSER
DOTH IN ALL HV-
MILITIE DEDI-
CATE, PRE-
SENT
AND CONSECRATE THESE
HIS LABOVRS TO LIVE
VVITH THE ETERNI-
TIE OF HER
FAME.

A
Letter of the Authors expounding his
whole intention in the course of this worke: which
for that it giveth great light to the Reader, for
the better understanding is hereunto
annexed.

To the Right noble, and Valorous, Sir Walter Raleigh knight,
Lo. Wardein of the Stanneryes, and her Majesties liefe-
tenaunt of the County of Cornewayll.

*SIr knowing how doubtfully all Allegories may be construed, and this
booke of mine, which I have entituled the Faery Queene, being a con-
tinued Allegory, or darke conceit, I have thought good aswell for
avoyding of gealous opinions and misconstructions, as also for your
better light in reading therof, (being so by you commanded,) to discover
unto you the general intention and meaning, which in the whole course
thereof I have fashioned, without expressing of any particular purposes
or by-accidents therein occasioned. The generall end therefore of all the
booke is to fashion a gentleman or noble person in vertuous and gentle
discipline: Which for that I conceived shoulde be most plausible and
pleasing, being coloured with an historicall fiction, the which the most
part of men delight to read, rather for variety of matter, then for profite
of the ensample: I chose the historye of king Arthure, as most fitte
for the excellency of his person, being made famous by many mens
former workes, and also furthest from the daunger of envy, and sus-
pition of present time. In which I have followed all the antique Poets
historicall, first Homere, who in the Persons of Agamemnon and Ulysses
hath ensampled a good governour and a vertuous man, the one in his
Ilias, the other in his Odysseis: then Virgil, whose like intention was
to doe in the person of Aeneas: after him Ariosto comprised them both*

in his Orlando: and lately Tasso dissevered them againe, and formed both parts in two persons, namely that part which they in Philosophy call Ethice, or vertues of a private man, coloured in his Rinaldo: The other named Politice in his Godfredo. By ensample of which excellente Poets, I labour to pourtraict in Arthure, before he was king, the image of a brave knight, perfected in the twelve private morall vertues, as Aristotle hath devised, the which is the purpose of these first twelve bookes: which if I finde to be well accepted, I may be perhaps encoraged, to frame the other part of pollitike vertues in his person, after that hee came to be king. To some I know this Methode will seeme displeasaunt, which had rather have good discipline delivered plainly in way of precepts, or sermoned at large, as they use, then thus clowdily enwrapped in Allegoricall devises. But such, me seeme, should be satisfide with the use of these dayes, seeing all things accounted by their showes, and nothing esteemed of, that is not delightfull and pleasing to commune sence. For this cause is Xenophon preferred before Plato, for that the one in the exquisite depth of his judgement, formed a Commune welth such as it should be, but the other in the person of Cyrus and the Persians fashioned a governement such as might best be: So much more profitable and gratious is doctrine by ensample, then by rule. So have I laboured to doe in the person of Arthure: whome I conceive after his long education by Timon, to whom he was by Merlin delivered to be brought up, so soone as he was borne of the Lady Igrayne, to have seene in a dream or vision the Faery Queen, with whose excellent beauty ravished, he awaking resolved to seeke her out, and so being by Merlin armed, and by Timon throughly instructed, he went to seeke her forth in Faerye land. In that Faery Queene I meane glory in my generall intention, but in my particular I conceive the most excellent and glorious person of our soveraine the Queene, and her kingdome in Faery land. And yet in some places els, I doe otherwise shadow her. For considering she beareth two persons, the one of a most royall Queene or Empresse, the other of a most vertuous and beautifull Lady, this latter part in some places I doe *expresse in Belphœbe, fashioning her name according to your owne excellent conceipt of Cynthia, (Phœbe and Cynthia being both names of Diana.) So in the person of Prince Arthure I sette forth magnificence in particular, which vertue for that (according to Aristotle and the rest) it is the perfection of all the rest, and conteineth in it them all, therefore in the whole course I mention the deedes of Arthure applyable to that vertue, which I write of in that booke. But of the xii. other vertues, I make xii. other knights the patrones, for the more variety of the history: Of which these three bookes contayn three, The first of the knight of the Redcrosse, in whome I expresse Holynes: The seconde of Sir Guyon, in whome I sette forth Temperaunce: The third of Britomartis a Lady knight, in whome I picture Chastity. But because the beginning of the whole worke seemeth abrupte and as depending upon other antecedents, it needs that ye know the occasion of these three knights severall adventures. For the Methode of a Poet historical is not such, as of an Historiographer. For an Historiographer discourseth of affayres orderly as they were donne, accounting as well the times as the actions, but a Poet thrusteth into the middest, even where it most concerneth him, and there recoursing to the thinges forepaste, and divining of thinges to come, maketh a pleasing Analysis of all. The beginning therefore of my history, if it were to be told by an Historio-grapher, should be the twelfth booke, which is the last, where I devise that the Faery Queene kept her Annuall feaste xii. dayes, uppon which xii. severall dayes, the occasions of the xii. severall adventures hapned, which being undertaken by xii. severall knights, are in these xii books severally handled and discoursed. The first was this. In the beginning of the feast, there presented him selfe a tall clownishe younge man, who falling before the Queen of Faries desired a boone (as the manner then was) which during that feast she might not refuse: which was that hee might have the atchievement of any adventure, which during that feaste should happen, that being graunted, he rested him on the floore, unfitte through his rusticity for a better place. Soone after entred a faire Ladye in mourning weedes, riding on a white Asse, with a*

*dwarfe behind her leading a warlike steed, that bore the Armes of a knight,
and his speare in the dwarfes hand. Shee falling before the Queene of
Faeries, complayned that her father and mother an ancient King and
Queene, had bene by an huge dragon many years shut up in a brasen Castle,
who thence suffred them not to yssew: and therefore besought the Faery
Queene to assygne her some one of her knights to take on him that
exployt. Presently that clownish person upstarting, desired that adventure: whereat the Queene much wondering, and the Lady much gainesay-
ing, yet he earnestly importuned his desire. In the end the Lady told him
that unlesse that armour which she brought, would serve him (that is the
armour of a Christian man specified by Saint Paul v. Ephes.) that he could
not succeed in that enterprise, which being forthwith put upon him with
dewe furnitures thereunto, he seemed the goodliest man in al that
company, and was well liked of the Lady. And eftesoones taking on him
knighthood, and mounting on that straunge Courser, he went forth
with her on that adventure: where beginneth the first booke, vz.*

A gentle knight was pricking on the playne, &c.

*The second day ther came in a Palmer bearing an Infant with
bloody hands, whose Parents he complained to have bene slayn by an
Enchaunteresse called Acrasia: and therfore craved of the Faery Queene,
to appoint him some knight, to performe that adventure, which being
assigned to Sir Guyon, he presently went forth with that same Palmer:
which is the beginning of the second booke and the whole subject thereof.
The third day there came in, a Groome who complained before the
Faery Queene, that a vile Enchaunter called Busirane had in hand a
most faire Lady called Amoretta, whom he kept in most grievous
torment, because she would not yield him the pleasure of her body.
Whereupon Sir Scudamour the lover of that Lady presently tooke
on him that adventure. But being unable to performe it by reason of the
hard Enchauntments, after long sorrow, in the end met with Britomartis,
who succoured him, and reskewed his love.*

*But by occasion hereof, many other adventures are intermedled,
but rather as Accidents, then intendments. As the love of Britomart,*

the overthrow of *Marinell*, the misery of *Florimell*, the *vertuousnes
of Belphœbe*, the lasciviousnes of *Hellenora*, and many the like.

Thus much Sir, I have briefly overronne to direct your understanding
to the wel-head of the History, that from thence gathering the whole
intention of the conceit, ye may as in a handfull gripe al the discourse,
which otherwise may happily seeme tedious and confused. So humbly
craving the continuaunce of your honorable favour towards me, and
th'eternall establishment of your happines, I humbly take leave.

23. *January*. 1589.

Yours most humbly affectionate.
Ed. Spenser.

THE FIRST

BOOKE OF THE

FAERIE QUEENE.

Contayning,

THE LEGENDE OF THE
KNIGHT OF THE RED CROSSE.

OR

Of Holinesse.

1   Lo I the man, whose Muse whilome did maske,
      As time her taught, in lowly Shepheards weeds,
      Am now enforst a far unfitter taske,
      For trumpets sterne to chaunge mine Oaten reeds,
      And sing of Knights and Ladies gentle deeds;
      Whose prayses having slept in silence long,
      Me, all too meane, the sacred Muse areeds
      To blazon broad emongst her learned throng:
   Fierce warres and faithfull loves shall moralize my song.

---

1. *whilome*: formerly. *weeds*: garments. *gentle*: noble. *meane*: lowly. *areeds*: (here) commands. *broad*: abroad.

2   Helpe then, O holy Virgin chiefe of nine,
        Thy weaker Novice to performe thy will,
        Lay forth out of thine everlasting scryne
        The antique rolles, which there lye hidden still,
        Of Faerie knights and fairest *Tanaquill,*
        Whom that most noble Briton Prince so long
        Sought through the world, and suffered so much ill,
        That I must rue his undeserved wrong:
    O helpe thou my weake wit, and sharpen my dull tong.

3   And thou most dreaded impe of highest *Jove,*
        Faire *Venus* sonne, that with thy cruell dart
        At that good knight so cunningly didst rove,
        That glorious fire it kindled in his hart,
        Lay now thy deadly Heben bow apart,
        And with thy mother milde come to mine ayde:
        Come both, and with you bring triumphant *Mart,*
        In loves and gentle jollities arrayd,
    After his murdrous spoiles and bloudy rage allayd.

4   And with them eke, O Goddesse heavenly bright,
        Mirrour of grace and Majestie divine,
        Great Lady of the greatest Isle, whose light
        Like *Phœbus* lampe throughout the world doth shine,
        Shed thy faire beames into my feeble eyne,
        And raise my thoughts too humble and too vile,
        To thinke of that true glorious type of thine,
        The argument of mine afflicted stile:
    The which to heare, vouchsafe, O dearest dred a-while.

2. *weaker*: too weak (see note).   *scryne*: chest, box for valuables.   *wit*: mind, intelligence.   *tong*: tongue.

3. *impe*: child (see note).   *rove*: shoot at.   *Heben*: ebony.   *Mart*: Mars (see note).

4. *eke*: also.   *eyne*: eyes.   *type*: see note.   *argument*: subject.   *afflicted*: low, humble.   *dred*: object of reverence, (here) Goddess.

Canto 1

The Patron of true Holinesse,
Foule Errour doth defeate:
Hypocrisie him to entrappe,
Doth to his home entreate.

1 A Gentle Knight was pricking on the plaine,   A
    Y cladd in mightie armes and silver shielde,   B
    Wherein old dints of deepe wounds did remaine, A
    The cruell markes of many' a bloudy fielde;   B
    Yet armes till that time did he never wield: B
    His angry steede did chide his foming bitt,   C
    As much disdayning to the curbe to yield: B
    Full jolly knight he seemd, and faire did sitt,   C
As one for knightly giusts and fierce encounters fitt. C

2 But on his brest a bloudie Crosse he bore,   A
    The deare remembrance of his dying Lord,   B
    For whose sweete sake that glorious badge he wore, A
    And dead as living ever him ador'd: B
    Upon his shield the like was also scor'd,   B
    For soveraine hope, which in his helpe he had: C
    Right faithfull true he was in deede and word, B
    But of his cheere did seeme too solemne sad;   C
Yet nothing did he dread, but ever was ydrad.   C

---

1. *Gentle*: noble and chivalrous. *pricking*: riding, spurring. *Y cladd*: clad (see Glossary under *y-*). *disdayning*: disliking. *jolly:* handsome. *giusts*: jousts.
2. *soveraine hope*: see note. *cheere*: countenance. *sad*: (here) serious. *ydrad*: feared, dreaded (see Glossary under *y-*).

3   Upon a great adventure he was bond,
        That greatest *Gloriana* to him gave,
        That greatest Glorious Queene of *Faerie* lond,
        To winne him worship, and her grace to have,
        Which of all earthly things he most did crave;
        And ever as he rode, his hart did earne
        To prove his puissance in battell brave
        Upon his foe, and his new force to learne;
    Upon his foe, a Dragon horrible and stearne.

4   A lovely Ladie rode him faire beside,
        Upon a lowly Asse more white then snow,
        Yet she much whiter, but the same did hide
        Under a vele, that wimpled was full low,
        And over all a blacke stole she did throw,
        As one that inly mournd: so was she sad,
        And heavie sat upon her palfrey slow:
        Seemed in heart some hidden care she had,
    And by her in a line a milke white lambe she lad.

5   So pure an innocent, as that same lambe,
        She was in life and every vertuous lore,
        And by descent from Royall lynage came
        Of ancient Kings and Queenes, that had of yore
        Their scepters stretcht from East to Westerne shore,
        And all the world in their subjection held;
        Till that infernall feend with foule uprore
        Forwasted all their land, and them expeld:
    Whom to avenge, she had this Knight from far compeld.

   3. *bond*: bound.   *worship*: honour.   *earne*: yearn.   *puissance*: strength, prowess.
stearne: grim, fierce.
   4. *then*: (here) than.   *vele*: veil.   *stole*: robe.   *inly*: inwardly.   *palfrey*: saddle-
horse (see glossary).
   5. *lynage*: lineage.   *uprore*: rebellion.   *Forwasted*: laid waste.

6   Behind her farre away a Dwarfe did lag,
    That lasie seemd in being ever last,
    Or wearied with bearing of her bag
    Of needments at his backe. Thus as they past,
    The day with cloudes was suddeine overcast,
    And angry *Jove* an hideous storme of raine
    Did poure into his Lemans lap so fast,
    That every wight to shrowd it did constrain,
And this faire couple eke to shroud themselves were fain.

7   Enforst to seeke some covert nigh at hand,
    A shadie grove not far away they spide,
    That promist ayde the tempest to withstand:
    Whose loftie trees yclad with sommers pride,
    Did spred so broad, that heavens light did hide,
    Not perceable with power of any starre:
    And all within were pathes and alleies wide,
    With footing worne, and leading inward farre:
Faire harbour that them seemes; so in they entred arre.

8   And foorth they passe, with pleasure forward led,
    Joying to heare the birdes sweete harmony,
    Which therein shrouded from the tempest dred,
    Seemd in their song to scorne the cruell sky.
    Much can they prayse the trees so straight and hy,
    The sayling Pine, the Cedar proud and tall,
    The vine-prop Elme, the Poplar never dry,
    The builder Oake, sole king of forrests all,
The Aspine good for staves, the Cypresse funerall.

---

6. *Lemans*: Lover's. *wight*: creature. ***shrowd***: *shroud*: shelter. *fain*: glad.
8. *can*: began (to).

9   The Laurell, meed of mightie Conquerors
         And Poets sage, the Firre that weepeth still,
         The Willow worne of forlorne Paramours,
         The Eugh obedient to the benders will,
         The Birch for shaftes, the Sallow for the mill,
         The Mirrhe sweete bleeding in the bitter wound,
         The warlike Beech, the Ash for nothing ill,
         The fruitfull Olive, and the Platane round,
     The carver Holme, the Maple seeldom inward sound.

10   Led with delight, they thus beguile the way,
         Untill the blustring storme is overblowne;
         When weening to returne, whence they did stray,
         They cannot finde that path, which first was showne,
         But wander too and fro in wayes unknowne,
         Furthest from end then, when they neerest weene,
         That makes them doubt, their wits be not their owne:
         So many pathes, so many turnings seene,
     That which of them to take, in diverse doubt they been.

11   At last resolving forward still to fare,
         Till that some end they finde or in or out,
         That path they take, that beaten seemd most bare,
         And like to lead the labyrinth about;
         Which when by tract they hunted had throughout,
         At length it brought them to a hollow cave,
         Amid the thickest woods. The Champion stout
         Eftsoones dismounted from his courser brave,
     And to the Dwarfe a while his needlesse spere he gave.

9. *meed*: reward. *Eugh*: yew. *Sallow*: kind of willow. *Platane*: plane-tree.
Holme: holm-oak.
   10. *weening*: thinking, intending.
   11. *or . . . or*: either . . . or. *tract*: track. *Eftsoones*: soon after, forthwith.

12   Be well aware, quoth then that Ladie milde,
      Least suddaine mischiefe ye too rash provoke:
      The danger hid, the place unknowne and wilde,
      Breedes dreadfull doubts: Oft fire is without smoke,
      And perill without show: therefore your stroke
      Sir knight with-hold, till further triall made.
      Ah Ladie (said he) shame were to revoke
      The forward footing for an hidden shade:
  Vertue gives her selfe light, through darkenesse for to wade.

13   Yea but (quoth she) the perill of this place
      I better wot then you, though now too late
      To wish you backe returne with foule disgrace,
      Yet wisedome warnes, whilest foot is in the gate,
      To stay the steppe, ere forced to retrate.
      This is the wandring wood, this *Errours den*,
      A monster vile, whom God and man does hate:
      Therefore I read beware. Fly fly (quoth then
  The fearefull Dwarfe:) this is no place for living men.

14   But full of fire and greedy hardiment,
      The youthfull knight could not for ought be staide,
      But forth unto the darksome hole he went,
      And looked in: his glistring armor made
      A litle glooming light, much like a shade,
      By which he saw the ugly monster plaine,
      Halfe like a serpent horribly displaide,
      But th'other halfe did womans shape retaine,
  Most lothsom, filthie, foule, and full of vile disdaine.

12. *Least*: lest.   *revoke*: see note.   *wade*: go.
13. *wot*: know.   *then*: (here) than.   *gate*: (here) way.   *retrate*: retreat.   *read*: advise.   *fearefull*: full of fear, frightened.
14. *greedy hardiment*: eager courage.   *disdaine*: (here) loathsomeness.

15 And as she lay upon the durtie ground,
　　Her huge long taile her den all overspred,
　　Yet was in knots and many boughtes upwound,
　　Pointed with mortall sting. Of her there bred
　　A thousand yong ones, which she dayly fed,
　　Sucking upon her poisonous dugs, eachone
　　Of sundry shapes, yet all ill favored:
　　Soone as that uncouth light upon them shone,
Into her mouth they crept, and suddain all were gone.

16 Their dam upstart, out of her den effraide,
　　And rushed forth, hurling her hideous taile
　　About her cursed head, whose folds displaid
　　Were stretcht now forth at length without entraile.
　　She lookt about, and seeing one in mayle
　　Armed to point, sought backe to turne againe;
　　For light she hated as the deadly bale,
　　Ay wont in desert darknesse to remaine,
Where plaine none might her see, nor she see any plaine.

17 Which when the valiant Elfe perceiv'd, he lept
　　As Lyon fierce upon the flying pray,
　　And with his trenchand blade her boldly kept
　　From turning backe, and forced her to stay:
　　Therewith enrag'd she loudly gan to bray,
　　And turning fierce, her speckled taile advaunst,
　　Threatning her angry sting, him to dismay:
　　Who nought aghast, his mightie hand enhaunst:
The stroke down from her head unto her shoulder glaunst.

15. *boughtes*: folds. *dugs*: breasts. *ill favored*: evil-looking (but see glossary). *uncouth*: unusual, strange.
16. *upstart*: leapt up. *effraide*: scared, frightened. *displaid*: extended. *entraile*: fold, coil. *Armed to point*: fully armed. *bale*: mischief, trouble. *Ay*: ever. *wont*: accustomed.
17. *Elfe*: see note. *trenchand*: sharp. *gan*: began. *enhaunst*: raised.

18 Much daunted with that dint, her sence was dazd,
       Yet kindling rage, her selfe she gathered round,
       And all attonce her beastly body raizd
       With doubled forces high above the ground:
       Tho wrapping up her wrethed sterne arownd,
       Lept fierce upon his shield, and her huge traine
       All suddenly about his body wound,
       That hand or foot to stirre he strove in vaine:
    God helpe the man so wrapt in *Errours* endlesse traine.

19 His Lady sad to see his sore constraint,
       Cride out, Now now Sir knight, shew what ye bee,
       Add faith unto your force, and be not faint:
       Strangle her, else she sure will strangle thee.
       That when he heard, in great perplexitie,
       His gall did grate for griefe and high disdaine,
       And knitting all his force got one hand free,
       Wherewith he grypt her gorge with so great paine,
    That soone to loose her wicked bands did her constraine.

20 Therewith she spewd out of her filthy maw
       A floud of poyson horrible and blacke,
       Full of great lumpes of flesh and gobbets raw,
       Which stunck so vildly, that it forst him slacke
       His grasping hold, and from her turne him backe:
       Her vomit full of bookes and papers was,
       With loathly frogs and toades, which eyes did lacke,
       And creeping sought way in the weedy gras:
    Her filthy parbreake all the place defiled has.

18. *Tho*: then. *traine*: tail.
19. *gall*: see note. *grate*: fret. *griefe*: pain. *disdaine*: angry indignation.
20. *gobbets*: lumps of flesh. *vildly*: vilely. *parbreake*: vomiting.

21 As when old father *Nilus* gins to swell
       With timely pride above the *Aegyptian* vale,
       His fattie waves do fertile slime outwell,
       And overflow each plaine and lowly dale:
       But when his later spring gins to avale,
       Huge heapes of mudd he leaves, wherein there breed
       Ten thousand kindes of creatures, partly male
       And partly female of his fruitfull seed;
    Such ugly monstrous shapes elsewhere may no man reed.

22 The same so sore annoyed has the knight,
       That welnigh choked with the deadly stinke,
       His forces faile, ne can no longer fight.
       Whose corage when the feend perceiv'd to shrinke,
       She poured forth out of her hellish sinke
       Her fruitfull cursed spawne of serpents small,
       Deformed monsters, fowle, and blacke as inke,
       Which swarming all about his legs did crall,
    And him encombred sore, but could not hurt at all.

23 As gentle Shepheard in sweete even-tide,
       When ruddy *Phœbus* gins to welke in west,
       High on an hill, his flocke to vewen wide,
       Markes which do byte their hasty supper best;
       A cloud of combrous gnattes do him molest,
       All striving to infixe their feeble stings,
       That from their noyance he no where can rest,
       But with his clownish hands their tender wings
    He brusheth oft, and oft doth mar their murmurings.

21. *gins*: begins.   *fattie*: rich, fertilizing.   *outwell*: pour forth.   *avale*: droop,
decline.   *reed*: see, perceive.
22. *ne*: nor.
23. *welke*: fade, grow dim.   *noyance*: annoyance.

24 Thus ill bestedd, and fearefull more of shame,
    Then of the certaine perill he stood in,
    Halfe furious unto his foe he came,
    Resolv'd in minde all suddenly to win,
    Or soone to lose, before he once would lin;
    And strooke at her with more then manly force,
    That from her body full of filthie sin
    He raft her hatefull head without remorse;
A streame of cole black bloud forth gushed from her corse.

25 Her scattred brood, soone as their Parent deare
    They saw so rudely falling to the ground,
    Groning full deadly, all with troublous feare,
    Gathred themselves about her body round,
    Weening their wonted entrance to have found
    At her wide mouth: but being there withstood
    They flocked all about her bleeding wound,
    And sucked up their dying mothers blood,
Making her death their life, and eke her hurt their good.

26 That detestable sight him much amazde,
    To see th'unkindly Impes of heaven accurst,
    Devoure their dam; on whom while so he gazd,
    Having all satisfide their bloudy thurst,
    Their bellies swolne he saw with fulnesse burst,
    And bowels gushing forth: well worthy end
    Of such as drunke her life, the which them nurst;
    Now needeth him no lenger labour spend,
His foes have slaine themselves, with whom he should
    contend.

24. *bestedd*: situated. *lin*: cease. *raft*: took away. *corse*: body.
25. *rudely*: roughly, heavily. *Weening*: thinking, intending. *eke*: also.
26. *unkindly*: see note. *Impes*: children, offspring. *lenger*: longer.

27 His Ladie seeing all, that chaunst, from farre
    Approcht in hast to greet his victorie,
    And said, Faire knight, borne under happy starre,
    Who see your vanquisht foes before you lye;
    Well worthy be you of that Armorie,
    Wherein ye have great glory wonne this day,
    And proov'd your strength on a strong enimie,
    Your first adventure: many such I pray,
And henceforth ever wish, that like succeed it may.

28 Then mounted he upon his Steede againe,
    And with the Lady backward sought to wend;
    That path he kept, which beaten was most plaine,
    Ne ever would to any by-way bend,
    But still did follow one unto the end,
    The which at last out of the wood them brought.
    So forward on his way (with God to frend)
    He passed forth, and new adventure sought;
Long way he travelled, before he heard of ought.

29 At length they chaunst to meet upon the way
    An aged Sire, in long blacke weedes yclad,
    His feete all bare, his beard all hoarie gray,
    And by his belt his booke he hanging had;
    Sober he seemde, and very sagely sad,
    And to the ground his eyes were lowly bent,
    Simple in shew, and voyde of malice bad,
    And all the way he prayed, as he went,
And often knockt his brest, as one that did repent.

---

27. *Armorie*: armour (see note).   28. *ne*: nor. *to frend*: as a friend.
29. *weedes*: garments.

30 He faire the knight saluted, louting low,
        Who faire him quited, as that courteous was:
        And after asked him, if he did know
        Of straunge adventures, which abroad did pas.
        Ah my deare Sonne (quoth he) how should, alas,
        Silly old man, that lives in hidden cell,
        Bidding his beades all day for his trespas,
        Tydings of warre and worldly trouble tell?
    With holy father sits not with such things to mell.

31 But if of daunger which hereby doth dwell,
        And homebred evill ye desire to heare,
        Of a straunge man I can you tidings tell,
        That wasteth all this countrey farre and neare.
        Of such (said he) I chiefly do inquere,
        And shall you well reward to shew the place,
        In which that wicked wight his dayes doth weare:
        For to all knighthood it is foule disgrace,
    That such a cursed creature lives so long a space.

32 Far hence (quoth he) in wastfull wildernesse
        His dwelling is, by which no living wight
        May ever passe, but thorough great distresse.
        Now (sayd the Lady) draweth toward night,
        And well I wote, that of your later fight
        Ye all forwearied be: for what so strong,
        But wanting rest will also want of might?
        The Sunne that measures heaven all day long,
    At night doth baite his steedes the *Ocean* waves emong.

30. *louting*: bowing. *quited*: (here) responded. *Silly*: simple, innocent.
Bidding his beades: saying his prayers. *sits not*: is not suitable, fitting. *mell*:
meddle.

31. *wight*: creature. *weare*: spend, pass.

32. *wastfull*: wild, like a waste. *thorough*: through. *wote*: know. *forwearied*:
exhausted. *baite*: feed, refresh.

33   Then with the Sunne take Sir, your timely rest,
      And with new day new worke at once begin:
      Untroubled night they say gives counsell best.
      Right well Sir knight ye have advised bin,
      (Quoth then that aged man;) the way to win
      Is wisely to advise: now day is spent;
      Therefore with me ye may take up your In
      For this same night. The knight was well content:
  So with that godly father to his home they went.

34   A little lowly Hermitage it was,
      Downe in a dale, hard by a forests side,
      Far from resort of people, that did pas
      In travell to and froe: a little wyde
      There was an holy Chappell edifyde,
      Wherein the Hermite dewly wont to say
      His holy things each morne and eventyde:
      Thereby a Christall streame did gently play,
  Which from a sacred fountaine welled forth alway.

35   Arrived there, the little house they fill,
      Ne looke for entertainement, where none was:
      Rest is their feast, and all things at their will;
      The noblest mind the best contentment has.
      With faire discourse the evening so they pas:
      For that old man of pleasing wordes had store,
      And well could file his tongue as smooth as glas;
      He told of Saintes and Popes, and evermore
  He strowd an *Ave-Mary* after and before.

---

33. *advise*: consider, reflect.   *In*: lodging.
34. *edifyde*: built.   *wont*: was accustomed.
35. *file*: polish, smoothe.

36 The drouping Night thus creepeth on them fast,
      And the sad humour loading their eye liddes,
      As messenger of *Morpheus* on them cast
      Sweet slombring deaw, the which to sleepe them biddes.
      Unto their lodgings then his guestes he riddes:
      Where when all drownd in deadly sleepe he findes,
      He to his study goes, and there amiddes
      His Magick bookes and artes of sundry kindes,
    He seekes out mighty charmes, to trouble sleepy mindes.

37 Then choosing out few wordes most horrible,
      (Let none them read) thereof did verses frame,
      With which and other spelles like terrible,
      He bad awake blacke *Plutoes* griesly Dame,
      And cursed heaven, and spake reprochfull shame
      Of highest God, the Lord of life and light;
      A bold bad man, that dar'd to call by name
      Great *Gorgon*, Prince of darknesse and dead night,
    At which *Cocytus* quakes, and *Styx* is put to flight.

38 And forth he cald out of deepe darknesse dred
      Legions of Sprights, the which like little flyes
      Fluttring about his ever damned hed,
      A-waite whereto their service he applyes,
      To aide his friends, or fray his enimies:
      Of those he chose out two, the falsest twoo,
      And fittest for to forge true-seeming lyes;
      The one of them he gave a message too,
    The other by him selfe staide other worke to doo.

---

36. *sad*: (here) heavy.   *humour*: moisture.   *deaw*: dew.   *riddes*: sends away.
amiddes: amidst.
      37. *griesly*: terrible.   38. *Sprights*: spirits.   *fray*: frighten.
EFQ

39   He making speedy way through spersed ayre,
        And through the world of waters wide and deepe,
        To *Morpheus* house doth hastily repaire.
        Amid the bowels of the earth full steepe,
        And low, where dawning day doth never peepe,
        His dwelling is; there *Tethys* his wet bed
        Doth ever wash, and *Cynthia* still doth steepe
        In silver deaw his ever-drouping hed,
  Whiles sad Night over him her mantle black doth spred.

40   Whose double gates he findeth locked fast,
        The one faire fram'd of burnisht Yvory,
        The other all with silver overcast;
        And wakefull dogges before them farre do lye,
        Watching to banish Care their enimy,
        Who oft is wont to trouble gentle Sleepe.
        By them the Sprite doth passe in quietly,
        And unto *Morpheus* comes, whom drowned deepe
  In drowsie fit he findes: of nothing he takes keepe.

41   And more, to lulle him in his slumber soft,
        A trickling streame from high rocke tumbling downe
        And ever-drizling raine upon the loft,
        Mixt with a murmuring winde, much like the sowne
        Of swarming Bees, did cast him in a swowne:
        No other noyse, nor peoples troublous cryes,
        As still are wont t'annoy the walled towne,
        Might there be heard: but carelesse Quiet lyes,
  Wrapt in eternall silence farre from enemyes.

39. *spersed*: dispersed.   *repaire*: make (his) way.   *deaw*: dew.
40. *takes keepe*: takes heed.
41. *upon the loft*: in the air.   *sowne*: sound.   *swowne*: swoon.   *carelesse*: free from care.

42   The messenger approching to him spake,
       But his wast wordes returnd to him in vaine:
       So sound he slept, that nought mought him awake.
       Then rudely he him thrust, and pusht with paine,
       Whereat he gan to stretch: but he againe
       Shooke him so hard, that forced him to speake.
       As one then in a dreame, whose dryer braine
       Is tost with troubled sights and fancies weake,
     He mumbled soft, but would not all his silence breake.

43   The Sprite then gan more boldly him to wake,
       And threatned unto him the dreaded name
       Of *Hecate*: whereat he gan to quake,
       And lifting up his lumpish head, with blame
       Halfe angry asked him, for what he came.
       Hither (quoth he) me *Archimago* sent,
       He that the stubborne Sprites can wisely tame,
       He bids thee to him send for his intent
     A fit false dreame, that can delude the sleepers sent.

44   The God obayde, and calling forth straight way
       A diverse dreame out of his prison darke,
       Delivered it to him, and down did lay
       His heavie head, devoide of carefull carke,
       Whose sences all were straight benumbd and starke.
       He backe returning by the Yvorie dore,
       Remounted up as light as chearefull Larke,
       And on his litle winges the dreame he bore
     In hast unto his Lord, where he him left afore.

42. *mought*: could.   *rudely*: roughly.   *tost*: troubled.
43. *gan*: began.   *sent*: perception, senses.
44. *diverse*: ?diverting (see note).   *carefull carke*: sorrowful grief.   *starke*: rigid, unfeeling.

45 Who all this while with charmes and hidden artes,
    Had made a Lady of that other Spright,
    And fram'd of liquid ayre her tender partes
    So lively, and so like in all mens sight,
    That weaker sence it could have ravisht quight:
    The maker selfe for all his wondrous witt,
    Was nigh beguiled with so goodly sight:
    Her all in white he clad, and over it
Cast a blacke stole, most like to seeme for *Una* fit.

46 Now when that ydle dreame was to him brought,
    Unto that Elfin knight he bad him fly,
    Where he slept soundly void of evill thought,
    And with false shewes abuse his fantasy,
    In sort as he him schooled privily:
    And that new creature borne without her dew,
    Full of the makers guile, with usage sly
    He taught to imitate that Lady trew,
Whose semblance she did carrie under feigned hew.

47 Thus well instructed, to their worke they hast,
    And comming where the knight in slomber lay,
    The one upon his hardy head him plast,
    And made him dreame of loves and lustfull play,
    That nigh his manly hart did melt away,
    Bathed in wanton blis and wicked joy:
    Then seemed him his Lady by him lay,
    And to him playnd, how that false winged boy
Her chast hart had subdewd, to learne Dame pleasures toy.

45. *lively*: life-like. *witt*: ability. *stole*: robe.
46. *ydle*: vain, empty. *Elfin*: see Glossary. *In sort as*: in the way that. *hew*: appearance.
47. *playnd*: complained. *toy*: amorous play.

48 And she her selfe of beautie soveraigne Queene,
      Faire *Venus* seemde unto his bed to bring
      Her, whom he waking evermore did weene
      To be the chastest flowre, that ay did spring
      On earthly braunch, the daughter of a king,
      Now a loose Leman to vile service bound:
      And eke the *Graces* seemed all to sing,
      Hymen iô Hymen, dauncing all around,
  Whilst freshest *Flora* her with Yvie girlond crownd.

49 In this great passion of unwonted lust,
      Or wonted feare of doing ought amis,
      He started up, as seeming to mistrust
      Some secret ill, or hidden foe of his:
      Loe there before his face his Lady is,
      Under blake stole hyding her bayted hooke,
      And as halfe blushing offred him to kis,
      With gentle blandishment and lovely looke,
  Most like that virgin true, which for her knight him took.

50 All cleane dismayd to see so uncouth sight,
      And halfe enraged at her shamelesse guise,
      He thought have slaine her in his fierce despight:
      But hasty heat tempring with sufferance wise,
      He stayde his hand, and gan himselfe advise
      To prove his sense, and tempt her faigned truth.
      Wringing her hands in wemens pitteous wise,
      Tho can she weepe, to stirre up gentle ruth,
  Both for her noble bloud, and for her tender youth.

---

48. *ay*: ever.   *Leman*: (here) loose woman.   *girlond*: garland.
50. *uncouth*: strange.   *despight*: anger.   *prove*; *tempt*: test.   *Tho*: then. *can*: began.   *ruth*: pity.

51 And said, Ah Sir, my liege Lord and my love,
        Shall I accuse the hidden cruell fate,
        And mightie causes wrought in heaven above,
        Or the blind God, that doth me thus amate,
        For hoped love to winne me certaine hate?
        Yet thus perforce he bids me do, or die.
        Die is my dew: yet rew my wretched state
        You, whom my hard avenging destinie
    Hath made judge of my life or death indifferently.

52 Your owne deare sake forst me at first to leave
        My Fathers kingdome, There she stopt with teares;
        Her swollen hart her speach seemd to bereave,
        And then againe begun, My weaker years
        Captiv'd to fortune and frayle worldly feares,
        Fly to your faith for succour and sure ayde:
        Let me not dye in languor and long teares.
        Why Dame (quoth he) what hath ye thus dismayd?
    What frayes ye, that were wont to comfort me affrayd?

53 Love of your selfe, she said, and deare constraint
        Lets me not sleepe, but wast the wearie night
        In secret anguish and unpittied plaint,
        Whiles you in carelesse sleepe are drowned quight.
        Her doubtfull words made that redoubted knight
        Suspect her truth: yet since no' untruth he knew,
        Her fawning love with foule disdainefull spight
        He would not shend, but said, Deare dame I rew,
    That for my sake unknowne such griefe unto you grew.

51. *amate*: subdue.   52. *languor*: sorrow.   *frayes*: frightens.
53. *disdainefull*: angry.   *shend*: (here) reproach.

54 Assure your selfe, it fell not all to ground;
   For all so deare as life is to my hart,
   I deeme your love, and hold me to you bound;
   Ne let vaine feares procure your needlesse smart,
   Where cause is none, but to your rest depart.
   Not all content, yet seemd she to appease
   Her mournefull plaintes, beguiled of her art,
   And fed with words, that could not chuse but please,
So slyding softly forth, she turnd as to her ease.

55 Long after lay he musing at her mood,
   Much griev'd to thinke that gentle Dame so light,
   For whose defence he was to shed his blood.
   At last dull wearinesse of former fight
   Having yrockt a sleepe his irkesome spright,
   That troublous dreame gan freshly tosse his braine,
   With bowres, and beds, and Ladies deare delight:
   But when he saw his labour all was vaine,
With that misformed spright he backe returnd againe.

Canto 2

The guilefull great Enchaunter parts
The Redcrosse Knight from Truth:
Into whose stead faire falshood steps,
And works him wofull ruth.

54. *all so*: just as. *appease*: cease.
55. *light*: wanton. *irkesome*: tired. *spright*: spirit. *tosse*: agitate, trouble.
Argument. *ruth*: (here) pitiable situation.

1   By this the Northerne wagoner had set
      His sevenfold teme behind the stedfast starre,
      That was in Ocean waves yet never wet,
      But firme is fixt, and sendeth light from farre
      To all, that in the wide deepe wandring arre:
      And chearefull Chaunticlere with his note shrill
      Had warned once, that *Phœbus* fiery carre
      In hast was climbing up the Easterne hill,
  Full envious that night so long his roome did fill.

2   When those accursed messengers of hell,
      That feigning dreame, and that faire-forged Spright
      Came to their wicked maister, and gan tell
      Their bootelesse paines, and ill succeeding night:
      Who all in rage to see his skilfull might
      Deluded so, gan threaten hellish paine
      And sad *Proserpines* wrath, them to affright.
      But when he saw his threatning was but vaine,
  He cast about, and searcht his balefull bookes againe.

3   Eftsoones he tooke that miscreated faire,
      And that false other Spright, on whom he spred
      A seeming body of the subtile aire,
      Like a young Squire, in loves and lusty-hed
      His wanton dayes that ever loosely led,
      Without regard of armes and dreaded fight:
      Those two he tooke, and in a secret bed,
      Covered with darknesse and misdeeming night,
  Them both together laid, to joy in vaine delight.

---

1. *Chaunticlere*: see note.   *carre*: chariot (see note).   *roome*: place.
2. *bootelesse*: unavailing.   *Deluded*: frustrated.   *balefull*: pernicious.
3. *Eftsoones*: soon after, forthwith.   *misdeeming*: misjudging.   *joy*: take joy (in).

4 Forthwith he runnes with feigned faithfull hast
    Unto his guest, who after troublous sights
    And dreames, gan now to take more sound repast,
    Whom suddenly he wakes with fearefull frights,
    As one aghast with feends or damned sprights,
    And to him cals, Rise rise unhappy Swaine,
    That here wex old in sleepe, whiles wicked wights
    Have knit themselves in *Venus* shamefull chaine;
Come see, where your false Lady doth her honour staine.

5 All in amaze he suddenly up start
    With sword in hand, and with the old man went;
    Who soone him brought into a secret part,
    Where that false couple were full closely ment
    In wanton lust and lewd embracement:
    Which when he saw, he burnt with gealous fire,
    The eye of reason was with rage yblent,
    And would have slaine them in his furious ire,
But hardly was restreined of that aged sire.

6 Returning to his bed in torment great,
    And bitter anguish of his guiltie sight,
    He could not rest, but did his stout heart eat,
    And wast his inward gall with deepe despight,
    Irkesome of life, and too long lingring night.
    At last faire *Hesperus* in highest skie
    Had spent his lampe, and brought forth dawning light
    Then up he rose, and clad him hastily;
The Dwarfe him brought his steed: so both away do fly.

4. *Swaine*: young man.   *wex*: grow.   *wights*: creatures, persons.
5. *up start*: leapt up.   *ment*: joined.   *yblent*: blinded.
6. *despight*: anger, hostility.   *Irkesome*: tired.

7   Now when the rosy-fingred Morning faire,
         Weary of aged *Tithones* saffron bed,
         Had spred her purple robe through deawy aire,
         And the high hils *Titan* discovered,
         The royall virgin shooke off drowsy-hed,
         And rising forth out of her baser bowre,
         Lookt for her knight, who far away was fled,
         And for her Dwarfe, that wont to wait each houre;
     Then gan she waile and weepe, to see that woefull stowre.

8   And after him she rode with so much speede
         As her slow beast could make; but all in vaine:
         For him so far had borne his light-foot steede,
         Pricked with wrath and fiery fierce disdaine,
         That him to follow was but fruitlesse paine;
         Yet she her weary limbes would never rest,
         But every hill and dale, each wood and plaine
         Did search, sore grieved in her gentle brest,
     He so ungently left her, whom she loved best.

9   But subtill *Archimago*, when his guests
         He saw divided into double parts,
         And *Una* wandring in woods and forrests,
         Th'end of his drift, he praisd his divelish arts,
         That had such might over true meaning harts;
         Yet rests not so, but other meanes doth make,
         How he may worke unto her further smarts:
         For her he hated as the hissing snake,
     And in her many troubles did most pleasure take.

7. *deawy*: dewy.   *stowre*: time of stress.
8. *Pricked*: spurred.   *disdaine*: angry indignation.
9. *drift*: aim, intention.

10   He then devisde himselfe how to disguise;
      For by his mightie science he could take
      As many formes and shapes in seeming wise,
      As ever *Proteus* to himselfe could make:
      Sometime a fowle, sometime a fish in lake,
      Now like a foxe, now like a dragon fell,
      That of himselfe he oft for feare would quake,
      And oft would flie away. O who can tell
  The hidden power of herbes, and might of Magicke spell?

11   But now seemde best, the person to put on
      Of that good knight, his late beguiled guest:
      In mighty armes he was yclad anon,
      And silver shield: upon his coward brest
      A bloudy crosse, and on his craven crest
      A bounch of haires discolourd diversly:
      Full jolly knight he seemde, and well addrest,
      And when he sate upon his courser free,
  Saint George himself ye would have deemed him to be.

12   But he the knight, whose semblaunt he did beare,
      The true *Saint George* was wandred far away,
      Still flying from his thoughts and gealous feare;
      Will was his guide, and griefe led him astray.
      At last him chaunst to meete upon the way
      A faithlesse Sarazin all arm'd to point,
      In whose great shield was writ with letters gay
      Sans foy: full large of limbe and every joint
  He was, and cared not for God or man a point.

10. *fell*: fierce.
11. *bounch*: bunch, cluster.   *jolly*: handsome, excellent.   *addrest*: dressed, fitted out.   *free*: noble.
12. *semblaunt*: semblance.   *arm'd to point*: fully armed.

13   He had a faire companion of his way,
        A goodly Lady clad in scarlot red,
        Purfled with gold and pearle of rich assay,
        And like a *Persian* mitre on her hed
        She wore, with crownes and owches garnished,
        The which her lavish lovers to her gave;
        Her wanton palfrey all was overspred
        With tinsell trappings, woven like a wave,
     Whose bridle rung with golden bels and bosses brave.

14   With faire disport and courting dalliaunce
        She intertainde her lover all the way:
        But when she saw the knight his speare advaunce,
        She soone left off her mirth and wanton play,
        And bad her knight addresse him to the fray:
        His foe was nigh at hand. He prickt with pride
        And hope to winne his Ladies heart that day,
        Forth spurred fast: adowne his coursers side
     The red bloud trickling staind the way, as he did ride.

15   The knight of the *Redcrosse* when him he spide,
        Spurring so hote with rage dispiteous,
        Gan fairely couch his speare, and towards ride:
        Soone meete they both, both fell and furious,
        That daunted with their forces hideous,
        Their steeds do stagger, and amazed stand,
        And eke themselves too rudely rigorous,
        Astonied with the stroke of their owne hand,
     Do backe rebut, and each to other yeeldeth land.

   13. *scarlot*: a rich cloth. *Purfled*: fringed. *assay*: proved value. *owches*:
ornaments. *palfrey*: saddle-horse. *tinsell*: glittering.
   14. *disport*: entertainment, diversion.
   15. *dispiteous*: cruel. *couch*: lower for attack. *fell*: fierce. *Astonied*: stunned,
astounded. *rebut*: recoil.

16 As when two rams stird with ambitious pride,
      Fight for the rule of the rich fleeced flocke,
      Their horned fronts so fierce on either side
      Do meete, that with the terrour of the shocke
      Astonied both, stand sencelesse as a blocke,
      Forgetfull of the hanging victory:
      So stood these twaine, unmoved as a rocke,
      Both staring fierce, and holding idely
  The broken reliques of their former cruelty.

17 The *Sarazin* sore daunted with the buffe
      Snatcheth his sword, and fiercely to him flies;
      Who well it wards, and quyteth cuff with cuff:
      Each others equal puissaunce envies,
      And through their iron sides with cruell spies
      Does seeke to perce: repining courage yields
      No foote to foe. The flashing fier flies
      As from a forge out of their burning shields,
  And streames of purple bloud new dies the verdant fields.

18 Curse on that Crosse (quoth then the *Sarazin*)
      That keepes thy body from the bitter fit;
      Dead long ygoe I wote thou haddest bin,
      Had not that charme from thee forwarned it:
      But yet I warne thee now assured sitt,
      And hide thy head. Therewith upon his crest
      With rigour so outrageous he smitt,
      That a large share it hewd out of the rest,
  And glauncing downe his shield, from blame him fairely
      blest.

16. *Astonied*: stunned. *hanging victory*: victory (being) in the balance.
17. *buffe*: blow. *quyteth*: repays. *puissaunce*: strength, valour. *repining*: fierce, furious.
18. *ygoe*: ago. *outrageous*: violent. *share*: piece. *blame*: injury. *blest*: protected(see note).

19 Who thereat wondrous wroth, the sleeping spark
      Of native vertue gan eftsoones revive,
      And at his haughtie helmet making mark,
      So hugely stroke, that it the steele did rive,
      And cleft his head. He tumbling downe alive,
      With bloudy mouth his mother earth did kis,
      Greeting his grave: his grudging ghost did strive
      With the fraile flesh; at last it flitted is,
   Whither the soules do fly of men, that live amis.

20 The Lady when she saw her champion fall,
      Like the old ruines of a broken towre,
      Staid not to waile his woefull funerall,
      But from him fled away with all her powre;
      Who after her as hastily gan scowre,
      Bidding the Dwarfe with him to bring away
      The *Sarazins* shield, signe of the conqueroure.
      Her soone he overtooke, and bad to stay,
   For present cause was none of dread her to dismay.

21 She turning backe with ruefull countenaunce,
      Cride, Mercy mercy Sir vouchsafe to show
      On silly Dame, subject to hard mischaunce,
      And to your mighty will. Her humblesse low
      In so ritch weedes and seeming glorious show,
      Did much emmove his stout heroïcke heart,
      And said, Deare dame, your suddein overthrow
      Much rueth me; but now put feare apart,
   And tell, both who ye be, and who that tooke your part.

19. *grudging*: complaining.   20. *scowre*: run fast.
21. *silly*: simple, innocent.   *humblesse*: humility.   *emmove*: move.

22 Melting in teares, then gan she thus lament;
  The wretched woman, whom unhappy howre
  Hath now made thrall to your commandement,
  Before that angry heavens list to lowre,
  And fortune false betraide me to your powre
  Was, (O what now availeth that I was!)
  Borne the sole daughter of an Emperour,
  He that the wide West under his rule has,
And high hath set his throne, where *Tiberis* doth pas.

23 He in the first flowre of my freshest age,
  Betrothed me unto the onely haire
  Of a most mighty king, most rich and sage;
  Was never Prince so faithfull and so faire,
  Was never Prince so meeke and debonaire;
  But ere my hoped day of spousall shone,
  My dearest Lord fell from high honours staire,
  Into the hands of his accursed fone,
And cruelly was slaine, that shall I ever mone.

24 His blessed body spoild of lively breath,
  Was afterward, I know not how, convaid
  And fro me hid: of whose most innocent death
  When tidings came to me unhappy maid,
  O how great sorrow my sad soule assaid.
  Then forth I went his woefull corse to find,
  And many yeares throughout the world I straid,
  A virgin widow, whose deepe wounded mind
With love, long time did languish as the striken hind.

22. *Before that*: before. *list*: wish, choose.
23. *debonaire*: gracious, courteous. *fone*: foes.
24. *spoild*: despoiled, robbed. *lively*: living. *assaid*: assailed. *corse*: body.

25   At last it chaunced this proud *Sarazin*
        To meete me wandring, who perforce me led
        With him away, but yet could never win
        The Fort, that Ladies hold in soveraigne dread.
        There lies he now with foule dishonour dead,
        Who whiles he liv'de, was called proud *Sans foy*,
        The eldest of three brethren, all three bred
        Of one bad sire, whose youngest is *Sans joy*,
     And twixt them both was borne the bloudy bold *Sans loy*.

26   In this sad plight, friendlesse, unfortunate,
        Now miserable I *Fidessa* dwell,
        Craving of you in pitty of my state,
        To do none ill, if please ye not do well.
        He in great passion all this while did dwell,
        More busying his quicke eyes, her face to view,
        Then his dull eares, to heare what she did tell;
        And said, Faire Lady hart of flint would rew
     The undeserved woes and sorrowes, which ye shew.

27   Henceforth in safe assuraunce may ye rest,
        Having both found a new friend you to aid,
        And lost an old foe, that did you molest:
        Better new friend then an old foe is said.
        With chaunge of cheare the seeming simple maid
        Let fall her eyen, as shamefast to the earth,
        And yeelding soft, in that she nought gain-said,
        So forth they rode, he feining seemely merth,
     And she coy lookes: so dainty they say maketh derth.

27. *cheare*: countenance.   *eyen*: eyes.   *shamefast*: modest.   *dainty*: fastidiousness (see note).

28   Long time they thus together traveiled,
     Till weary of their way, they came at last,
     Where grew two goodly trees, that faire did spred
     Their armes abroad, with gray mosse overcast,
     And their greene leaves trembling with every blast,
     Made a calme shadow far in compasse round:
     The fearefull Shepheard often there aghast
     Under them never sat, ne wont there sound
His mery oaten pipe, but shund th'unlucky ground.

29   But this good knight soone as he them can spie,
     For the coole shade him thither hastly got:
     For golden *Phœbus* now ymounted hie,
     From fiery wheeles of his faire chariot
     Hurled his beame so scorching cruell hot,
     That living creature mote it not abide;
     And his new Lady it endured not.
     There they alight, in hope themselves to hide
From the fierce heat, and rest their weary limbs a tide.

30   Faire seemely pleasaunce each to other makes,
     With goodly purposes there as they sit:
     And in his falsed fancy he her takes
     To be the fairest wight, that lived yit;
     Which to expresse, he bends his gentle wit,
     And thinking of those braunches greene to frame
     A girlond for her dainty forehead fit,
     He pluckt a bough; out of whose rift there came
Small drops of gory bloud, that trickled downe the same.

29. *can spie*: spied. *mote*: could.
30. *purposes*: conversation. *falsed*: deceived. *yit*: yet. *girlond*: garland.
F*F*Q

31   Therewith a piteous yelling voyce was heard,
           Crying, O spare with guilty hands to teare
           My tender sides in this rough rynd embard,
           But fly, ah fly far hence away, for feare
           Least to you hap, that happened to me heare,
           And to this wretched Lady, my deare love,
           O too deare love, love bought with death too deare.
           Astond he stood, and up his haire did hove,
      And with that suddein horror could no member move.

32   At last whenas the dreadfull passion
           Was overpast, and manhood well awake,
           Yet musing at the straunge occasion,
           And doubting much his sence, he thus bespake;
           What voyce of damned Ghost from *Limbo* lake,
           Or guilefull spright wandring in empty aire,
           Both which fraile men do oftentimes mistake,
           Sends to my doubtfull eares these speaches rare,
      And ruefull plaints, me bidding guiltlesse bloud to spare?

33   Then groning deepe, Nor damned Ghost, (quoth he,)
           Nor guilefull sprite to thee these wordes doth speake,
           But once a man *Fradubio*, now a tree,
           Wretched man, wretched tree; whose nature weake,
           A cruell witch her cursed will to wreake,
           Hath thus transformd, and plast in open plaines,
           Where *Boreas* doth blow full bitter bleake,
           And scorching Sunne does dry my secret vaines:
      For though a tree I seeme, yet cold and heat me paines.

   31. embard: confined, enclosed.   *Least*: lest.   *Astond*: astonished.   *hove*: stand
on end.   *member*: limb

34 Say on *Fradubio* then, or man, or tree,
     Quoth then the knight, by whose mischievous arts
     Art thou misshaped thus, as now I see?
     He oft finds med'cine, who his griefe imparts;
     But double griefs afflict concealing harts,
     As raging flames who striveth to suppresse.
     The author then (said he) of all my smarts,
     Is one *Duessa* a false sorceresse,
That many errant knights hath brought to wretchednesse.

35 In prime of youthly yeares, when corage hot
     The fire of love and joy of chevalree
     First kindled in my brest, it was my lot
     To love this gentle Lady, whom ye see,
     Now not a Lady, but a seeming tree;
     With whom as once I rode accompanyde,
     Me chaunced of a knight encountred bee,
     That had a like faire Lady by his syde,
Like a faire Lady, but did fowle *Duessa* hyde.

36 Whose forged beauty he did take in hand,
     All other Dames to have exceeded farre;
     I in defence of mine did likewise stand,
     Mine, that did then shine as the Morning starre:
     So both to battell fierce arraunged arre,
     In which his harder fortune was to fall
     Under my speare: such is the dye of warre:
     His Lady left as a prise martiall,
Did yield her comely person, to be at my call.

34. *or . . . or*: either . . . or.   *errant*: wandering.
35. *youthly*: youthful.   36. *dye*: hazard, chance.

37 So doubly lov'd of Ladies unlike faire,
      Th'one seeming such, the other such indeede,
      One day in doubt I cast for to compare,
      Whether in beauties glorie did exceede;
      A Rosy girlond was the victors meede:
      Both seemde to win, and both seemde won to bee,
      So hard the discord was to be agreede.
      Frælissa was as faire, as faire mote bee,
    And ever false *Duessa* seemde as faire as shee.

38 The wicked witch now seeing all this while
      The doubtfull ballaunce equally to sway,
      What not by right, she cast to win by guile,
      And by her hellish science raisd streight way
      A foggy mist, that overcast the day,
      And a dull blast, that breathing on her face,
      Dimmed her former beauties shining ray,
      And with foule ugly forme did her disgrace:
    Then was she faire alone, when none was faire in place.

39 Then cride she out, Fye, fye, deformed wight,
      Whose borrowed beautie now appeareth plaine
      To have before bewitched all mens sight;
      O leave her soone, or let her soone be slaine.
      Her loathly visage viewing with disdaine,
      Eftsoones I thought her such, as she me told,
      And would have kild her; but with faigned paine,
      The false witch did my wrathfull hand withhold;
    So left her, where she now is turnd to treen mould.

---

37. *cast*: resolved, planned.   *Whether*: which.   *meede*: reward.   *mote*: could.
38. *disgrace*: (here) disfigure.
39. *disdaine*: angry indignation.   *treen mould*: the shape of a tree.

40   Thens forth I tooke *Duessa* for my Dame,
      And in the witch unweeting joyd long time,
      Ne ever wist, but that she was the same,
      Till on a day (that day is every Prime,
      When Witches wont do penance for their crime)
      I chaunst to see her in her proper hew,
      Bathing her selfe in origane and thyme:
      A filthy foule old woman I did vew,
   That ever to have toucht her, I did deadly rew.

41   Her neather partes misshapen, monstruous,
      Were hidd in water, that I could not see,
      But they did seeme more foule and hideous,
      Then womans shape man would beleeve to bee.
      Thens forth from her most beastly companie
      I gan refraine, in minde to slip away,
      Soone as appeard safe opportunitie:
      For danger great, if not assur'd decay
   I saw before mine eyes, if I were knowne to stray.

42   The divelish hag by chaunges of my cheare
      Perceiv'd my thought, and drownd in sleepie night,
      With wicked herbes and ointments did besmeare
      My bodie all, through charmes and magicke might,
      That all my senses were bereaved quight:
      Then brought she me into this desert waste,
      And by my wretched lovers side me pight,
      Where now enclosd in wooden wals full faste,
   Banisht from living wights, our wearie dayes we waste.

40. *unweeting*: not knowing, unwitting. *wist*: knew. *Prime*: springtime.
origane: wild marjoram.
41. *decay*: destruction, death.
42. *cheare*: countenance. *pight*: placed.

43   But how long time, said then the Elfin knight,
          Are you in this misformed house to dwell?
          We may not chaunge (quoth he) this evil plight,
          Till we be bathed in a living well;
          That is the terme prescribed by the spell.
          O how, said he, mote I that well out find,
          That may restore you to your wonted well?
          Time and suffised fates to former kynd
      Shall us restore, none else from hence may us unbynd.

44   The false *Duessa*, now *Fidessa* hight,
          Heard how in vaine *Fradubio* did lament,
          And knew well all was true. But the good knight
          Full of sad feare and ghastly dreriment,
          When all this speech the living tree had spent,
          The bleeding bough did thrust into the ground,
          That from the bloud he might be innocent,
          And with fresh clay did close the wooden wound:
      Then turning to his Lady, dead with feare her found.

45   Her seeming dead he found with feigned feare,
          As all unweeting of that well she knew,
          And paynd himselfe with busie care to reare
          Her out of carelesse swowne. Her eylids blew
          And dimmed sight with pale and deadly hew
          At last she up gan lift: with trembling cheare
          Her up he tooke, too simple and too trew,
          And oft her kist. At length all passed feare,
      He set her on her steede, and forward forth did beare.

    43. *mote*: might, can.   *well* (l.7): well-being.   *suffised*: satisfied.
    44. *hight*: called.   *dreriment*: sorrow.
    45. *unweeting*: unconscious.   *swowne*: swoon.   *all passed feare*: (her) fear all
passed.

Canto 3

Forsaken Truth long seekes her love,
And makes the Lyon mylde,
Marres blind Devotions mart, and fals
In hand of leachour vylde.

1   Nought is there under heav'ns wide hollownesse,
    That moves more deare compassion of mind,
    Then beautie brought t'unworthy wretchednesse
    Through envies snares or fortunes freakes unkind:
    I, whether lately through her brightnesse blind,
    Or through alleageance and fast fealtie,
    Which I do owe unto all woman kind,
    Feele my heart perst with so great agonie,
When such I see, that all for pittie I could die.

2   And now it is empassioned so deepe,
    For fairest *Unaes* sake, of whom I sing,
    That my fraile eyes these lines with teares do steepe,
    To thinke how she through guilefull handeling,
    Though true as touch, though daughter of a king,
    Though faire as ever living wight was faire,
    Though nor in word nor deede ill meriting,
    Is from her knight divorced in despaire
And her due loves deriv'd to that vile witches share.

Argument.   *mart*: business, pursuits.   *vylde*: vile.
1. *freakes*: whims, caprices.
2. *empassioned*: (deeply) moved.   *deriv'd*: transferred.   *share*: portion.

3   Yet she most faithfull Ladie all this while
        Forsaken, wofull, solitarie mayd
        Farre from all peoples prease, as in exile,
        In wildernesse and wastfull deserts strayd,
        To seeke her knight; who subtilly betrayd
        Through that late vision, which th'Enchaunter wrought,
        Had her abandon. She of nought affrayd,
        Through woods and wastnesse wide him daily sought;
    Yet wished tydings none of him unto her brought.

4   One day nigh wearie of the yrkesome way,
        From her unhastie beast she did alight,
        And on the grasse her daintie limbes did lay
        In secret shadow, farre from all mens sight:
        From her faire head her fillet she undight,
        And laid her stole aside. Her angels face
        As the great eye of heaven shyned bright,
        And made a sunshine in the shadie place;
    Did never mortall eye behold such heavenly grace.

5   It fortuned out of the thickest wood
        A ramping Lyon rushed suddainly,
        Hunting full greedie after salvage blood;
        Soone as the royall virgin he did spy,
        With gaping mouth at her ran greedily,
        To have attonce devour'd her tender corse:
        But to the pray when as he drew more ny,
        His bloudie rage asswaged with remorse,
    And with the sight amazd, forgat his furious forse.

3. *prease*: press, throng.   *wastfull*: waste.
4. *yrkesome*: painful.   *undight*: unfastened.
5. *ramping*: bounding.   *salvage*: wild, savage.   *corse*: body.   *remorse*: pity.

6 In stead thereof he kist her wearie feet,
     And lickt her lilly hands with fawning tong,
     As he her wronged innocence did weet.
     O how can beautie maister the most strong,
     And simple truth subdue avenging wrong?
     Whose yeelded pride and proud submission,
     Still dreading death, when she had marked long,
     Her hart gan melt in great compassion,
  And drizling teares did shed for pure affection.

7 The Lyon Lord of everie beast in field,
     Quoth she, his princely puissance doth abate,
     And mightie proud to humble weake does yield,
     Forgetfull of the hungry rage, which late
     Him prickt, in pittie of my sad estate:
     But he my Lyon, and my noble Lord,
     How does he find in cruell hart to hate
     Her that him lov'd, and ever most adord,
  As the God of my life? why hath he me abhord?

8 Redounding teares did choke th'end of her plaint,
     Which softly ecchoed from the neighbour wood;
     And sad to see her sorrowfull constraint
     The kingly beast upon her gazing stood;
     With pittie calmd, downe fell his angry mood.
     At last in close hart shutting up her paine,
     Arose the virgin borne of heavenly brood,
     And to her snowy Palfrey got againe,
  To seeke her strayed Champion, if she might attaine.

6. *As*: as if. *weet*: know of.   8. *Redounding*: overflowing.

9 The Lyon would not leave her desolate,
    But with her went along, as a strong gard
    Of her chast person, and a faithfull mate
    Of her sad troubles and misfortunes hard:
    Still when she slept, he kept both watch and ward,
    And when she wakt, he waited diligent,
    With humble service to her will prepard:
    From her faire eyes he tooke commaundement,
And ever by her lookes conceived her intent.

10 Long she thus traveiled through deserts wyde,
    By which she thought her wandring knight shold pas,
    Yet never shew of living wight espyde;
    Till that at length she found the troden gras,
    In which the tract of peoples footing was,
    Under the steepe foot of a mountaine hore;
    The same she followes, till at last she has
    A damzell spyde slow footing her before,
That on her shoulders sad a pot of water bore.

11 To whom approching she to her gan call,
    To weet, if dwelling place were nigh at hand;
    But the rude wench her answer'd nought at all,
    She could not heare, nor speake, nor understand;
    Till seeing by her side the Lyon stand,
    With suddaine feare her pitcher downe she threw,
    And fled away: for never in that land
    Face of faire Ladie she before did vew,
And that dread Lyons looke her cast in deadly hew.

10. *tract*: track.   *hore*: hoary, grey.   *sad*: (here) firm.
11. *weet*: know.   *rude*: simple, unsophisticated.

12 Full fast she fled, ne ever lookt behynd,
       As if her life upon the wager lay,
       And home she came, whereas her mother blynd
       Sate in eternall night: nought could she say,
       But suddaine catching hold, did her dismay
       With quaking hands, and other signes of feare:
       Who full of ghastly fright and cold affray,
       Gan shut the dore. By this arrived there
    Dame *Una*, wearie Dame, and entrance did requere.

13 Which when none yeelded, her unruly Page
       With his rude clawes the wicket open rent,
       And let her in; where of his cruell rage
       Nigh dead with feare, and faint astonishment,
       She found them both in darkesome corner pent;
       Where that old woman day and night did pray
       Upon her beades devoutly penitent;
       Nine hundred *Pater nosters* every day,
    And thrise nine hundred *Aves* she was wont to say.

14 And to augment her painefull pennance more,
       Thrise every weeke in ashes she did sit,
       And next her wrinkled skin rough sackcloth wore,
       And thrise three times did fast from any bit:
       But now for feare her beads she did forget.
       Whose needlesse dread for to remove away,
       Faire *Una* framed words and count'nance fit:
       Which hardly doen, at length she gan them pray,
    That in their cotage small, that night she rest her may.

12. *upon the wager lay*: lay in the balance. *whereas*: (to) where. *affray*: terror.
Gan shut: shut.
13. *rude*: rough.   14. *bit*: morsel of food. *doen*: done.

15 The day is spent, and commeth drowsie night,
       When every creature shrowded is in sleepe;
       Sad *Una* downe her laies in wearie plight,
       And at her feet the Lyon watch doth keepe:
       In stead of rest, she does lament, and weepe
       For the late losse of her deare loved knight,
       And sighes, and grones, and evermore does steepe
       Her tender brest in bitter teares all night,
   All night she thinks too long, and often lookes for light.

16 Now when *Aldeboran* was mounted hie
       Above the shynie *Cassiopeias* chaire,
       And all in deadly sleepe did drowned lie,
       One knocked at the dore, and in would fare;
       He knocked fast, and often curst, and sware,
       That readie entrance was not at his call:
       For on his backe a heavy load he bare
       Of nightly stelths and pillage severall,
   Which he had got abroad by purchase criminall.

17 He was to weete a stout and sturdie thiefe,
       Wont to robbe Churches of their ornaments,
       And poore mens boxes of their due reliefe,
       Which given was to them for good intents;
       The holy Saints of their rich vestiments
       He did disrobe, when all men carelesse slept,
       And spoild the Priests of their habiliments,
       Whiles none the holy things in safety kept;
   Then he by cunning sleights in at the window crept.

16. *purchase*: robbery.
17. *to weete*: to wit.   *spoild*: robbed.   *habiliments*: attire.

18   And all that he by right or wrong could find,
          Unto this house he brought, and did bestow
          Upon the daughter of this woman blind,
          Abessa daughter of *Corceca* slow,
          With whom he whoredome usd, that few did know,
          And fed her fat with feast of offerings,
          And plentie, which in all the land did grow;
          Ne spared he to give her gold and rings:
      And now he to her brought part of his stolen things.

19   Thus long the dore with rage and threats he bet,
          Yet of those fearefull women none durst rize,
          The Lyon frayed them, him in to let:
          He would no longer stay him to advize,
          But open breakes the dore in furious wize,
          And entring is; when that disdainfull beast
          Encountring fierce, him suddaine doth surprize,
          And seizing cruell clawes on trembling brest,
      Under his Lordly foot him proudly hath supprest.

20   Him booteth not resist, nor succour call,
          His bleeding hart is in the vengers hand,
          Who streight him rent in thousand peeces small,
          And quite dismembred hath: the thirstie land
          Drunke up his life; his corse left on the strand.
          His fearefull friends weare out the wofull night,
          Ne dare to weepe, nor seeme to understand
          The heavie hap, which on them is alight,
      Affraid, least to themselves the like mishappen might.

19.   *bet*: beat.   *frayed*: frightened.   *advize* (him): consider, reflect.   *disdainfull*: angry.
20.   *Him booteth not*: it avails him not.   *least*: lest.   *mishappen*: happen amiss.

21 Now when broad day the world discovered has,
        Up *Una* rose, up rose the Lyon eke,
        And on their former journey forward pas,
        In wayes unknowne, her wandring knight to seeke,
        With paines farre passing that long wandring *Greeke*,
        That for his love refused deitie;
        Such were the labours of this Lady meeke,
        Still seeking him, that from her still did flie,
    Then furthest from her hope, when most she weened nie.

22 Soone as she parted thence, the fearefull twaine,
        That blind old woman and her daughter deare
        Came forth, and finding *Kirkrapine* there slaine,
        For anguish great they gan to rend their heare,
        And beat their brests, and naked flesh to teare.
        And when they both had wept and wayld their fill,
        Then forth they ranne like two amazed deare,
        Halfe mad through malice, and revenging will,
    To follow her, that was the causer of their ill.

23 Whom overtaking, they gan loudly bray,
        With hollow howling, and lamenting cry,
        Shamefully at her rayling all the way,
        And her accusing of dishonesty,
        That was the flowre of faith and chastity;
        And still amidst her rayling, she did pray,
        That plagues, and mischiefs, and long misery
        Might fall on her, and follow all the way,
    And that in endlesse error she might ever stray.

24 But when she saw her prayers nought prevaile,
      She backe returned with some labour lost;
      And in the way as she did weepe and waile,
      A knight her met in mighty armes embost,
      Yet knight was not for all his bragging bost,
      But subtill *Archimag*, that *Una* sought
      By traynes into new troubles to have tost:
      Of that old woman tydings he besought,
  If that of such a Ladie she could tellen ought.

25 Therewith she gan her passion to renew,
      And cry, and curse, and raile, and rend her heare,
      Saying, that harlot she too lately knew,
      That causd her shed so many a bitter teare,
      And so forth told the story of her feare:
      Much seemed he to mone her haplesse chaunce,
      And after for that Ladie did inquere;
      Which being taught, he forward gan advaunce
  His fair enchaunted steed, and eke his charmed launce.

26 Ere long he came, where *Una* traveild slow,
      And that wilde Champion wayting her besyde:
      Whom seeing such, for dread he durst not show
      Himselfe too nigh at hand, but turned wyde
      Unto an hill; from whence when she him spyde,
      By his like seeming shield, her knight by name
      She weend it was, and towards him gan ryde:
      Approching nigh, she wist it was the same,
  And with faire fearefull humblesse towards him shee came.

24. *embost*: enclosed. *bost*: boast. *traynes*: tricks, snares.
26. *wayting*: watching. *wist*: knew. *humblesse*: humility.

27 And weeping said, Ah my long lacked Lord,
  Where have ye been thus long out of my sight?
  Much feared I to have bene quite abhord,
  Or ought have done, that ye displeasen might,
  That should as death unto my deare hart light:
  For since mine eye your joyous sight did mis,
  My chearefull day is turnd to chearelesse night,
  And eke my night of death the shadow is;
But welcome now my light, and shining lampe of blis.

28 He thereto meeting said, My dearest Dame,
  Farre be it from your thought, and fro my will,
  To thinke that knighthood I so much should shame,
  As you to leave, that have me loved still,
  And chose in Faery court of meere goodwill,
  Where noblest knights were to be found on earth:
  The earth shall sooner leave her kindly skill
  To bring forth fruit, and make eternall derth,
Then I leave you, my liefe, yborne of heavenly berth.

29 And sooth to say, why I left you so long,
  Was for to seeke adventure in strange place,
  Where *Archimago* said a felon strong
  To many knights did daily worke disgrace;
  But knight he now shall never more deface:
  Good cause of mine excuse; that mote ye please
  Well to accept, and evermore embrace
  My faithfull service, that by land and seas
Have vowd you to defend, now then your plaint appease.

28. *chose*: choose. *meere*: complete. *kindly*: natural. *liefe*: beloved, darling.
29. *sooth*: truth. *disgrace*: mischief, harm. *deface*: daunt, destroy. *mote*: may, might. *appease*: subdue, cease.

30 His lovely words her seemd due recompence
Of all her passed paines: one loving howre
For many yeares of sorrow can dispence:
A dram of sweet is worth a pound of sowre:
She has forgot, how many a wofull stowre
For him she late endur'd; she speakes no more
Of past: true is, that true love hath no powre
To looken backe; his eyes be fixt before.
Before her stands her knight, for whom she toyld so sore.

31 Much like, as when the beaten marinere,
That long hath wandred in the *Ocean* wide,
Oft soust in swelling *Tethys* saltish teare,
And long time having tand his tawney hide
With blustring breath of heaven, that none can bide,
And scorching flames of fierce *Orions* hound,
Soone as the port from farre he has espide,
His chearefull whistle merrily doth sound,
And *Nereus* crownes with cups; his mates him pledg around.

32 Such joy made *Una*, when her knight she found;
And eke th'enchaunter joyous seemd no lesse,
Then the glad marchant, that does vew from ground
His ship farre come from watrie wildernesse,
He hurles out vowes, and *Neptune* oft doth blesse:
So forth they past, and all the way they spent
Discoursing of her dreadfull late distresse,
In which he askt her, what the Lyon ment:
Who told her all that fell in journey as she went.

30. *stowre*: time of anxiety, of stress.   31. *soust*: drenched.

G 2

33   They had not ridden farre, when they might see
    One pricking towards them with hastie heat,
    Full strongly armd, and on a courser free,
    That through his fiercenesse fomed all with sweat,
    And the sharpe yron did for anger eat,
    When his hot ryder spurd his chauffed side;
    His looke was sterne, and seemed still to threat
    Cruell revenge, which he in hart did hyde,
And on his shield *Sans loy* in bloudie lines was dyde.

34   When nigh he drew unto this gentle payre
    And saw the Red-crosse, which the knight did beare,
    He burnt in fire, and gan eftsoones prepare
    Himselfe to battell with his couched speare.
    Loth was that other, and did faint through feare,
    To taste th'untryed dint of deadly steele;
    But yet his Lady did so well him cheare,
    That hope of new good hap he gan to feele;
So bent his speare, and spurnd his horse with yron heele.

35   But that proud Paynim forward came so fierce,
    And full of wrath, that with his sharp-head speare
    Through vainely crossed shield he quite did pierce,
    And had his staggering steede not shrunke for feare,
    Through shield and bodie eke he should him beare:
    Yet so great was the puissance of his push,
    That from his saddle quite he did him beare:
    He tombling rudely downe to ground did rush,
And from his gored wound a well of bloud did gush.

33. *chauffed*: chafed.   34. *couched*: lowered for attack.
35. *Paynim*: pagan, heathen.   *rudely*: (here) awkwardly, heavily.

36 Dismounting lightly from his loftie steed,
    He to him lept, in mind to reave his life,
    And proudly said, Lo there the worthie meed
    Of him, that slew *Sansfoy* with bloudie knife;
    Henceforth his ghost freed from repining strife,
    In peace may passen over *Lethe* lake,
    When mourning altars purgd with enemies life,
    The blacke infernall *Furies* doen aslake:
Life from *Sansfoy* thou tookst, *Sansloy* shall from thee take.

37 Therewith in haste his helmet gan unlace,
    Till *Una* cride, O hold that heavie hand,
    Deare Sir, what ever that thou be in place:
    Enough is, that thy foe doth vanquisht stand
    Now at thy mercy: Mercie not withstand:
    For he is one the truest knight alive,
    Though conquered now he lie on lowly land,
    And whilest him fortune favour, faire did thrive
In bloudie field: therefore of life him not deprive.

38 Her piteous words might not abate his rage,
    But rudely rending up his helmet, would
    Have slaine him straight: but when he sees his age,
    And hoarie head of *Archimago* old,
    His hastie hand he doth amazed hold,
    And halfe ashamed, wondred at the sight:
    For the old man well knew he, though untold,
    In charmes and magicke to have wondrous might,
Ne ever wont in field, ne in round lists to fight.

36. *reave*: take away (by violence).   *meed*: reward.   *repining*: restless, discontented.   *doen*: do.   *aslake*: pacify.
38. *rudely*: roughly.

39   And said, Why *Archimago*, lucklesse syre,
        What doe I see? what hard mishap is this,
        That hath thee hither brought to taste mine yre?
        Or thine the fault, or mine the error is,
        In stead of foe to wound my friend amis?
        He answered nought, but in a traunce still lay,
        And on those guilefull dazed eyes of his
        The cloud of death did sit. Which doen away,
     He left him lying so, ne would no lenger stay.

40   But to the virgin comes, who all this while
        Amased stands, her selfe so mockt to see
        By him, who has the guerdon of his guile,
        For so misfeigning her true knight to bee:
        Yet is she now in more perplexitie,
        Left in the hand of that same Paynim bold,
        From whom her booteth not at all to flie;
        Who by her cleanly garment catching hold,
     Her from her Palfrey pluckt, her visage to behold.

41   But her fierce servant full of kingly awe
        And high disdaine, whenas his soveraine Dame
        So rudely handled by her foe he sawe,
        With gaping jawes full greedy at him came,
        And ramping on his shield, did weene the same
        Have reft away with his sharpe rending clawes.
        But he was stout, and lust did now inflame
        His corage more, that from his griping pawes
     He hath his shield redeem'd, and foorth his swerd he drawes.

39. *lenger*: longer.
40. *guerdon*: reward.   *Paynim*: pagan.   *her booteth not*: it avails her not.
41. *ramping*: with fore-paws up.   *reft away*: (here) torn away.

42 O then too weake and feeble was the forse
    Of salvage beast, his puissance to withstand:
    For he was strong, and of so mightie corse,
    As ever wielded speare in warlike hand,
    And feates of armes did wisely understand.
    Eftsoones he perced through his chaufed chest
    With thrilling point of deadly yron brand,
    And launcht his Lordly hart: with death opprest
He roar'd aloud, whiles life forsooke his stubborne brest.

43 Who now is left to keepe the forlorne maid
    From raging spoile of lawlesse victors will?
    Her faithfull gard remov'd, her hope dismaid,
    Her selfe a yeelded pray to save or spill.
    He now Lord of the field, his pride to fill,
    With foule reproches, and disdainfull spight
    Her vildly entertaines, and will or nill,
    Beares her away upon his courser light:
Her prayers nought prevaile, his rage is more of might.

44 And all the way, with great lamenting paine,
    And piteous plaints she filleth his dull eares,
    That stony hart could riven have in twaine,
    And all the way she wets with flowing teares:
    But he enrag'd with rancor, nothing heares.
    Her servile beast yet would not leave her so,
    But followes her farre off, ne ought he feares,
    To be partaker of her wandring woe,
More mild in beastly kind, then that her beastly foe.

42. *salvage*: savage, fierce. *chaufed*: heated. *thrilling*: piercing. *brand*: sword.
launcht: ran through, pierced.
    43. *spill*: destroy. *vildly*: vilely. *will or nill*: willy-nilly. *more of might*: the
greater.

Canto 4

To sinfull house of Pride, Duessa
guides the faithfull knight,
Where brothers death to wreak Sansjoy
doth chalenge him to fight.

1 Young knight, what ever that dost armes professe,
  And through long labours huntest after fame,
  Beware of fraud, beware of ficklenesse,
  In choice, and change of thy deare loved Dame,
  Least thou of her beleeve too lightly blame,
  And rash misweening doe thy hart remove:
  For unto knight there is no greater shame,
  Then lightnesse and inconstancie in love;
That doth this *Redcrosse* knights ensample plainly prove.

2 Who after that he had fair *Una* lorne,
  Through light misdeeming of her loialtie,
  And false *Duessa* in her sted had borne,
  Called *Fidess'*, and so supposd to bee;
  Long with her traveild, till at last they see
  A goodly building, bravely garnished,
  The house of mightie Prince it seemd to bee:
  And towards it a broad high way that led,
All bare through peoples feet, which thither traveiled.

1. *misweening*: mistaking.   *ensample*: example.
2. *after that*: after.   *misdeeming*: misjudging.

3   Great troupes of people traveild thitherward
     Both day and night, of each degree and place,
     But few returned, having scaped hard,
     With balefull beggerie, or foule disgrace,
     Which ever after in most wretched case,
     Like loathsome lazars, by the hedges lay.
     Thither *Duessa* bad him bend his pace:
     For she is wearie of the toilesome way,
  And also nigh consumed is the lingring day.

4   A stately Pallace built of squared bricke,
     Which cunningly was without morter laid,
     Whose wals were high, but nothing strong, nor thick,
     And golden foile all over them displaid,
     That purest skye with brightnesse they dismaid:
     High lifted up were many loftie towres,
     And goodly galleries farre over laid,
     Full of faire windowes, and delightfull bowres;
  And on the top a Diall told the timely howres.

5   It was a goodly heape for to behould,
     And spake the praises of the workmans wit;
     But full great pittie, that so faire a mould
     Did on so weake foundation ever sit:
     For on a sandie hill, that still did flit,
     And fall away, it mounted was full hie,
     That every breath of heaven shaked it:
     And all the hinder parts, that few could spie,
  Were ruinous and old, but painted cunningly.

3. *scaped*: escaped. *balefull*: miserable. *lazars*: lepers.
5. *heape*: building. *mould*: shape. *flit*: give way.

6   Arrived there they passed in forth right;
    For still to all the gates stood open wide,
    Yet charge of them was to a Porter hight
    Cald *Malvenù*, who entrance none denide:
    Thence to the hall, which was on every side
    With rich array and costly arras dight:
    Infinite sorts of people did abide
    There waiting long, to win the wished sight
Of her, that was the Lady of that Pallace bright.

7   By them they passe, all gazing on them round,
    And to the Presence mount; whose glorious vew
    Their frayle amazed senses did confound:
    In living Princes court none ever knew
    Such endlesse richesse, and so sumptuous shew;
    Ne *Persia* selfe, the nourse of pompous pride
    Like ever saw. And there a noble crew
    Of Lordes and Ladies stood on every side,
Which with their presence faire, the place much beautifide.

8   High above all a cloth of State was spred,
    And a rich throne, as bright as sunny day,
    On which there sate most brave embellished
    With royall robes and gorgeous array,
    A mayden Queene, that shone as *Titans* ray,
    In glistring gold, and peerelesse pretious stone:
    Yet her bright blazing beautie did assay
    To dim the brightnesse of her glorious throne,
As envying her selfe, that too exceeding shone.

6. *forth right*: at once. *hight*: entrusted. *arras*: tapestry (see note). *dight*: decorated.
8. *assay*: attempt.

9   Exceeding shone, like *Phœbus* fairest childe,
         That did presume his fathers firie wayne,
         And flaming mouthes of steedes unwonted wilde
         Through highest heaven with weaker hand to rayne;
         Proud of such glory and advancement vaine,
         While flashing beames do daze his feeble eyen,
         He leaves the welkin way most beaten plaine,
         And rapt with whirling wheeles, inflames the skyen,
     With fire not made to burne, but fairely for to shyne.

10   So proud she shyned in her Princely state,
         Looking to heaven; for earth she did disdayne,
         And sitting high; for lowly she did hate:
         Lo underneath her scornefull feete, was layne
         A dreadfull Dragon with an hideous trayne,
         And in her hand she held a mirrhour bright,
         Wherein her face she often vewed fayne,
         And in her selfe-lov'd semblance tooke delight;
     For she was wondrous faire, as any living wight.

11   Of griesly *Pluto* she the daughter was,
         And sad *Proserpina* the Queene of hell;
         Yet did she thinke her pearelesse worth to pas
         That parentage, with pride so did she swell,
         And thundring *Jove*, that high in heaven doth dwell,
         And wield the world, she claymed for her syre,
         Or if that any else did *Jove* excell:
         For to the highest she did still aspyre,
     Or if ought higher were then that, did it desyre.

9. *presume*: venture in.   *wayne*: waggon, chariot.   *welkin way*: way through
the sky (see note).   *rapt*: carried away.   *skyen*: skies.
10. *trayne*: tail.   *fayne*: glad, pleased.
11. *griesly*: grim, terrible.

12 And proud *Lucifera* men did her call,
        That made her selfe a Queene, and crownd to be,
        Yet rightfull kingdome she had none at all,
        Ne heritage of native soveraintie,
        But did usurpe with wrong and tyrannie
        Upon the scepter, which she now did hold:
        Ne ruld her Realmes with lawes, but pollicie,
        And strong advizement of six wisards old,
    That with their counsels bad her kingdome did uphold.

13 Soone as the Elfin knight in presence came,
        And false *Duessa* seeming Lady faire,
        A gentle Husher, *Vanitie* by name
        Made rowme, and passage for them did prepaire:
        So goodly brought them to the lowest staire
        Of her high throne, where they on humble knee
        Making obeyssance, did the cause declare,
        Why they were come, her royall state to see,
    To prove the wide report of her great Majestee.

14 With loftie eyes, halfe loth to looke so low,
        She thanked them in her disdainefull wise,
        Ne other grace vouchsafed them to show
        Of Princesse worthy, scarse them bad arise.
        Her Lordes and Ladies all this while devise
        Themselves to setten forth to straungers sight:
        Some frounce their curled haire in courtly guise,
        Some prancke their ruffes, and others trimly dight
    Their gay attire: each others greater pride does spight.

---

12. *pollicie*: statecraft. *advizement*: counsel, advice.
13. *Husher*: usher.
14. *frounce*: wave, wrinkle. *prancke*: show off. *dight*: arrange.

15 Goodly they all that knight do entertaine,
        Right glad with him to have increast their crew:
        But to *Duess'* each one himselfe did paine
        All kindnesse and faire courtesie to shew;
        For in that court whylome her well they knew;
        Yet the stout Faerie mongst the middest crowd
        Thought all their glorie vaine in knightly vew,
        And that great Princesse too exceeding prowd,
    That to strange knight no better countenance allowd.

16 Suddein upriseth from her stately place
        The royall Dame, and for her coche doth call:
        All hurtlen forth, and she with Princely pace,
        As faire *Aurora* in her purple pall,
        Out of the East the dawning day doth call:
        So forth she comes: her brightnesse brode doth blaze;
        The heapes of people thronging in the hall,
        Do ride each other, upon her to gaze:
    Her glorious glitterand light doth all mens eyes amaze.

17 So forth she comes, and to her coche does clyme,
        Adorned all with gold, and girlonds gay,
        That sccmd as frcsh as *Flora* in her prime,
        And strove to match, in royall rich array,
        Great *Junoes* golden chaire, the which they say
        The Gods stand gazing on, when she does ride
        To *Joves* high house through heavens braspaved way
        Drawne of faire Pecocks, that excell in pride,
    And full of *Argus* eyes their tailes dispredden wide.

15. *whylome*: formerly.
16. *coche*: coach (also 17).   *hurtlen*: jostle.   *pall*: cloak, robe.   *brode*: abroad.
glitterand: glittering.
17. *dispredden*: spread.

18 But this was drawne of six unequall beasts,
　　On which her six sage Counsellours did ryde,
　　Taught to obay their bestiall beheasts,
　　With like conditions to their kinds applyde:
　　Of which the first, that all the rest did guyde,
　　Was sluggish *Idlenesse* the nourse of sin;
　　Upon a slouthfull Asse he chose to ryde,
　　Arayd in habit blacke, and amis thin,
Like to an holy Monck, the service to begin.

19 And in his hand his Portesse still he bare,
　　That much was worne, but therein little red,
　　For of devotion he had little care,
　　Still drownd in sleepe, and most of his dayes ded;
　　Scarse could he once uphold his heavie hed,
　　To looken, whether it were night or day:
　　May seeme the wayne was very evill led,
　　When such an one had guiding of the way,
That knew not, whether right he went, or else astray.

20 From worldly cares himselfe he did esloyne,
　　And greatly shunned manly exercise,
　　From every worke he chalenged essoyne,
　　For contemplation sake: yet otherwise,
　　His life he led in lawlesse riotise;
　　By which he grew to grievous malady;
　　For in his lustlesse limbs through evill guise
　　A shaking fever raignd continually:
Such one was *Idlenesse*, first of this company.

18. *beheasts*: behests, commands. *amis*: amice, priestly vestment.
19. *Portesse*: breviary. *wayne*: chariot.
20. *esloyne*: remove, detach. *chalenged essoyne*: claimed exemption. *riotise*: riotousness. *lustlesse*: listless, feeble.

21 And by his side rode loathsome *Gluttony*,
    Deformed creature, on a filthie swyne,
    His belly was up-blowne with luxury,
    And eke with fatnesse swollen were his eyne,
    And like a Crane his necke was long and fyne,
    With which he swallowed up excessive feast,
    For want whereof poore people oft did pyne;
    And al the way, most like a brutish beast,
He spued up his gorge, that all did him deteast.

22 In greene vine leaves he was right fitly clad;
    For other clothes he could not weare for heat,
    And on his head an yvie girland had,
    From under which fast trickled downe the sweat:
    Still as he rode, he somewhat still did eat,
    And in his hand did beare a bouzing can,
    Of which he supt so oft, that on his seat
    His dronken corse he scarse upholden can,
In shape and life more like a monster, then a man.

23 Unfit he was for any worldly thing,
    And eke unhable once to stirre or go,
    Not meet to be of counsell to a king,
    Whose mind in meat and drinke was drowned so,
    That from his friend he seldome knew his fo:
    Full of diseases was his carcas blew,
    And a dry dropsie through his flesh did flow:
    Which by misdiet daily greater grew:
Such one was *Gluttony*, the second of that crew.

---

21. *up-blowne*: swollen. *eyne*: eyes. *pyne*: waste away. *deteast*: detest.
23. *unhable*: unable. *go*: walk. *dry dropsie*: ?dropsy causing thirst. *misdiet*: wrong feeding.

24 And next to him rode lustfull *Lechery*,
        Upon a bearded Goat, whose rugged haire,
        And whally eyes (the signe of gelosy,)
        Was like the person selfe, whom he did beare:
        Who rough, and blacke, and filthy did appeare,
        Unseemely man to please faire Ladies eye;
        Yet he of Ladies oft was loved deare,
        When fairer faces were bid standen by:
O who does know the bent of womens fantasy?

25 In a greene gowne he clothed was full faire,
        Which underneath did hide his filthinesse,
        And in his hand a burning hart he bare,
        Full of vaine follies, and new fanglenesse:
        For he was false, and fraught with ficklenesse,
        And learned had to love with secret lookes,
        And well could daunce, and sing with ruefulnesse,
        And fortunes tell, and read in loving bookes,
And thousand other wayes, to bait his fleshly hookes.

26 Inconstant man, that loved all he saw,
        And lusted after all, that he did love,
        Ne would his looser life be tide to law,
        But joyd weake wemens hearts to tempt and prove
        If from their loyall loves he might them move;
        Which lewdnesse fild him with reprochfull paine
        Of that fowle evill, which all men reprove,
        That rots the marrow, and consumes the braine:
Such one was *Lecherie*, the third of all this traine.

24. *whally*: ?glaring, ?greenish.
25. *new fanglenesse*: novelty, innovation.   *ruefulnesse*: dolefulness.
26. *prove*: test.

27   And greedy *Avarice* by him did ride,
    Upon a Camell loaden all with gold;
    Two iron coffers hong on either side,
    With precious mettall full, as they might hold,
    And in his lap an heape of coine he told;
    For of his wicked pelfe his God he made,
    And unto hell him selfe for money sold;
    Accursed usurie was all his trade,
And right and wrong ylike in equall ballaunce waide.

28   His life was nigh unto deaths doore yplast,
    And thred-bare cote, and cobled shoes he ware,
    Ne scarse good morsell all his life did tast,
    But both from backe and belly still did spare,
    To fill his bags, and richesse to compare;
    Yet chylde ne kinsman living had he none
    To leave them to; but thorough daily care
    To get, and nightly feare to lose his owne,
He led a wretched life unto him selfe unknowne.

29   Most wretched wight, whom nothing might suffise,
    Whose greedy lust did lacke in greatest store,
    Whose need had end, but no end covetise,
    Whose wealth was want, whose plenty made him pore,
    Who had enough, yet wished ever more;
    A vile disease, and ckc in foote and hand
    A grievous gout tormented him full sore,
    That well he could not touch, nor go, nor stand:
Such one was *Avarice*, the fourth of this faire band.

27. *told*: counted.   *ylike*: alike.   28. *compare*: acquire.
29. *covetise*: covetousness.   *go*: walk.

30   And next to him malicious *Envie* rode,
        Upon a ravenous wolfe, and still did chaw
        Betweene his cankred teeth a venemous tode,
        That all the poison ran about his chaw;
        But inwardly he chawed his owne maw
        At neighbours wealth, that made him ever sad;
        For death it was, when any good he saw,
        And wept, that cause of weeping none he had,
    But when he heard of harme, he wexed wondrous glad.

31   All in a kirtle of discolourd say
        He clothed was, ypainted full of eyes;
        And in his bosome secretly there lay
        An hatefull Snake, the which his taile uptyes
        In many folds, and mortall sting implyes.
        Still as he rode, he gnasht his teeth, to see
        Those heapes of gold with griple Covetyse,
        And grudged at the great felicitie
    Of proud *Lucifera*, and his owne companie.

32   He hated all good workes and vertuous deeds,
        And him no lesse, that any like did use,
        And who with gracious bread the hungry feeds,
        His almes for want of faith he doth accuse;
        So every good to bad he doth abuse:
        And eke the verse of famous Poets witt
        He does backebite, and spightfull poison spues
        From leprous mouth on all, that ever writt:
    Such one vile *Envie* was, that fifte in row did sitt.

    30. *did chaw*: chewed.   *chaw*: jaw.   *wexed*: grew, became.
      31. *kirtle*: tunic.   *say*: fine-textured cloth.   *implyes*: enfolds, conceals.   *griple*:
grasping.   *Covetyse*: covetousness.

33 And him beside rides fierce revenging *Wrath*,
        Upon a Lion, loth for to be led;
        And in his hand a burning brond he hath,
        The which he brandisheth about his hed;
        His eyes did hurle forth sparkles fiery red,
        And stared sterne on all, that him beheld,
        As ashes pale of hew and seeming ded;
        And on his dagger still his hand he held,
    Trembling through hasty rage, when choler in him sweld.

34 His ruffin raiment all was staind with blood,
        Which he had spilt, and all to rags yrent,
        Through unadvized rashnesse woxen wood;
        For of his hands he had no governemen.,
        Ne car'd for bloud in his avengement:
        But when the furious fit was overpast,
        His cruell facts he often would repent;
        Yet wilfull man he never would forecast,
    How many mischieves should ensue his heedlesse hast.

35 Full many mischiefes follow cruell *Wrath*;
        Abhorred bloudshed, and tumultuous strife,
        Unmanly murder, and unthrifty scath,
        Bitter despight, with rancours rusty knife,
        And fretting griefe the enemy of life;
        All these, and many evils moe haunt ire,
        The swelling Splene, and Frenzy raging rife,
        The shaking Palsey, and Saint *Fraunces* fire:
    Such one was *Wrath*, the last of this ungodly tire.

33. *brond*: brand, burning piece of wood.
34. *ruffin*: ruffianly, disordered. *woxen*: grown, become. *wood*: mad. *avengement*: revenge. *facts*: evil deeds. *forecast*: think beforehand.
35. *scath*: hurt, harm. *despight*: spite. *moe*: more. *Saint Fraunces fire*: see note. *tire*: ?train, ?mob.

36   And after all, upon the wagon beame
        Rode *Sathan*, with a smarting whip in hand,
        With which he forward lasht the laesie teme,
        So oft as *Slowth* still in the mire did stand.
        Huge routs of people did about them band,
        Showting for joy, and still before their way
        A foggy mist had covered all the land;
        And underneath their feet, all scattered lay
  Dead sculs and bones of men, whose life had gone astray.

37   So forth they marchen in this goodly sort,
        To take the solace of the open aire,
        And in fresh flowring fields themselves to sport;
        Emongst the rest rode that false Lady faire,
        The fowle *Duessa*, next unto the chaire
        Of proud *Lucifera*, as one of the traine:
        But that good knight would not so nigh repaire,
        Him selfe estraunging from their joyaunce vaine,
  Whose fellowship seemd far unfit for warlike swaine.

38   So having solaced themselves a space
        With pleasaunce of the breathing fields yfed,
        They backe returned to the Princely Place;
        Whereas an errant knight in armes ycled,
        And heathnish shield, wherein with letters red
        Was writ *Sans joy*, they new arrived find:
        Enflam'd with fury and fiers hardy-hed,
        He seemd in hart to harbour thoughts unkind,
  And nourish bloudy vengeaunce in his bitter mind.

---

37. *repaire*: make (his) way, approach.   *joyaunce*: delight.   *swaine*: young man.
38. *Whereas*: where.   *errant*: wandering.   *hardy-hed*: boldness.

39 Who when the shamed shield of slaine *Sans foy*
    He spide with that same Faery champions page,
    Bewraying him, that did of late destroy
    His eldest brother, burning all with rage
    He to him leapt, and that same envious gage
    Of victors glory from him snatcht away:
    But th'Elfin knight, which ought that warlike wage,
    Disdaind to loose the meed he wonne in fray,
And him rencountring fierce, reskewd the noble pray.

40 Therewith they gan to hurtlen greedily,
    Redoubted battaile ready to darrayne,
    And clash their shields, and shake their swords on hy,
    That with their sturre they troubled all the traine;
    Till that great Queene upon eternall paine
    Of high displeasure, that ensewen might,
    Commaunded them their fury to refraine,
    And if that either to that shield had right,
In equall lists they should the morrow next it fight.

41 Ah dearest Dame, (quoth then the Paynim bold,)
    Pardon the errour of enraged wight,
    Whom great griefe made forget the raines to hold
    Of reasons rule, to see this recreant knight,
    No knight, but treachour full of false despight
    And shamefull treason, who through guile hath slayn
    The prowest knight, that ever field did fight,
    Even stout *Sans foy* (O who can then refrayn?)
Whose shield he beares renverst, the more to heape disdayn.

39. *Bewraying*: accusing. *gage*: pledge, token. *ought*: possessed. *wage*: reward (see note). *rencountring*: engaging in battle.
40. *greedily*: eagerly, fiercely. *Redoubted*: fierce, terrible. *darrayne*: offer, engage in.
41. *Paynim*: pagan. *treachour*: traitor, deceiver. *prowest*: bravest. *renverst*: reversed, upside down (see note).

42 And to augment the glorie of his guile,
   His dearest love the faire *Fidessa* loe
   Is there possessed of the traytour vile,
   Who reapes the harvest sowen by his foe,
   Sowen in bloudy field, and bought with woe:
   That brothers hand shall dearely well requight
   So be, O Queene, you equall favour showe.
   Him litle answerd th'angry Elfin knight;
He never meant with words, but swords to plead his right.

43 But threw his gauntlet as a sacred pledge,
   His cause in combat the next day to try:
   So been they parted both, with harts on edge,
   To be aveng'd each on his enimy.
   That night they pas in joy and jollity,
   Feasting and courting both in bowre and hall;
   For Steward was excessive *Gluttonie*,
Which doen, the Chamberlain *Slowth* did to rest them call.

44 Now whenas darkesome night had all displayd
   Her coleblacke curtein over brightest skye,
   The warlike youthes on dayntie couches layd,
   Did chace away sweet sleepe from sluggish eye,
   To muse on meanes of hoped victory.
   But whenas *Morpheus* had with leaden mace
   Arrested all that courtly company,
   Up-rose *Duessa* from her resting place,
And to the Paynims lodging comes with silent pace.

43. *doen*: done.
44. *displayd*: spread out. *Arrested*: charmed to sleep (see note).

45 Whom broad awake she finds, in troublous fit,
   Forecasting, how his foe he might annoy,
   And him amoves with speaches seeming fit:
   Ah deare *Sans joy*, next dearest to *Sans foy*,
   Cause of my new griefe, cause of my new joy,
   Joyous, to see his ymage in mine eye,
   And greev'd, to thinke how foe did him destroy,
   That was the flowre of grace and chevalrye;
Lo his *Fidessa* to thy secret faith I flye.

46 With gentle wordes he can her fairely greet,
   And bad say on the secret of her hart.
   Then sighing soft, I learne that litle sweet
   Oft tempred is (quoth she) with muchell smart:
   For since my brest was launcht with lovely dart
   Of deare *Sansfoy*, I never joyed howre,
   But in eternall woes my weaker hart
   Have wasted, loving him with all my powre,
And for his sake have felt full many an heavie stowre.

47 At last when perils all I weened past,
   And hop'd to reape the crop of all my care,
   Into new woes unweeting I was cast,
   By this false faytor, who unworthy ware
   His worthy shield, whom he with guilefull snare
   Entrapped slew, and brought to shamefull grave.
   Me silly maid away with him he bare,
   And ever since hath kept in darksome cave,
For that I would not yeeld, that to *Sans-foy* I gave.

45. *Forecasting*: planning. *amoves*: moves.
46. *bad say on*: bade her tell. *muchell*: great, much. *launcht*: pierced. *stowre*: anxious time.
47. *unweeting*: unwitting. *faytor*: deceiver, villain. *silly*: simple, innocent.

48 But since faire Sunne hath sperst that lowring clowd,
    And to my loathed life now shewes some light,
    Under your beames I will me safely shrowd,
    From dreaded storme of his disdainfull spight:
    To you th'inheritance belongs by right
    Of brothers prayse, to you eke longs his love.
    Let not his love, let not his restlesse spright
    Be unreveng'd, that calles to you above
From wandring *Stygian* shores, where it doth endlesse move.

49 Thereto said he, Faire Dame be nought dismaid
    For sorrowes past; their griefe is with them gone:
    Ne yet of present perill be affraid;
    For needlesse feare did never vantage none,
    And helplesse hap it booteth not to mone.
    Dead is *Sans-foy*, his vitall paines are past,
    Though greeved ghost for vengeance deepe do grone:
    He lives, that shall him pay his dewties last,
And guiltie Elfin bloud shall sacrifice in hast.

50 O but I feare the fickle freakes (quoth shee)
    Of fortune false, and oddes of armes in field.
    Why dame (quoth he) what oddes can ever bee,
    Where both do fight alike, to win or yield?
    Yea but (quoth she) he beares a charmed shield,
    And eke enchaunted armes, that none can perce,
    Ne none can wound the man, that does them wield.
    Charmd or enchaunted (answerd he then ferce)
I no whit reck, ne you the like need to reherce.

48. *sperst*: dispersed.   *longs*: belongs.
49. *vantage*: profit.   *vitall*: life's, relating to life.
50. *freakes*: whims.   *reherce*: tell.

51 But faire *Fidessa*, sithens fortunes guile,
    Or enimies powre hath now captived you,
    Returne from whence ye came, and rest a while
    Till morrow next, that I the Elfe subdew,
    And with *Sans-foyes* dead dowry you endew.
    Ay me, that is a double death (she said)
    With proud foes sight my sorrow to renew:
    Where ever yet I be, my secrete aid
Shall follow you. So passing forth she him obaid.

Canto 5

The faithfull knight in equall field
subdewes his faithlesse foe,
Whom false Duessa saves, and for
his cure to hell does goe.

1 The noble hart, that harbours vertuous thought,
    And is with child of glorious great intent,
    Can never rest, untill it forth have brought
    Th'eternall brood of glorie excellent:
    Such restlesse passion did all night torment
    The flaming corage of that Faery knight,
    Devizing, how that doughtie turnament
    With greatest honour he atchieven might;
Still did he wake, and still did watch for dawning light.

51. *sithens*: since, seeing that.

2 At last the golden Orientall gate
      Of greatest heaven gan to open faire,
      And *Phœbus* fresh, as bridegrome to his mate,
      Came dauncing forth, shaking his deawie haire:
      And hurld his glistring beames through gloomy aire.
      Which when the wakeful Elfe perceiv'd, streight way
      He started up, and did him selfe prepaire,
      In sun-bright armes, and battailous array:
  For with that Pagan proud he combat will that day.

3 And forth he comes into the commune hall,
      Where earely waite him many a gazing eye,
      To weet what end to straunger knights may fall.
      There many Minstrales maken melody,
      To drive away the dull melancholy,
      And many Bardes, that to the trembling chord
      Can tune their timely voyces cunningly,
      And many Chroniclers, that can record
  Old loves, and warres for Ladies doen by many a Lord.

4 Soone after comes the cruell Sarazin,
      In woven maile all armed warily,
      And sternly lookes at him, who not a pin
      Does care for looke of living creatures eye.
      They bring them wines of *Greece* and *Araby*,
      And daintie spices fetcht from furthest *Ynd*,
      To kindle heat of corage privily:
      And in the wine a solemne oth they bynd
  T'observe the sacred lawes of armes, that are assynd.

3. *weet*: know.

5 At last forth comes that far renowmed Queene,
     With royall pomp and Princely majestie;
     She is ybrought unto a paled greene,
     And placed under stately canapee,
     The warlike feates of both those knights to see.
     On th'other side in all mens open vew
     Duessa placed is, and on a tree
     Sans-foy his shield is hangd with bloudy hew:
  Both those the lawrell girlonds to the victor dew.

6 A shrilling trompet sownded from on hye,
     And unto battaill bad them selves addresse:
     Their shining shieldes about their wrestes they tye,
     And burning blades about their heads do blesse,
     The instruments of wrath and heavinesse:
     With greedy force each other doth assayle,
     And strike so fiercely, that they do impresse
     Deepe dinted furrowes in the battred mayle;
  The yron walles to ward their blowes are weake and fraile.

7 The Sarazin was stout, and wondrous strong,
     And heaped blowes like yron hammers great:
     For after bloud and vengeance he did long.
     The knight was fiers, and full of youthly heat:
     And doubled strokes, like dreaded thunders threat:
     For all for prayse and honour he did fight.
     Both stricken strike, and beaten both do beat,
     That from their shields forth flyeth firie light,
  And helmets hewen deepe, shew marks of eithers might.

---

5. *far renowmed*: renowned afar, famous.   *paled greene*: see note.   *Sans-foy his shield*: Sansfoy's shield.
6. *wrestes*: wrists.   *blesse*: brandish.   *greedy*: eager.

8 So th'one for wrong, the other strives for right:
   As when a Gryfon seized of his pray,
   A Dragon fiers encountreth in his flight,
   Through widest ayre making his ydle way,
   That would his rightfull ravine rend away:
   With hideous horrour both together smight,
   And souce so sore, that they the heavens affray:
   The wise Southsayer seeing so sad sight,
   Th'amazed vulgar tels of warres and mortall fight.

9 So th'one for wrong, the other strives for right,
   And each to deadly shame would drive his foe:
   The cruell steele so greedily doth bight
   In tender flesh, that streames of bloud down flow,
   With which the armes, that earst so bright did show,
   Into a pure vermillion now are dyde:
   Great ruth in all the gazers harts did grow,
   Seeing the gored woundes to gape so wyde.
   That victory they dare not wish to either side.

10 At last the Paynim chaunst to cast his eye,
   His suddein eye, flaming with wrathfull fyre,
   Upon his brothers shield, which hong thereby:
   Therewith redoubled was his raging yre,
   And said, Ah wretched sonne of wofull syre,
   Doest thou sit wayling by black *Stygian* lake,
   Whilest here thy shield is hangd for victors hyre,
   And sluggish german doest thy forces slake,
   To after-send his foe, that him may overtake?

8. *Gryfon*: griffin (see note). *ravine*: prey. *souce*: strike heavy blows. *affray*: frighten. *Southsayer*: soothsayer. *vulgar*: common people.
   9. *earst*: previously.
   10. *hyre*: reward. *german*: brother.

11 Goe caytive Elfe, him quickly overtake,
        And soone redeeme from his long wandring woe;
        Goe guiltie ghost, to him my message make,
        That I his shield have quit from dying foe.
        Therewith upon his crest he stroke him so,
        That twise he reeled, readie twise to fall;
        End of the doubtfull battell deemed tho
        The lookers on, and lowd to him can call
    The false *Duessa*, Thine the shield, and I, and all.

12 Soone as the Faerie heard his Ladie speake,
        Out of his swowning dreame he gan awake,
        And quickning faith, that earst was woxen weake,
        The creeping deadly cold away did shake:
        Tho mov'd with wrath, and shame, and Ladies sake,
        Of all attonce he cast avengd to bee,
        And with so'exceeding furie at him strake,
        That forced him to stoupe upon his knee;
    Had he not stouped so, he should have cloven bee,

13 And to him said, Goe now proud Miscreant,
        Thy selfe thy message doe to german deare,
        Alone he wandring thee too long doth want:
        Goe say, his foe thy shield with his doth beare.
        Therewith his heavie hand he high gan reare,
        Him to have slaine; when loe a darkesome clowd
        Upon him fell: he no where doth appeare,
        But vanisht is. The Elfe him cals alowd,
    But answer none receives: the darknes him does shrowd.

11. *quit*: freed, recovered.
12. *earst was woxen weake*: previously had grown weak.   *Tho*: then.
13. *german*: brother.

14 In haste *Duessa* from her place arose,
        And to him running said, O prowest knight,
        That ever Ladie to her love did chose,
        Let now abate the terror of your might,
        And quench the flame of furious despight,
        And bloudie vengeance; lo th'infernall powres
        Covering your foe with cloud of deadly night,
        Have borne him hence to *Plutoes* balefull bowres.
    The conquest yours, I yours, the shield, and glory yours.

15 Not all so satisfide, with greedie eye
        He sought all round about, his thirstie blade
        To bath in bloud of faithlesse enemy;
        Who all that while lay hid in secret shade:
        He stands amazed, how he thence should fade.
        At last the trumpets Triumph sound on hie,
        And running Heralds humble homage made,
        Greeting him goodly with new victorie,
    And to him brought the shield, the cause of enmitie.

16 Wherewith he goeth to that soveraine Queene,
        And falling her before on lowly knee,
        To her makes present of his service seene:
        Which she accepts, with thankes, and goodly gree,
        Greatly advauncing his gay chevalree.
        So marcheth home, and by her takes the knight,
        Whom all the people follow with great glee,
        Shouting, and clapping all their hands on hight,
    That all the aire it fils, and flyes to heaven bright.

14. *prowest*: most valiant.   *chose*: choose.   *balefull*: grim.
16. *gree*: goodwill.   *advauncing*: praising.   *glee*: joy.   *on hight*: on high.

17 Home is he brought, and laid in sumptuous bed:
      Where many skilfull leaches him abide,
      To salve his hurts, that yet still freshly bled.
      In wine and oyle they wash his woundes wide,
      And softly can embalme on every side.
      And all the while, most heavenly melody
      About the bed sweet musicke did divide,
      Him to beguile of griefe and agony:
    And all the while *Duessa* wept full bitterly.

18 As when a wearie traveller that strayes
      By muddy shore of broad seven-mouthed *Nile*,
      Unweeting of the perillous wandring wayes,
      Doth meet a cruell craftie Crocodile,
      Which in false griefe hyding his harmefull guile,
      Doth weepe full sore, and sheddeth tender teares:
      The foolish man, that pitties all this while
      His mournefull plight, is swallowd up unwares,
    Forgetfull of his owne, that mindes anothers cares.

19 So wept *Duessa* untill eventide,
      That shyning lampes in *Joves* high house were light:
      Then forth she rose, ne lenger would abide,
      But comes unto the place, where th'Hethen knight
      In slombring swownd nigh voyd of vitall spright,
      Lay cover'd with inchaunted cloud all day:
      Whom when she found, as she him left in plight,
      To wayle his woefull case she would not stay,
    But to the easterne coast of heaven makes speedy way.

17. *leaches*: physicians.   *divide*: see note.
19. *swownd*: swoon.   *vitall spright*: spirit of life.

20 Where griesly *Night*, with visage deadly sad,
   That *Phœbus* chearefull face durst never vew,
   And in a foule blacke pitchie mantle clad,
   She findes forth comming from her darkesome mew,
   Where she all day did hide her hated hew.
   Before the dore her yron charet stood,
   Alreadie harnessed for journey new;
   And coleblacke steedes yborne of hellish brood,
 That on their rustie bits did champ, as they were wood.

21 Who when she saw *Duessa* sunny bright,
   Adornd with gold and jewels shining cleare,
   She greatly grew amazed at the sight,
   And th'unacquainted light began to feare:
   For never did such brightnesse there appeare,
   And would have backe retyred to her cave,
   Untill the witches speech she gan to heare,
   Saying, Yet O thou dreaded Dame, I crave
 Abide, till I have told the message, which I have.

22 She stayd, and foorth *Duessa* can proceede,
   O thou most auncient Grandmother of all,
   More old then *Jove*, whom thou at first didst breede,
   Or that great house of Gods cælestiall,
   Which wast begot in *Dæmogorgons* hall,
   And sawst the secrets of the world unmade,
   Why suffredst thou thy Nephewes deare to fall
   With Elfin sword, most shamefully betrade?
 Lo where the stout *Sansjoy* doth sleepe in deadly shade.

20. *mew*: den, place of confinement. *charet*: chariot. *wood*: mad.
21. *unacquainted*: unfamiliar.
22. *Nephewes*: descendants, grandchildren.

23   And him before, I saw with bitter eyes
        The bold *Sansfoy* shrinke underneath his speare;
        And now the pray of fowles in field he lyes,
        Nor wayld of friends, nor laid on groning beare,
        That whylome was to me too dearely deare.
        O what of Gods then boots it to be borne,
        If old *Aveugles* sonnes so evill heare?
        Or who shall not great *Nightes* children scorne,
     When two of three her Nephews are so fowle forlorne.

24   Up then, up dreary Dame, of darknesse Queene,
        Go gather up the reliques of thy race,
        Or else goe them avenge, and let be seene,
        That dreaded *Night* in brightest day hath place,
        And can the children of faire light deface.
        Her feeling speeches some compassion moved
        In hart, and chaunge in that great mothers face:
        Yet pittie in her hart was never proved
     Till then: for evermore she hated, never loved.

25   And said, Deare daughter rightly may I rew
        The fall of famous children borne of mee,
        And good successes, which their foes ensew:
        But who can turne the streame of destince,
        Or breake the chayne of strong necessitee,
        Which fast is tyde to *Joves* eternall seat?
        The sonnes of Day he favoureth, I see,
        And by my ruines thinkes to make them great:
     To make one great by others losse, is bad excheat.

---

23. *groning*: sorrowful.   *so evill heare*: fare so evilly.   *Nephews*: see 22.
24. *dreary*: grim and gloomy.   *deface*: put out of countenance, destroy.
25. *excheat*: gain, exchange.

26 Yet shall they not escape so freely all;
        For some shall pay the price of others guilt:
        And he the man that made *Sansfoy* to fall,
        Shall with his owne bloud price that he hath spilt.
        But what art thou, that telst of Nephews kilt?
        I that do seeme not I, *Duessa* am,
        (Quoth she) how ever now in garments gilt,
        And gorgeous gold arayd I to thee came;
    Duessa I, the daughter of Deceipt and Shame.

27 Then bowing downe her aged backe, she kist
        The wicked witch, saying; In that faire face
        The false resemblance of Deceipt, I wist
        Did closely lurke; yet so true-seeming grace
        It carried, that I scarce in darkesome place
        Could it discerne, though I the mother bee
        Of falshood, and root of *Duessaes* race.
        O welcome child, whom I have longd to see,
    And now have seene unwares. Lo now I go with thee.

28 Then to her yron wagon she betakes,
        And with her beares the fowle welfavourd witch:
        Through mirkesome aire her readie way she makes.
        Her twyfold Teme, of which two blacke as pitch,
        And two were browne, yet each to each unlich,
        Did softly swim away, ne ever stampe,
        Unlesse she chaunst their stubborne mouths to twitch;
        Then foming tarre, their bridles they would champe,
    And trampling the fine element, would fiercely rampe.

---

26. *price*: pay for. *kilt*: killed.
    28. *welfavourd*: good-looking. *mirkesome*: murky. *twyfold*: twofold. *unlich*:
unlike. *rampe*: prance.

29 So well they sped, that they be come at length
   Unto the place, whereas the Paynim lay,
   Devoid of outward sense, and native strength,
   Coverd with charmed cloud from vew of day,
   And sight of men, since his late luckelesse fray.
   His cruell wounds with cruddy bloud congealed,
   They binden up so wisely, as they may,
   And handle softly, till they can be healed:
So lay him in her charet, close in night concealed.

30 And all the while she stood upon the ground,
   The wakefull dogs did never cease to bay,
   As giving warning of th'unwonted sound,
   With which her yron wheeles did them affray,
   And her darke griesly looke them much dismay;
   The messenger of death, the ghastly Owle
   With drearie shriekes did also her bewray;
   And hungry Wolves continually did howle,
At her abhorred face, so filthy and so fowle.

31 Thence turning backe in silence soft they stole,
   And brought the heavie corse with easie pace
   To yawning gulfe of deepe *Avernus* hole.
   By that same hole an entrance darke and bace
   With smoake and sulphure hiding all the place,
   Descends to hell: there creature never past,
   That backe returned without heavenly grace;
   But dreadfull Furies, which their chaines have brast,
And damned sprights sent forth to make ill men aghast.

      29. *whereas*: where.   *cruddy*: curdled.   *charet*: chariot.
      30. *drearie*: doleful.   *bewray*: betray (her presence).
      31. *brast*: burst.   *ill*: evil, wicked.

32 By that same way the direfull dames doe drive
    Their mournefull charet, fild with rusty blood,
    And downe to *Plutoes* house are come bilive:
    Which passing through, on every side them stood
    The trembling ghosts with sad amazed mood,
    Chattring their yron teeth, and staring wide
    With stonie eyes; and all the hellish brood
    Of feends infernall flockt on every side,
To gaze on earthly wight, that with the Night durst ride.

33 They pas the bitter waves of *Acheron*,
    Where many soules sit wailing woefully,
    And come to fiery flood of *Phlegeton*,
    Whereas the damned ghosts in torments fry,
    And with sharpe shrilling shriekes doe bootlesse cry,
    Cursing high *Jove*, the which them thither sent.
    The house of endlesse paine is built thereby,
    In which ten thousand sorts of punishment
The cursed creatures doe eternally torment.

34 Before the threshold dreadfull *Cerberus*
    His three deformed heads did lay along,
    Curled with thousand adders venemous,
    And lilled forth his bloudie flaming tong:
    At them he gan to reare his bristles strong,
    And felly gnarre, untill dayes enemy
    Did him appease; then downe his taile he hong
    And suffered them to passen quietly:
For she in hell and heaven had power equally.

32. *rusty*: rust-coloured.   *bilive*: quickly, forthwith.
33. *bootlesse*: unavailingly.
34. *lilled*: lolled.   *felly gnarre*: snarl fiercely.

35   There was *Ixion* turned on a wheele,
      For daring tempt the Queene of heaven to sin;
      And *Sisyphus* an huge round stone did reele
      Against an hill, ne might from labour lin;
      There thirstie *Tantalus* hong by the chin;
      And *Tityus* fed a vulture on his maw;
      Typhœus joynts were stretched on a gin,
      Theseus condemned to endlesse slouth by law,
  And fifty sisters water in leake vessels draw.

36   They all beholding worldly wights in place,
      Leave off their worke, unmindfull of their smart,
      To gaze on them; who forth by them doe pace,
      Till they be come unto the furthest part:
      Where was a Cave ywrought by wondrous art,
      Deepe, darke, uneasie, dolefull, comfortlesse,
      In which sad *Æsculapius* farre a part
      Emprisond was in chaines remedilesse,
  For that *Hippolytus* rent corse he did redresse.

37   *Hippolytus* a jolly huntsman was,
      That wont in charet chace the foming Bore;
      He all his Peeres in beautie did surpas,
      But Ladies love as losse of time forbore:
      His wanton stepdame loved him the more,
      But when she saw her offred sweets refused
      Her love she turnd to hate, and him before
      His father fierce of treason false accused,
  And with her gealous termes his open eares abused.

---

35. *reele*: roll. *lin*: cease. *gin*: instrument (of torture). *leake*: leaky.
36. *uneasie*: uncomfortable. *redresse*: restore, cure.
37. *termes*: words, language.

38   Who all in rage his Sea-god syre besought,
       Some cursed vengeance on his sonne to cast:
       From surging gulf two monsters straight were brought,
       With dread whereof his chasing steedes aghast,
       Both charet swift and huntsman overcast.
       His goodly corps on ragged cliffs yrent,
       Was quite dismembred, and his members chast
       Scattered on every mountaine, as he went,
That of *Hippolytus* was left no moniment.

39   His cruell stepdame seeing what was donne,
       Her wicked dayes with wretched knife did end,
       In death avowing th'innocence of her sonne.
       Which hearing his rash Syre, began to rend
       His haire, and hastie tongue, that did offend:
       Tho gathering up the relicks of his smart
       By *Dianes* meanes, who was *Hippolyts* frend,
       Them brought to *Æsculape*, that by his art
Did heale them all againe, and joyned every part.

40   Such wondrous science in mans wit to raine
       When *Jove* avizd, that could the dead revive,
       And fates expired could renew againe,
       Of endlesse life he might him not deprive,
       But unto hell did thrust him downe alive,
       With flashing thunderbolt ywounded sore:
       Where long remaining, he did alwaies strive
       Himselfe with salves to health for to restore,
And slake the heavenly fire, that raged evermore.

38. *members*: limbs.   40. *avizd*: considered.

41   There auncient Night arriving, did alight
        From her nigh wearie waine, and in her armes
        To *Æsculapius* brought the wounded knight:
        Whom having softly disarayd of armes,
        Tho gan to him discover all his harmes,
        Beseeching him with prayer, and with praise,
        If either salves, or oyles, or herbes, or charmes
        A fordonne wight from dore of death mote raise,
    He would at her request prolong her nephews daies.

42   Ah Dame (quoth he) thou temptest me in vaine,
        To dare the thing, which daily yet I rew,
        And the old cause of my continued paine
        With like attempt to like end to renew.
        Is not enough, that thrust from heaven dew
        Here endlesse penance for one fault I pay,
        But that redoubled crime with vengeance new
        Thou biddest me to eeke? Can Night defray
    The wrath of thundring *Jove*, that rules both night and day?

43   Not so (quoth she) but sith that heavens king
        From hope of heaven hath thee excluded quight,
        Why fearest thou, that canst not hope for thing,
        And fearest not, that more thee hurten might,
        Now in the powre of everlasting Night?
        Goe to then, O thou farre renowmed sonne
        Of great *Apollo*, shew thy famous might
        In medicine, that else hath to thee wonne
    Great paines, and greater praise, both never to be donne.

---

41. *fordonne*: exhausted, ruined.
42. *eeke*: increase.   *defray*: appease.
43. *sith that*: since, seeing that.   *farre renowmed*: far-famed.

44 Her words prevaild: And then the learned leach
       His cunning hand gan to his wounds to·lay,
       And all things else, the which his art did teach:
       Which having seene, from thence arose away
       The mother of dread darknesse, and let stay
       Aveugles sonne there in the leaches cure,
       And backe returning tooke her wonted way,
       To runne her timely race, whilst *Phœbus* pure
   In westerne waves his wearie wagon did recure.

45 The false *Duessa* leaving noyous Night,
       Returnd to stately pallace of dame Pride:
       Where when she came, she found the Faery knight
       Departed thence, albe his woundes wide
       Not throughly heald, unreadie were to ride.
       Good cause he had to hasten thence away;
       For on a day his wary Dwarfe had spide,
       Where in a dongeon deepe huge numbers lay
   Of caytive wretched thrals, that wayled night and day.

46 A ruefull sight, as could be seene with eie;
       Of whom he learned had in secret wise
       The hidden cause of their captivitie,
       How mortgaging their lives to *Covetise*,
       Through wastfull Pride, and wanton Riotise,
       They were by law of that proud Tyrannesse
       Provokt with *Wrath*, and *Envies* false surmise,
       Condemned to that Dongeon mercilesse,
   Where they should live in woe, and die in wretchednesse.

44. *leach*: physician.   *cure*: care.   *recure*: restore to health.
45. *noyous*: harmful, irksome.   *albe*: although.   *throughly*: thoroughly,
completely.   *caytive*: captive.
46. *Tyrannesse*: female tyrant.

47   There was that great proud king of *Babylon*,
      That would compell all nations to adore,
      And him as onely God to call upon,
      Till through celestiall doome throwne out of dore,
      Into an Oxe he was transform'd of yore:
      There also was king *Cræsus*, that enhaunst
      His heart too high through his great riches store;
      And proud *Antiochus*, the which advaunst
His cursed hand gainst God, and on his altars daunst.

48   And them long time before, great *Nimrod* was,
      That first the world with sword and fire warrayd;
      And after him old *Ninus* farre did pas
      In princely pompe, of all the world obayd;
      There also was that mightie Monarch layd
      Low under all, yet above all in pride,
      That name of native syre did fowle upbrayd,
      And would as *Ammons* sonne be magnifide,
Till scornd of God and man a shamefull death he dide.

49   All these together in one heape were throwne,
      Like carkases of beasts in butchers stall.
      And in another corner wide were strowne
      The antique ruines of the *Romaines* fall:
      Great *Romulus* the Grandsyre of them all,
      Proud *Tarquin*, and too lordly *Lentulus*,
      Stout *Scipio*, and stubborne *Hanniball*,
      Ambitious *Sulla*, and sterne *Marius*,
High *Cæsar*, great *Pompey*, and fierce *Antonius*.

---

47. *enhaunst*: raised up.   48. *warrayd*: harrassed with war.

50   Amongst these mighty men were wemen mixt,
         Proud wemen, vaine, forgetfull of their yoke:
         The bold *Semiramis*, whose sides transfixt
         With sonnes owne blade, her fowle reproches spoke;
         Faire *Sthenobœa*, that her selfe did choke
         With wilfull cord, for wanting of her will;
         High minded *Cleopatra*, that with stroke
         Of Aspes sting her selfe did stoutly kill:
      And thousands moe the like, that did that dongeon fill.

51   Besides the endlesse routs of wretched thralles,
         Which thither were assembled day by day,
         From all the world after their wofull falles,
         Through wicked pride, and wasted wealthes decay.
         But most of all, which in that Dongeon lay
         Fell from high Princes courts, or Ladies bowres,
         Where they in idle pompe, or wanton play,
         Consumed had their goods, and thriftlesse howres,
      And lastly throwne themselves into these heavy stowres.

52   Whose case when as the carefull Dwarfe had tould,
         And made ensample of their mournefull sight
         Unto his maister, he no lenger would
         There dwell in perill of like painefull plight,
         But early rose, and ere that dawning light
         Disovered had the world to heaven wyde,
         He by a privie Posterne tooke his flight,
         That of no envious eyes he mote be spyde:
      For doubtlesse death ensewd, if any him descryde.

            50. *moe*: more.
            52. *ensample*: example.   *Posterne*: small back gate.

53 Scarse could he footing find in that fowle way,
        For many corses, like a great Lay-stall
        Of murdred men which therein strowed lay,
        Without remorse, or decent funerall:
        Which all through that great Princesse pride did fall
        And came to shamefull end. And them beside
        Forth ryding underneath the castell wall,
        A donghill of dead carkases he spide,
    The dreadfull spectacle of that sad house of *Pride*.

Canto 6

From lawlesse lust by wondrous grace
fayre Una is releast:
Whom salvage nation does adore,
and learnes her wise beheast.

1   As when a ship, that flyes faire under saile,
        An hidden rocke escaped hath unwares,
        That lay in waite her wrack for to bewaile,
        The Marriner yet halfe amazed stares
        At perill past, and yet in doubt ne dares
        To joy at his foole-happie oversight:
        So doubly is distrest twixt joy and cares
        The dreadlesse courage of this Elfin knight,
    Having escapt so sad cnsamples in his sight.

53. *Lay-stall*: refuse-tip. *remorse*: pity.
Argument. *beheast*: behest, bidding.
  1. *bewaile*: (here) cause, bring about. *doubt*: fear. *joy*: rejoice. *fool-happie*:
fortunate.

2 Yet sad he was that his too hastie speed
       The faire *Duess'* had forst him leave behind;
       And yet more sad, that *Una* his deare dreed
       Her truth had staind with treason so unkind;
       Yet crime in her could never creature find,
       But for his love, and for her owne selfe sake,
       She wandred had from one to other *Ynd*,
       Him for to seeke, ne ever would forsake,
   Till her unwares the fierce *Sansloy* did overtake.

3 Who after *Archimagoes* fowle defeat,
       Led her away into a forrest wilde,
       And turning wrathfull fire to lustfull heat,
       With beastly sin thought her to have defilde,
       And made the vassall of his pleasures vilde.
       Yet first he cast by treatie, and by traynes,
       Her to perswade, that stubborne fort to yilde:
       For greater conquest of hard love he gaynes,
   That workes it to his will, then he that it constraines.

4 With fawning wordes he courted her a while,
       And looking lovely, and oft sighing sore,
       Her constant hart did tempt with diverse guile:
       But wordes, and lookes, and sighes she did abhore,
       As rocke of Diamond stedfast evermore.
       Yet for to feed his fyrie lustfull eye,
       He snatcht the vele, that hong her face before;
       Then gan her beautie shine, as brightest skye,
   And burnt his beastly hart t'efforce her chastitye.

2. *dreed*: object of reverence, loved one.
3. *cast*: tried.   *treatie*: entreaty.   *traynes*: tricks, wiles.
4. *vele*: veil.   *efforce*: gain by force.

5   So when he saw his flatt'ring arts to fayle,
    And subtile engines bet from batteree,
    With greedy force he gan the fort assayle,
    Whereof he weend possessed soone to bee,
    And win rich spoile of ransackt chastetee.
    Ah heavens, that do this hideous act behold,
    And heavenly virgin thus outraged see,
    How can ye vengeance just so long withhold,
And hurle not flashing flames upon that Paynim bold?

6   The pitteous maiden carefull comfortlesse,
    Does throw out thrilling shriekes, and shrieking cryes,
    The last vaine helpe of womens great distresse,
    And with loud plaints importuneth the skyes,
    That molten starres do drop like weeping eyes;
    And *Phœbus* flying so most shamefull sight,
    His blushing face in foggy cloud implyes,
    And hides for shame. What wit of mortall wight
Can now devise to quit a thrall from such a plight?

7   Eternall providence excceding thought,
    Where none appeares can make her selfe a way:
    A wondrous way it for this Lady wrought,
    From Lyons clawes to pluck the griped pray.
    Her shrill outcryes and shriekes so loud did bray,
    That all the woodes and forestes did resownd;
    A troupe of *Faunes* and *Satyres* far away
    Within the wood were dauncing in a rownd,
Whiles old *Sylvanus* slept in shady arber sownd.

    5. *bet from batteree*: beaten off.
    6. *thrilling*: piercing.   *implyes*: enfolds, hides.   *quit*: free.

8 Who when they heard that pitteous strained voice,
   In hast forsooke their rurall meriment,
   And ran towards the far rebownded noyce,
   To weet, what wight so loudly did lament.
   Unto the place they come incontinent:
   Whom when the raging Sarazin espide,
   A rude, misshapen, monstrous rablement,
   Whose like he never saw, he durst not bide,
But got his ready steed, and fast away gan ride.

9 The wyld woodgods arrived in the place,
   There find the virgin dolefull desolate,
   With ruffled rayments, and faire blubbred face,
   As her outrageous foe had left her late,
   And trembling yet through feare of former hate;
   All stand amazed at so uncouth sight,
   And gin to pittie her unhappie state,
   All stand astonied at her beautie bright,
In their rude eyes unworthie of so wofull plight.

10 She more amaz'd, in double dread doth dwell;
   And every tender part for feare does shake:
   As when a greedie Wolfe through hunger fell
   A seely Lambe farre from the flocke does take,
   Of whom he meanes his bloudie feast to make,
   A Lyon spyes fast running towards him,
   The innocent pray in hast he does forsake,
   Which quit from death yet quakes in every lim
With chaunge of feare, to see the Lyon looke so grim.

8. *incontinent*: straight away.   *rablement*: rabble.
9. *outrageous*: violent.   *uncouth*: strange.
10. *fell*: fierce.   *seely*: innocent.

11   Such fearefull fit assaid her trembling hart,
        Ne word to speake, ne joynt to move she had:
        The salvage nation feele her secret smart,
        And read her sorrow in her count'nance sad;
        Their frowning forheads with rough hornes yclad,
        And rusticke horror all a side doe lay,
        And gently grenning, shew a semblance glad
        To comfort her, and feare to put away,
     Their backward bent knees teach her humbly to obay.

12   The doubtfull Damzell dare not yet commit
        Her single person to their barbarous truth,
        But still twixt feare and hope amazd does sit,
        Late learnd what harme to hastie trust ensu'th,
        They in compassion of her tender youth,
        And wonder of her beautie soveraine,
        Are wonne with pitty and unwonted ruth,
        And all prostrate upon the lowly plaine,
     Do kisse her feete, and fawne on her with count'nance faine.

13   Their harts she ghesseth by their humble guise,
        And yieldes her to extremitie of time;
        So from the ground she fearelesse doth arise,
        And walketh forth without suspect of crime:
        They all as glad, as birdes of joyous Prime,
        Thence lead her forth, about her dauncing round,
        Shouting, and singing all a shepheards ryme,
        And with greene braunches strowing all the ground,
     Do worship her, as Queene, with olive girlond cround.

---

11. *horror*: roughness.   *grenning*: grinning.   12. *learnd*: taught.
13. *ghesseth*: guesses, judges.   *Prime*: springtime.

14   And all the way their merry pipes they sound,
      That all the woods with doubled Eccho ring,
      And with their horned feet do weare the ground,
      Leaping like wanton kids in pleasant Spring.
      So towards old *Sylvanus* they her bring;
      Who with the noyse awaked, commeth out,
      To weet the cause, his weake steps governing,
      And aged limbs on Cypresse stadle stout,
And with an yvie twyne his wast is girt about.

15   Far off he wonders, what them makes so glad,
      Or *Bacchus* merry fruit they did invent,
      Or *Cybeles* franticke rites have made them mad;
      They drawing nigh, unto their God present
      That flowre of faith and beautie excellent.
      That God himselfe vewing that mirrhour rare,
      Stood long amazd, and burnt in his intent;
      His owne faire *Dryope* now he thinkes not faire,
And *Pholoe* fowle, when her to this he doth compaire.

16   The woodborne people fall before her flat,
      And worship her as Goddesse of the wood;
      And old *Sylvanus* selfe bethinkes not, what
      To thinke of wight so faire, but gazing stood,
      In doubt to deeme her borne of earthly brood;
      Sometimes Dame *Venus* selfe he seemes to see,
      But *Venus* never had so sober mood;
      Sometimes *Diana* he her takes to bee,
But misseth bow, and shaftes, and buskins to her knee.

14. *stadle*: staff (see note).   15. *invent*: find (see note).

17 By vew of her he ginneth to revive
    His ancient love, and dearest *Cyparisse*,
    And calles to mind his pourtraiture alive,
    How faire he was, and yet not faire to this,
    And how he slew with glauncing dart amisse
    A gentle Hynd, the which the lovely boy
    Did love as life, above all worldly blisse;
    For griefe whereof the lad n'ould after joy,
But pynd away in anguish and selfe-wild annoy.

18 The wooddy Nymphes, faire *Hamadryades*
    Her to behold do thither runne apace,
    And all the troupe of light-foot *Naiades*,
    Flocke all about to see her lovely face:
    But when they vewed have her heavenly grace,
    They envie her in their malitious mind,
    And fly away for feare of fowle disgrace:
    But all the *Satyres* scorne their woody kind,
And henceforth nothing faire, but her on earth they find.

19 Glad of such lucke, the luckelesse lucky maid,
    Did her content to please their feeble eyes,
    And long time with that salvage people staid,
    To gather breath in many miseries.
    During which time her gentle wit she plyes,
    To teach them truth, which worshipt her in vaine,
    And made her th'Image of Idolatryes;
    But when their bootlesse zeale she did restraine
From her own worship, they her Asse would worship fayn.

17. *n'ould*: would not. *joy*: be glad. *annoy*: annoyance, vexation.
19. *would worship fayn*: would fain worship, wanted to worship.

20 It fortuned a noble warlike knight
        By just occasion to that forrest came,
        To seeke his kindred, and the lignage right,
        From whence he tooke his well deserved name:
        He had in armes abroad wonne muchell fame,
        And fild far landes with glorie of his might,
        Plaine, faithfull, true, and enimy of shame,
        And ever lov'd to fight for Ladies right,
    But in vaine glorious frayes he litle did delight.

21 A Satyres sonne yborne in forrest wyld,
        By straunge adventure as it did betyde,
        And there begotten of a Lady myld,
        Faire *Thyamis* the daughter of *Labryde*,
        That was in sacred bands of wedlocke tyde
        To *Therion*, a loose unruly swayne;
        Who had more joy to raunge the forrest wyde,
        And chase the salvage beast with busie payne,
    Then serve his Ladies love, and wast in pleasures vayne.

22 The forlorne mayd did with loves longing burne,
        And could not lacke her lovers company,
        But to the wood she goes, to serve her turne,
        And seeke her spouse, that from her still does fly,
        And followes other game and venery:
        A Satyre chaunst her wandring for to find,
        And kindling coles of lust in brutish eye,
        The loyall links of wedlocke did unbind,
    And made her person thrall unto his beastly kind.

20. *lignage*: lineage.   *muchell*: much, great.   22. *venery*: prey.

23 So long in secret cabin there he held
    Her captive to his sensuall desire,
    Till that with timely fruit her belly sweld,
    And bore a boy unto that salvage sire:
    Then home he suffred her for to retire,
    For ransome leaving him the late borne childe;
    Whom till to ryper yeares he gan aspire,
    He noursled up in life and manners wilde,
Emongst wild beasts and woods, from lawes of men exilde.

24 For all he taught the tender ymp, was but
    To banish cowardize and bastard feare;
    His trembling hand he would him force to put
    Upon the Lyon and the rugged Beare,
    And from the she Beares teats her whelps to teare;
    And eke wyld roring Buls he would him make
    To tame, and ryde their backes not made to beare;
    And the Robuckes in flight to overtake,
That every beast for feare of him did fly and quake.

25 Thereby so fearelesse, and so fell he grew,
    That his owne sire and maister of his guise
    Did often tremble at his horrid vew,
    And oft for dread of hurt would him advise,
    The angry beasts not rashly to despise,
    Nor too much to provoke; for he would learne
    The Lyon stoup to him in lowly wise,
    (A lesson hard) and make the Libbard sterne
Leave roaring, when in rage he for revenge did earne.

23. *noursled up*: reared, brought up.
25. *horrid*: terrible. *learne*: teach. *Libbard*: leopard. *sterne*: fierce. *earne*: yearn.

26   And for to make his powre approved more,
        Wyld beasts in yron yokes he would compell;
        The spotted Panther, and the tusked Bore,
        The Pardale swift, and the Tigre cruell;
        The Antelope, and Wolfe both fierce and fell;
        And them constraine in equall teme to draw.
        Such joy he had, their stubborne harts to quell,
        And sturdie courage tame with dreadfull aw,
     That his beheast they feared, as a tyrans law.

27   His loving mother came upon a day
        Unto the woods, to see her little sonne;
        And chaunst unwares to meet him in the way,
        After his sportes, and cruell pastime donne,
        When after him a Lyonesse did runne,
        That roaring all with rage, did lowd requere
        Her children deare, whom he away had wonne:
        The Lyon whelpes she saw how he did beare,
     And lull in rugged armes, withouten childish feare.

28   The fearefull Dame all quaked at the sight,
        And turning backe, gan fast to fly away,
        Untill with love revokt from vaine affright,
        She hardly yet perswaded was to stay,
        And then to him these womanish words gan say;
        Ah *Satyrane*, my dearling, and my joy,
        For love of me leave off this dreadfull play;
        To dally thus with death, is no fit toy,
     Go find some other play-fellowes, mine own sweet boy.

26. *approved*: proved, demonstrated.   *Pardale*: leopard.   *tyrans*: tyrant's.
28. *revokt*: called back.   *toy*: sport, amusement.

29 In these and like delights of bloudy game
        He trayned was, till ryper yeares he raught,
        And there abode, whilst any beast of name
        Walkt in that forest, whom he had not taught
        To feare his force: and then his courage haught
        Desird of forreine foemen to be knowne,
        And far abroad for straunge adventures sought:
        In which his might was never overthrowne,
    But through all Faery lond his famous worth was blown.

30 Yet evermore it was his manner faire,
        After long labours and adventures spent,
        Unto those native woods for to repaire,
        To see his sire and ofspring auncient.
        And now he thither came for like intent;
        Where he unwares the fairest *Una* found,
        Straunge Lady, in so straunge habiliment,
        Teaching the Satyres, which her sat around,
    Trew sacred lore, which from her sweet lips did redound.

31 He wondred at her wisedome heavenly rare,
        Whose like in womens wit he never knew;
        And when her curteous deeds he did compare,
        Gan her admire, and her sad sorrowes rew,
        Blaming of Fortune, which such troubles threw,
        And joyd to make proofe of her crueltie
        On gentle Dame, so hurtlesse, and so trew:
        Thenceforth he kept her goodly company,
    And learnd her discipline of faith and veritie.

---

           29. *raught*: reached.   *haught*: proud, haughty.
           30. *ofspring*: origin.   *redound*: proceed.

32   But she all vowd unto the *Redcrosse* knight,
     His wandring perill closely did lament,
     Ne in this new acquaintaunce could delight,
     But her deare heart with anguish did torment,
     And all her wit in secret counsels spent,
     How to escape. At last in privie wise
     To *Satyrane* she shewed her intent;
     Who glad to gain such favour, gan devise,
How with that pensive Maid he best might thence arise.

33   So on a day when Satyres all were gone,
     To do their service to *Sylvanus* old,
     The gentle virgin left behind alone
     He led away with courage stout and bold.
     Too late it was, to Satyres to be told,
     Or ever hope recover her againe:
     In vaine he seekes that having cannot hold.
     So fast he carried her with carefull paine,
That they the woods are past, and come now to the plaine.

34   The better part now of the lingring day,
     They traveild had, when as they farre espide
     A wearie wight forwandring by the way,
     And towards him they gan in hast to ride,
     To weet of newes, that did abroad betide,
     Or tydings of her knight of the *Redcrosse*.
     But he them spying, gan to turne aside,
     For feare as seemd, or for some feigned losse;
More greedy they of newes, fast towards him do crosse.

---

34. *forwandring*: wandering astray.

35 A silly man, in simple weedes forworne,
    And soild with dust of the long dried way;
    His sandales were with toilesome travell torne,
    And face all tand with scorching sunny ray,
    As he had traveild many a sommers day,
    Through boyling sands of *Arabie* and *Ynde*;
    And in his hand a *Jacobs* staffe, to stay
    His wearie limbes upon: and eke behind,
His scrip did hang, in which his needments he did bind.

36 The knight approching nigh, of him inquerd
    Tydings of warre, and of adventures new;
    But warres, nor new adventures none he herd.
    Then *Una* gan to aske, if ought he knew,
    Or heard abroad of that her champion trew,
    That in his armour bare a croslet red.
    Aye me, Deare dame (quoth he) well may I rew
    To tell the sad sight, which mine eies have red:
These eyes did see that knight both living and eke ded.

37 That cruell word her tender hart so thrild,
    That suddein cold did runne through every vaine,
    And stony horrour all her sences fild
    With dying fit, that downe she fell for paine.
    The knight her lightly reared up againe,
    And comforted with curteous kind reliefe:
    Then wonne from death, she bad him tellen plaine
    The further processe of her hidden griefe;
The lesser pangs can beare, who hath endur'd the chiefe.

---

35. *forworne*: worn out.   *stay*: rest, support.   *scrip*: small bag.
36. *croslet*: small cross.
37. *thrild*: pierced.   *With dying fit*: with a death-like fit.

38   Then gan the Pilgrim thus, I chaunst this day,
         This fatall day, that shall I ever rew,
         To see two knights in travell on my way
         (A sory sight) arraung'd in battall new,
         Both breathing vengeaunce, both of wrathfull hew:
         My fearefull flesh did tremble at their strife,
         To see their blades so greedily imbrew,
         That drunke with bloud, yet thristed after life:
     What more? the *Redcrosse* knight was slaine with Paynim
         knife.

39   Ah dearest Lord (quoth she) how might that bee.
         And he the stoutest knight, that ever wonne?
         Ah dearest dame (quoth he) how might I see
         The thing, that might not be, and yet was donne?
         Where is (said *Satyrane*) that Paynims sonne,
         That him of life, and us of joy hath reft?
         Not far away (quoth he) he hence doth wonne
         Foreby a fountaine, where I late him left
     Washing his bloudy wounds, that through the steele were
         cleft.

40   Therewith the knight thence marched forth in hast,
         Whiles *Una* with huge heavinesse opprest,
         Could not for sorrow follow him so fast;
         And soone he came, as he the place had ghest,
         Whereas that *Pagan* proud him selfe did rest,
         In secret shadow by a fountaine side:
         Even he it was, that earst would have supprest
         Faire *Una*: whom when *Satyrane* espide,
     With fowle reprochfull words he boldly him defide.

38. *imbrew*: be soaked (in blood).   *thristed*: thirsted.
39. *wonne*: fought, conquered.   *wonne* (l. 7): dwell.   *Foreby*: close by.
40. *ghest*: guessed.

41 And said, Arise thou cursed Miscreaunt,
  That hast with knightlesse guile and trecherous train
  Faire knighthood fowly shamed, and doest vaunt
  That good knight of the *Redcrosse* to have slain:
  Arise, and with like treason now maintain
  Thy guilty wrong, or else thee guilty yield.
  The Sarazin this hearing, rose amain,
  And catching up in hast his three square shield,
 And shining helmet, soone him buckled to the field.

42 And drawing nigh him said, Ah misborne Elfe,
  In evil houre thy foes thee hither sent,
  Anothers wrongs to wreake upon thy selfe:
  Yet ill thou blamest me, for having blent
  My name with guile and traiterous intent;
  That *Redcrosse* knight, perdie, I never slew,
  But had he beene, where earst his armes were lent,
  Th'enchaunter vaine his errour should not rew:
 But thou his errour shalt, I hope now proven trew.

43 Therewith they gan, both furious and fell,
  To thunder blowes, and fiersly to assaile
  Each other bent his enimy to quell,
  That with their force they perst both plate and maile,
  And made wide furrowes in their fleshes fraile,
  That it would pitty any living eie.
  Large floods of bloud adowne their sides did raile;
  But floods of bloud could not them satisfie:
 Both hungred after death: both chose to win, or die.

42. *blent*: ?connected, ?tainted. *perdie*: (a mild oath). *earst*: previously.
43. *raile*: flow.

44 So long they fight, and fell revenge pursue,
   That fainting each, themselves to breathen let,
   And oft refreshed, battell oft renue:
   As when two Bores with rancling malice met,
   Their gory sides fresh bleeding fiercely fret,
   Til breathlesse both them selves aside retire,
   Where foming wrath, their cruell tuskes they whet,
   And trample th'earth, the whiles they may respire;
Then backe to fight againe, new breathed and entire.

45 So fiersly, when these knights had breathed once,
   They gan to fight returne, increasing more
   Their puissant force, and cruell rage attonce,
   With heaped strokes more hugely, then before,
   That with their drerie wounds and bloudy gore
   They both deformed, scarsely could be known.
   By this sad *Una* fraught with anguish sore,
   Led with their noise, which through the aire was thrown,
Arriv'd, where they in erth their fruitles bloud had sown.

46 Whom all so soone as that proud Sarazin
   Espide, he gan revive the memory
   Of his lewd lusts, and late attempted sin,
   And left the doubtfull battell hastily,
   To catch her, newly offred to his eie:
   But *Satyrane* with strokes him turning, staid,
   And sternely bad him other businesse plie,
   Then hunt the steps of pure unspotted Maid:
Wherewith he all enrag'd, these bitter speaches said.

45. *puissant*: powerful. *drerie*: bloody.

47   O foolish faeries sonne, what furie mad
        Hath thee incenst, to hast thy dolefull fate?
        Were it not better, I that Lady had,
        Then that thou hadst repented it too late?
        Most sencelesse man he, that himselfe doth hate,
        To love another. Lo then for thine ayd
        Here take thy lovers token on thy pate.
        So they to fight; the whiles the royall Mayd
Fled farre away, of that proud Paynim sore afrayd.

48   But that false *Pilgrim*, which that leasing told,
        Being in deed old *Archimage*, did stay
        In secret shadow, all this to behold,
        And much rejoyced in their bloudy fray:
        But when he saw the Damsell passe away
        He left his stond, and her pursewd apace,
        In hope to bring her to her last decay,
        But for to tell her lamentable cace,
And eke this battels end, will need another place.

Canto 7

The Redcrosse knight is captive made
By Gyaunt proud opprest,
Prince Arthur meets with Una great-
ly with those newes distrest.

47. *they to fight*: they began to fight.
48. *leasing*: falsehood, lie.   *stond*: stand.   *last decay*: final ruin.

1   What man so wise, what earthly wit so ware,
     As to descry the crafty cunning traine,
     By which deceipt doth maske in visour faire,
     And cast her colours dyed deepe in graine,
     To seeme like Truth, whose shape she well can faine,
     And fitting gestures to her purpose frame,
     The guiltlesse man with guile to entertaine?
     Great maistresse of her art was that false Dame,
   The false *Duessa*, cloked with *Fidessaes* name.

2   Who when returning from the drery *Night*,
     She fownd not in that perilous house of *Pryde*,
     Where she had left, the noble *Redcrosse* knight,
     Her hoped pray, she would no lenger bide,
     But forth she went, to seeke him far and wide.
     Ere long she fownd, whereas he wearie sate,
     To rest him selfe, foreby a fountaine side,
     Disarmed all of yron-coted Plate,
   And by his side his steed the grassy forage ate.

3   He feedes upon the cooling shade, and bayes
     His sweatie forehead in the breathing wind,
     Which through the trembling leaves full gently playes
     Wherein the cherefull birds of sundry kind
     Do chaunt sweet musick, to delight his mind:
     The Witch approching gan him fairely greet,
     And with reproch of carelesnesse unkind
     Upbrayd, for leaving her in place unmeet,
   With fowle words tempring faire, soure gall with hony
     sweet.

---

1. *ware*: aware. *visour*: mask, disguise. *in graine*: in a fast colour, thoroughly. *faine*: feign.
  2. *drery*: grim and gloomy. *foreby*: close by.   3. *bayes*: bathes.

4   Unkindnesse past, they gan of solace treat,
        And bathe in pleasaunce of the joyous shade,
        Which shielded them against the boyling heat,
        And with greene boughes decking a gloomy glade,
        About the fountaine like a girlond made;
        Whose bubbling wave did ever freshly well,
        Ne ever would through fervent sommer fade:
        The sacred Nymph, which therein wont to dwell,
    Was out of *Dianes* favour, as it then befell.

5   The cause was this: one day when *Phœbe* fayre
        With all her band was following the chace,
        This Nymph, quite tyr'd with heat of scorching ayre
        Sat downe to rest in middest of the race:
        The goddesse wroth gan fowly her disgrace,
        And bad the waters, which from her did flow,
        Be such as she her selfe was then in place.
        Thenceforth her waters waxed dull and slow,
    And all that drunke thereof, did faint and feeble grow.

6   Hereof this gentle knight unweeting was,
        And lying downe upon the sandie graile,
        Drunke of the streame, as cleare as cristall glas;
        Eftsoones his manly forces gan to faile,
        And mightie strong was turnd to feeble fraile.
        His chaunged powres at first themselves not felt,
        Till crudled cold his corage gan assaile,
        And chearefull bloud in faintnesse chill did melt,
    Which like a fever fit through all his body swelt.

4. *fervent*: hot.
6. *graile*: gravel.   *at first . . . felt*: at first did not feel themselves changed.
crudled: curdled, frozen.   *swelt*: burned.

7   Yet goodly court he made still to his Dame,
        Pourd out in loosnesse on the grassy grownd,
        Both carelesse of his health, and of his fame:
        Till at the last he heard a dreadfull sownd,
        Which through the wood loud bellowing, did rebownd,
        That all the earth for terrour seemd to shake,
        And trees did tremble. Th'Elfe therewith astownd,
        Upstarted lightly from his looser make,
    And his unready weapons gan in hand to take.

8   But ere he could his armour on him dight,
        Or get his shield, his monstrous enimy
        With sturdie steps came stalking in his sight,
        An hideous Geant horrible and hye,
        That with his talnesse seemd to threat the skye,
        The ground eke groned under him for dreed;
        His living like saw never living eye,
        Ne durst behold: his stature did exceed
    The hight of three the tallest sonnes of mortall seed.

9   The greatest Earth his uncouth mother was,
        And blustring *Æolus* his boasted sire,
        Who with his breath, which through the world doth pas,
        Her hollow womb did secretly inspire,
        And fild her hidden caves with stormie yre,
        That she conceiv'd; and trebling the dew time,
        In which the wombes of women do expire,
        Brought forth this monstrous masse of earthly slime,
    Puft up with emptie wind, and fild with sinfull crime.

----

7. *astownd*: astonished.   *make*: companion.
8. *on him dight*: dress himself in.
9. *inspire*: quicken, make fertile.   *expire*: (here) give birth.

10 So growen great through arrogant delight
  Of th'high descent, whereof he was yborne,
  And through presumption of his matchlesse might,
  All other powres and knighthood he did scorne.
  Such now he marcheth to this man forlorne,
  And left to losse: his stalking steps are stayde
  Upon a snaggy Oke, which he had torne
  Out of his mothers bowelles, and it made
His mortall mace, wherewith his foemen he dismayde.

11 That when the knight he spide, he gan advance
  With huge force and insupportable mayne,
  And towards him with dreadfull fury praunce;
  Who haplesse, and eke hopelesse, all in vaine
  Did to him pace, sad battaile to darrayne,
  Disarmd, disgrast, and inwardly dismayde,
  And eke so faint in every joynt and vaine,
  Through that fraile fountaine, which him feeble made,
That scarsely could he weeld his bootlesse single blade.

12 The Geant strooke so maynly mercilesse,
  That could have overthrowne a stony towre,
  And were not heavenly grace, that him did blesse,
  He had beene pouldred all, as thin as flowre:
  But he was wary of that deadly stowre,
  And lightly lept from underneath the blow:
  Yet so exceeding was the villeins powre,
  That with the wind it did him overthrow,
And all his sences stound, that still he lay full low.

 10. *snaggy*: knotty.
 11. *mayne*: strength. *praunce*: swagger. *darrayne*: offer (battle).
 12. *maynly*: mightily. *were not*: had it not been for. *pouldred*: pulverized.
stound: stunned.

13 As when that divelish yron Engin wrought
      In deepest Hell, and framd by *Furies* skill,
      With windy Nitre and quick Sulphur fraught,
      And ramd with bullet round, ordaind to kill,
      Conceiveth fire, the heavens it doth fill
      With thundring noyse, and all the ayre doth choke,
      That none can breath, nor see, nor heare at will,
      Through smouldry cloud of duskish stincking smoke,
  That th'onely breath him daunts, who hath escapt the stroke.

14 So daunted when the Geaunt saw the knight,
      His heavie hand he heaved up on hye,
      And him to dust thought to have battred quight,
      Until *Duessa* loud to him gan crye;
      O great *Orgoglio*, greatest under skye,
      O hold thy mortall hand for Ladies sake,
      Hold for my sake, and do him not to dye,
      But vanquisht thine eternall bondslave make,
  And me thy worthy meed unto thy Leman take.

15 He hearkned, and did stay from further harmes,
      To gayne so goodly guerdon, as she spake:
      So willingly she came into his armes,
      Who her as willingly to grace did take,
      And was possessed of his new found make.
      Then up he tooke the slombred sencelesse corse,
      And ere he could out of his swowne awake,
      Him to his castle brought with hastie forse,
  And in a Dongeon deepe him threw without remorse.

  13. *windy*: ?airy, light. *fraught*: filled. *conceiveth fire*: ignites. *th'onely breath*:
the breath alone.
  14. *do him not to dye*: do not kill him; (lit.) cause him not to die.
  15. *guerdon*: reward. *make*: companion, mate.

16 From that day forth *Duessa* was his deare,
      And highly honourd in his haughtie eye,
      He gave her gold and purple pall to weare,
      And triple crowne set on her head full hye,
      And her endowd with royall majestye:
      Then for to make her dreaded more of men,
      And peoples harts with awfull terrour tye,
      A monstrous beast ybred in filthy fen
   He chose, which he had kept long time in darksome den.

17 Such/one it was, as that renowmed Snake
      Which great *Alcides* in *Stremona* slew,
      Long fostred in the filth of *Lerna* lake,
      Whose many heads out budding ever new,
      Did breed him endlesse labour to subdew:
      But this same Monster much more ugly was;
      For seven great heads out of his body grew,
      An yron brest, and backe of scaly bras,
   And all embrewd in bloud, his eyes did shine as glas.

18 His tayle was stretched out in wondrous length,
      That to the house of heavenly gods it raught,
      And with extorted powre, and borrow'd strength,
      The ever-burning lamps from thence it brought,
      And prowdly threw to ground, as things of nought;
      And underneath his filthy feet did tread
      The sacred things, and holy heasts foretaught.
      Upon this dreadfull Beast with sevenfold head
   He set the false *Duessa*, for more aw and dread.

16. *pall*: cloak, robe.   17. *embrewd*: soaked.
18. *raught*: reached.   *heasts*: commands.

19 The wofull Dwarfe, which saw his maisters fall,
      Whiles he had keeping of his grasing steed,
      And valiant knight become a caytive thrall,
      When all was past, tooke up his forlorne weed,
      His mightie armour, missing most at need;
      His silver shield, now idle maisterlesse;
      His poynant speare, that many made to bleed,
      The ruefull moniments of heavinesse,
And with them all departes, to tell his great distresse.

20 He had not travaild long, when on the way
      He wofull Ladie, wofull *Una* met,
      Fast flying from the Paynims greedy pray,
      Whilest *Satyrane* him from pursuit did let:
      Who when her eyes she on the Dwarfe had set,
      And saw the signes, that deadly tydings spake,
      She fell to ground for sorrowfull regret,
      And lively breath her sad brest did forsake,
Yet might her pitteous hart be seene to pant and quake.

21 The messenger of so unhappie newes
      Would faine have dyde: dead was his hart within,
      Yet outwardly some little comfort shewes:
      At last recovering hart, he does begin
      To rub her temples, and to chaufe her chin,
      And every tender part does tosse and turne:
      So hardly he the flitted life does win,
      Unto her native prison to retourne:
Then gins her grieved ghost thus to lament and mourne.

19. *caytive*: captive.   *forlorne weed*: abandoned attire.   *poynant*: sharp.
20. *let*: prevent.   21. *chaufe*: rub.

22 Ye dreary instruments of dolefull sight,
  That doe this deadly spectacle behold,
  Why do ye lenger feed on loathed light,
  Or liking find to gaze on earthly mould,
  Sith cruell fates the carefull threeds unfould,
  The which my life and love together tyde?
  Now let the stony dart of senselesse cold
  Perce to my hart, and pas through every side,
And let eternall night so sad sight fro me hide.

23 O lightsome day, the lampe of highest *Jove*,
  First made by him, mens wandring wayes to guyde,
  When darknesse he in deepest dongeon drove,
  Henceforth thy hated face for ever hyde,
  And shut up heavens windowes shyning wyde:
  For earthly sight can nought but sorrow breed,
  And late repentance, which shall long abyde.
  Mine eyes no more on vanitie shall feed,
But seeled up with death, shall have their deadly meed.

24 Then downe againe she fell unto the ground;
  But he her quickly reared up againe:
  Thrise did she sinke adowne in deadly swownd,
  And thrise he her reviv'd with busie paine:
  At last when life recover'd had the raine,
  And over-wrestled his strong enemie,
  With foltring tong, and trembling every vaine,
  Tell on (quoth she) the wofull Tragedie,
The which these reliques sad present unto mine eie.

22. *mould*: form. *Sith*: seeing that, since.
23. *seeled up with*: made blind by.
24. *raine*: rule, mastery. *foltring*: stammering.

L_FQ

25 Tempestuous fortune hath spent all her spight,
  And thrilling sorrow throwne his utmost dart;
  Thy sad tongue cannot tell more heavy plight,
  Then that I feele, and harbour in mine hart:
  Who hath endur'd the whole, can beare each part.
  If death it be, it is not the first wound,
  That launched hath my brest with bleeding smart.
  Begin, and end the bitter balefull stound;
If lesse, then that I feare, more favour I have found.

26 Then gan the Dwarfe the whole discourse declare,
  The subtill traines of *Archimago* old;
  The wanton loves of false *Fidessa* faire,
  Bought with the bloud of vanquisht Paynim bold:
  The wretched payre transform'd to treen mould;
  The house of Pride, and perils round about;
  The combat, which he with *Sansjoy* did hould;
  The lucklesse conflict with the Gyant stout,
Wherein captiv'd, of life or death he stood in doubt.

27 She heard with patience all unto the end,
  And strove to maister sorrowfull assay,
  Which greater grew, the more she did contend,
  And almost rent her tender hart in tway;
  And love fresh coles unto her fire did lay:
  For greater love, the greater is the losse.
  Was never Ladie loved dearer day,
  Then she did love the knight of the *Redcrosse*;
For whose deare sake so many troubles her did tosse.

25. *stound*: time of sorrow.   26. *treen mould*: the shape of trees.
27. *sorrowfull assay*: the assault of sorrow. *in tway*: in two.

28 At last when fervent sorrow slaked was,
    She up arose, resolving him to find
    Alive or dead: and forward forth doth pas,
    All as the Dwarfe the way to her assynd:
    And evermore in constant carefull mind
    She fed her wound with fresh renewed bale;
    Long tost with stormes, and bet with bitter wind,
    High over hils, and low adowne the dale,
  She wandred many a wood, and measurd many a vale

29 At last she chaunced by good hap to meet
    A goodly knight, faire marching by the way
    Together with his Squire, arayed meet:
    His glitterand armour shined farre away,
    Like glauncing light of *Phœbus* brightest ray;
    From top to toe no place appeared bare,
    That deadly dint of steele endanger may:
    Athwart his brest a bauldrick brave he ware,
  That shynd, like twinkling stars, with stons most pretious
      rare.

30 And in the midst thereof one pretious stone
    Of wondrous worth, and eke of wondrous mights,
    Shapt like a Ladies head, exceeding shone,
    Like *Hesperus* emongst the lesser lights,
    And strove for to amaze the weaker sights;
    Thereby his mortall blade full comely hong
    In yvory sheath, ycarv'd with curious slights;
    Whose hilts were burnisht gold, and handle strong
  Of mother pearle, and buckled with a golden tong.

28. *bale*: grief.　*bet*: beaten.
29. *glitterand*: glittering.　*bauldrick*: baldric, belt.
30. *curious slights*: skilfully wrought designs.　*mother pearle*: mother-of-pearl.

31 His haughtie helmet, horrid all with gold,
        Both glorious brightnesse, and great terrour bred;
        For all the crest a Dragon did enfold
        With greedie pawes, and over all did spred
        His golden wings: his dreadfull hideous hed
        Close couched on the bever, seem'd to throw
        From flaming mouth bright sparkles fierie red,
        That suddeine horror to faint harts did show;
    And scaly tayle was stretcht adowne his backe full low.

32 Upon the top of all his loftie crest,
        A bunch of haires discolourd diversly,
        With sprincled pearle, and gold full richly drest,
        Did shake, and seem'd to daunce for jollity,
        Like to an Almond tree ymounted hye
        On top of greene *Selinis* all alone,
        With blossomes brave bedecked daintily;
        Whose tender locks do tremble every one
    At every little breath, that under heaven is blowne.

33 His warlike shield all closely cover'd was,
        Ne might of mortall eye be ever seene;
        Not made of steele, nor of enduring bras,
        Such earthly mettals soone consumed bene:
        But all of Diamond perfect pure and cleene
        It framed was, one massie entire mould,
        Hewen out of Adamant rocke with engines keene,
        That point of speare it never percen could,
    Ne dint of direfull sword divide the substance would.

    31. *haughtie*: proud.   *horrid*: bristling.   *Close couched*: set close.   *bever*: beaver
(see glossary).
    33. *massie*: massive.

34   The same to wight he never wont disclose,
       But when as monsters huge he would dismay,
       Or daunt unequall armies of his foes,
       Or when the flying heavens he would affray;
       For so exceeding shone his glistring ray,
       That *Phœbus* golden face it did attaint,
       As when a cloud his beames doth over-lay;
       And silver *Cynthia* wexed pale and faint,
    As when her face is staynd with magicke arts constraint.

35   No magicke arts hereof had any might,
       Nor bloudie wordes of bold Enchaunters call,
       But all that was not such, as seemd in sight,
       Before that shield did fade, and suddeine fall:
       And when him list the raskall routes appall,
       Men into stones therewith he could transmew,
       And stones to dust, and dust to nought at all;
       And when him list the prouder lookes subdew,
    He would them gazing blind, or turne to other hew.

36   Ne let it seeme, that credence this exceedes,
       For he that made the same, was knowne right well
       To have done much more admirable deedes.
       It *Merlin* was, which whylome did excell
       All living wightes in might of magicke spell:
       Both shield, and sword, and armour all he wrought
       For this young Prince, when first to armes he fell;
       But when he dyde, the Faerie Queene it brought
    To Faerie lond, where yet it may be seene, if sought.

---

    34. *affray*: frighten.   *attaint*: sully, make dim.
    35. *when him list*: when it pleases him.   *raskall*: base, worthless.   *appall*:
subdue.   *transmew*: transmute, change.

37 A gentle youth, his dearely loved Squire
        His speare of heben wood behind him bare,
        Whose harmefull head, thrice heated in the fire,
        Had riven many a brest with pikehead square;
        A goodly person, and could menage faire
        His stubborne steed with curbed canon bit,
        Who under him did trample as the aire,
        And chauft, that any on his backe should sit;
    The yron rowels into frothy fome he bit.

38 When as this knight nigh to the Ladie drew,
        With lovely court he gan her entertaine;
        But when he heard her answeres loth, he knew
        Some secret sorrow did her heart distraine:
        Which to allay, and calme her storming paine,
        Faire feeling words he wisely gan display,
        And for her humour fitting purpose faine,
        To tempt the cause it selfe for to bewray;
    Wherewith emmov'd, these bleeding words she gan to say.

39 What worlds delight, or joy of living speach
        Can heart, so plung'd in sea of sorrowes deepe,
        And heaped with so huge misfortunes, reach?
        The carefull cold beginneth for to creepe,
        And in my heart his yron arrow steepe,
        Soone as I thinke upon my bitter bale:
        Such helplesse harmes yts better hidden keepe,
        Then rip up griefe, where it may not availe,
    My last left comfort is, my woes to weepe and waile.

37. *heben*: ebony. *menage*: handle. *canon bit*: smooth, round bit.
38. *distraine*: oppress, afflict. *purpose*: conversation. *faine*: feign. *bewray*: reveal. *emmov'd*: moved (with emotion).

40 Ah Ladie deare, quoth then the gentle knight,
    Well may I weene, your griefe is wondrous great;
    For wondrous great griefe groneth in my spright,
    Whiles thus I heare you of your sorrowes treat.
    But wofull Ladie let me you intrete,
    For to unfold the anguish of your hart:
    Mishaps are maistred by advice discrete,
    And counsell mittigates the greatest smart;
Found never helpe, who never would his hurts impart.

41 O but (quoth she) great griefe will not be tould,
    And can more easily be thought, then said.
    Right so; (quoth he) but he, that never would,
    Could never: will to might gives greatest aid.
    But griefe (quoth she) does greater grow displaid,
    If then it find not helpe, and breedes despaire.
    Despaire breedes not (quoth he) where faith is staid.
    No faith so fast (quoth she) but flesh does paire.
Flesh may empaire (quoth he) but reason can repaire.

42 His goodly reason, and well guided speach
    So deepe did settle in her gratious thought,
    That her perswaded to disclose the breach,
    Which love and fortune in her heart had wrought,
    And said; Faire Sir, I hope good hap hath brought
    You to inquire the secrets of my griefe,
    Or that your wisedome will direct my thought,
    Or that your prowesse can me yield reliefe:
Then heare the storie sad, which I shall tell you briefe.

40. *discrete*: suitable, wise.
41. *staid*: constant.   *paire*: weaken (it).   *empaire*: weaken.

43   The forlorne Maiden, whom your eyes have seene
     The laughing stocke of fortunes mockeries,
     Am th'only daughter of a King and Queene,
     Whose parents deare, whilest equall destinies
     Did runne about, and their felicities
     The favourable heavens did not envy,
     Did spread their rule through all the territories,
     Which *Phison* and *Euphrates* floweth by,
And *Gehons* golden waves doe wash continually.

44   Till that their cruell cursed enemy,
     An huge great Dragon horrible in sight,
     Bred in the loathly lakes of *Tartary*,
     With murdrous ravine, and devouring might
     Their kingdome spoild, and countrey wasted quight:
     Themselves, for feare into his jawes to fall,
     He forst to castle strong to take their flight,
     Where fast embard in mightie brasen wall,
He has them now foure yeres besiegd to make them thrall.

45   Full many knights adventurous and stout
     Have enterprizd that Monster to subdew;
     From every coast that heaven walks about,
     Have thither come the noble Martiall crew,
     That famous hard atchievements still pursew,
     Yet never any could that girlond win,
     But all still shronke, and still he greater grew:
     All they for want of faith, or guilt of sin,
The pitteous pray of his fierce crueltie have bin.

---

44. *Till that*: until.   *ravine*: plunder.   45. *enterprizd*: endeavoured.

46   At last yledd with farre reported praise,
       Which flying fame throughout the world had spred,
       Of doughtie knights, whom Faery land did raise,
       That noble order hight of Maidenhed,
       Forthwith to court of *Gloriane* I sped,
       Of *Gloriane* great Queene of glory bright,
       Whose kingdomes seat *Cleopolis* is red,
       There to obtaine some such redoubted knight,
   That Parents deare from tyrants powre deliver might.

47   It was my chance (my chance was faire and good)
       There for to find a fresh unproved knight,
       Whose manly hands imbrew'd in guiltie blood
       Had never bene, ne ever by his might
       Had throwne to ground the unregarded right:
       Yet of his prowesse proofe he since hath made
       (I witnesse am) in many a cruell fight;
       The groning ghosts of many one dismaide
   Have felt the bitter dint of his avenging blade.

48   And ye the forlorne reliques of his powre,
       His byting sword, and his devouring speare,
       Which have endured many a dreadfull stowre,
       Can speake his prowesse, that did earst you beare,
       And well could rule: now he hath left you heare,
       To be the record of his ruefull losse,
       And of my dolefull disaventurous deare:
       O heavie record of the good *Redcrosse*,
   Where have you left your Lord, that could so well you
      tosse?

46. *hight*: is called.   *red*: named, called   47. *imbrew'd*: bathed, steeped.
48. *disaventurous*: unfortunate.   *deare*: hurt, injury.

49 Well hoped I, and faire beginnings had,
    That he my captive langour should redeeme,
    Till all unweeting, an Enchaunter bad
    His sence abusd, and made him to misdeeme
    My loyalty, not such as it did seeme;
    That rather death desire, then such despight.
    Be judge ye heavens, that all things right esteeme,
    How I him lov'd, and love with all my might,
So thought I eke of him, and thinke I thought aright.

50 Thenceforth me desolate he quite forsooke,
    To wander, where wilde fortune would me lead,
    And other bywaies he himselfe betooke,
    Where never foot of living wight did tread,
    That brought not backe the balefull body dead;
    In which him chaunced false *Duessa* meete,
    Mine onely foe, mine onely deadly dread,
    Who with her witchcraft and misseeming sweete,
Inveigled him to follow her desires unmeete.

51 At last by subtill sleights she him betraid
    Unto his foe, a Gyant huge and tall,
    Who him disarmed, dissolute, dismaid,
    Unwares surprised, and with mightie mall
    The monster mercilesse him made to fall,
    Whose fall did never foe before behold;
    And now in darkesome dungeon, wretched thrall,
    Remedilesse, for aie he doth him hold;
This is my cause of griefe, more great, then may be told.

49. *langour*: sorrowful plight (see note).   *misdeeme*: misjudge.
50. *balefull*: (here)? doomed.   *misseeming*: false show.
51. *dissolute*: weak.   *mall*: club.

52 Ere she had ended all, she gan to faint:
    But he her comforted and faire bespake,
    Certes, Madame, ye have great cause of plaint,
    That stoutest heart, I weene, could cause to quake.
    But be of cheare, and comfort to you take:
    For till I have acquit your captive knight,
    Assure your selfe, I will you not forsake.
    His chearefull words reviv'd her chearelesse spright,
So forth they went, the Dwarfe them guiding ever right.

Canto 8

*Faire virgin to redeeme her deare
    brings Arthur to the fight:
Who slayes the Gyant, wounds the beast,
    and strips Duessa quight.*

1   Ay me, how many perils doe enfold
    The righteous man, to make him daily fall?
    Were not, that heavenly grace doth him uphold,
    And stedfast truth acquite him out of all.
    Her love is firme, her care continuall,
    So oft as he through his owne foolish pride,
    Or weakenesse is to sinfull bands made thrall:
    Else should this *Redcrosse* knight in bands have dyde,
For whose deliverance she this Prince doth thither guide.

52. *Certes*: indeed, certainly.   *acquit*: released.   1. *acquite*: release.

2   They sadly traveild thus, untill they came
       Nigh to a castle builded strong and hie:
       Then cryde the Dwarfe, lo yonder is the same,
       In which my Lord my liege doth lucklesse lie,
       Thrall to that Gyants hatefull tyrannie:
       Therefore, deare Sir, your mightie powres assay.
       The noble knight alighted by and by
       From loftie steede, and bad the Ladie stay,
    To see what end of fight should him befall that day.

3   So with the Squire, th'admirer of his might,
       He marched forth towards that castle wall;
       Whose gates he found fast shut, ne living wight
       To ward the same, nor answere commers call.
       Then tooke that Squire an horne of bugle small,
       Which hong adowne his side in twisted gold,
       And tassels gay. Wyde wonders over all
       Of that same hornes great vertues weren told,
    Which had approved bene in uses manifold.

4   Was never wight, that heard that shrilling sound,
       But trembling feare did feele in every vaine;
       Three miles it might be easie heard around,
       And Ecchoes three answerd it selfe againe:
       No false enchauntment, nor deceiptfull traine
       Might once abide the terror of that blast,
       But presently was voide and wholly vaine:
       No gate so strong, no locke so firme and fast,
    But with that percing noise flew open quite, or brast.

3. *ward*: guard.   *bugle*: wild ox (see note).   4. *brast*: shattered.

5   The same before the Geants gate he blew,
     That all the castle quaked from the ground,
     And every dore of freewill open flew.
     The Gyant selfe dismaied with that sownd,
     Where he with his *Duessa* dalliance fownd,
     In hast came rushing forth from inner bowre,
     With staring countenance sterne, as one astownd,
     And staggering steps, to weet, what suddein stowre
    Had wrought that horror strange, and dar'd his dreaded
       powre.

6   And after him the proud *Duessa* came,
     High mounted on her manyheaded beast,
     And every head with fyrie tongue did flame,
     And every head was crowned on his creast,
     And bloudie mouthed with late cruell feast.
     That when the knight beheld, his mightie shild
     Upon his manly arme he soone addrest,
     And at him fiercely flew, with courage fild,
    And eger greedinesse through every member thrild.

7   Therewith the Gyant buckled him to fight,
     Inflam'd with scornefull wrath and high disdaine,
     And lifting up his dreadfull club on hight,
     All arm'd with ragged snubbes and knottie graine,
     Him thought at first encounter to have slaine.
     But wise and warie was that noble Pere,
     And lightly leaping from so monstrous maine,
     Did faire avoide the violence him nere;
    It booted nought, to thinke, such thunderbolts to beare.

5. *astownd*: amazed, astounded.   6. *creast*: crest.   *addrest*: fixed.
7. *snubbes*: stubs.   *Pere*: champion.   *maine*: might.

8   Ne shame he thought to shunne so hideous might:
         The idle stroke, enforcing furious way,
         Missing the marke of his misaymed sight
         Did fall to ground, and with his heavie sway
         So deepely dinted in the driven clay,
         That three yardes deepe a furrow up did throw:
         The sad earth wounded with so sore assay,
         Did grone full grievous underneath the blow,
    And trembling with strange feare, did like an earthquake
         show.

9   As when almightie *Jove* in wrathfull mood,
         To wreake the guilt of mortall sins is bent,
         Hurles forth his thundring dart with deadly food,
         Enrold in flames, and smouldring dreriment,
         Through riven cloudes and molten firmament;
         The fierce threeforked engin making way,
         Both loftie towres and highest trees hath rent,
         And all that might his angrie passage stay,
    And shooting in the earth, casts up a mount of clay.

10   His boystrous club, so buried in the ground,
         He could not rearen up againe so light,
         But that the knight him at avantage found,
         And whiles he strove his combred clubbe to quight
         Out of the earth, with blade all burning bright
         He smote off his left arme, which like a blocke
         Did fall to ground, depriv'd of native might;
         Large streames of bloud out of the truncked stocke
    Forth gushed, like fresh water streame from riven rocke.

8. *idle*: useless.   *assay*: attack.
9. *food*: feud.   *dreriment*: (here) terror.
10. *boystrous*: rough and massive.   *quight*: free, release.

11 Dismaied with so desperate deadly wound,
        And eke impatient of unwonted paine,
        He loudly brayd with beastly yelling sound,
        That all the fields rebellowed againe;
        As great a noyse, as when in Cymbrian plaine
        An heard of Bulles, whom kindly rage doth sting,
        Do for the milkie mothers want complaine,
        And fill the fields with troublous bellowing,
    The neighbour woods around with hollow murmur ring.

12 That when his deare *Duessa* heard, and saw
        The evill stownd, that daungerd her estate,
        Unto his aid she hastily did draw
        Her dreadfull beast, who swolne with bloud of late
        Came ramping forth with proud presumpteous gate,
        And threatned all his heads like flaming brands.
        But him the Squire made quickly to retrate,
        Encountring fierce with single sword in hand,
    And twixt him and his Lord did like a bulwarke stand.

13 The proud *Duessa* full of wrathfull spight,
        And fierce disdaine, to be affronted so,
        Enforst her purple beast with all her might
        That stop out of the way to overthroe,
        Scorning the let of so unequall foe:
        But nathemore would that courageous swayne
        To her yeeld passage, gainst his Lord to goe,
        But with outrageous strokes did him restraine,
    And with his bodie bard the way atwixt them twaine.

11. *impatient*: intolerant. *rebellowed*: re-echoed loudly. *kindly rage*: natural feeling.
12. *stownd*: peril. *ramping*: prancing. *retrate*: retreat.
13. *let*: hindrance. *nathemore*: not the more. *outrageous*: mighty

14   Then tooke the angrie witch her golden cup,
        Which still she bore, replete with magick artes;
        Death and despeyre did many thereof sup,
        And secret poyson through their inner parts,
        Th'eternall bale of heavie wounded harts;
        Which after charmes and some enchauntments said,
        She lightly sprinkled on his weaker parts;
        Therewith his sturdie courage soone was quayd,
And all his senses were with suddeine dread dismayd.

15   So downe he fell before the cruell beast,
        Who on his necke his bloudie clawes did seize,
        That life nigh crusht out of his panting brest:
        No powre he had to stirre, nor will to rize.
        That when the carefull knight gan well avise,
        He lightly left the foe, with whom he fought,
        And to the beast gan turne his enterprise;
        For wondrous anguish in his hart it wrought,
To see his loved Squire into such thraldome brought.

16   And high advauncing his bloud-thirstie blade,
        Stroke one of those deformed heads so sore,
        That of his puissance proud ensample made;
        His monstrous scalpe downe to his teeth it tore,
        And that misformed shape mis-shaped more:
        A sea of bloud gusht from the gaping wound,
        That her gay garments staynd with filthy gore,
        And overflowed all the field around;
That over shoes in bloud he waded on the ground.

14. *quayd*: subdued.   15. *avise*: consider.

17   Thereat he roared for exceeding paine,
        That to have heard, great horror would have bred,
        And scourging th'emptie ayre with his long traine,
        Through great impatience of his grieved hed
        His gorgeous ryder from her loftie sted
        Would have cast downe, and trod in durtie myre,
        Had not the Gyant soone her succoured;
        Who all enrag'd with smart and franticke yre,
    Came hurtling in full fierce, and forst the knight retyre.

18   The force, which wont in two to be disperst,
        In one alone left hand he now unites,
        Which is through rage more strong then both were erst;
        With which his hideous club aloft he dites,
        And at his foe with furious rigour smites,
        That strongest Oake might seeme to overthrow:
        The stroke upon his shield so heavie lites,
        That to the ground it doubleth him full low:
    What mortall wight could ever beare so monstrous blow?

19   And in his fall his shield, that covered was,
        Did loose his vele by chaunce, and open flew:
        The light whereof, that heavens light did pas,
        Such blazing brightnesse through the aier threw,
        That eye mote not the same endure to vew.
        Which when the Gyaunt spyde with staring eye,
        He downe let fall his arme, and soft withdrew
        His weapon huge, that heaved was on hye
    For to have slaine the man, that on the ground did lye.

17. *impatience*: want of endurance.   *grieved*: injured.   *sted*: place.
18. *dites*: raises.   19. *his vele*: its covering.

20   And eke the fruitfull-headed beast, amaz'd
          At flashing beames of that sunshiny shield,
          Became starke blind, and all his senses daz'd,
          That downe he tumbled on the durtie field,
          And seem'd himselfe as conquered to yield.
          Whom when his maistresse proud perceiv'd to fall,
          Whiles yet his feeble feet for faintnesse reeld,
          Unto the Gyant loudly she gan call,
      O helpe *Orgoglio*, helpe, or else we perish all.

21   At her so pitteous cry was much amoov'd
          Her champion stout, and for to ayde his frend,
          Againe his wonted angry weapon proov'd:
          But all in vaine: for he has read his end
          In that bright shield, and all their forces spend
          Themselves in vaine: for since that glauncing sight,
          He hath no powre to hurt, nor to defend;
          As where th'Almighties lightning brond does light,
      It dimmes the dazed eyen, and daunts the senses quight.

22   Whom when the Prince, to battell new addrest,
          And threatning high his dreadfull stroke did see,
          His sparkling blade about his head he blest,
          And smote off quite his right leg by the knee,
          That downe he tombled; as an aged tree,
          High growing on the top of rocky clift,
          Whose hartstrings with keene steele nigh hewen be,
          The mightie trunck halfe rent, with ragged rift
      Doth roll adowne the rocks, and fall with fearefull drift.

---

21. *amoov'd*: moved.   *proov'd*: tried out.   *brond*: brand.
22. *blest*: brandished.   *clift*: cliff.

23 Or as a Castle reared high and round,
     By subtile engins and malitious slight
     Is undermined from the lowest ground,
     And her foundation forst, and feebled quight,
     At last downe falles, and with her heaped hight
     Her hastie ruine does more heavie make,
     And yields it selfe unto the victours might;
     Sich was this Gyaunts fall, that seemd to shake
The stedfast globe of earth, as it for feare did quake.

24 The knight then lightly leaping to the pray,
     With mortall steele him smot againe so sore,
     That headlesse his unweldy bodie lay,
     All wallowd in his owne fowle bloudy gore,
     Which flowed from his wounds in wondrous store.
     But soone as breath out of his breast did pas,
     That huge great body, which the Gyaunt bore,
     Was vanisht quite, and of that monstrous mas
Was nothing left, but like an emptie bladder was.

25 Whose grievous fall, when false *Duessa* spide,
     Her golden cup she cast unto the ground,
     And crowned mitre rudely threw aside;
     Such piercing griefe her stubborne hart did wound,
     That she could not endure that dolefull stound,
     But leaving all behind her, fled away:
     The light-foot Squire her quickly turnd around,
     And by hard meanes enforcing her to stay,
So brought unto his Lord, as his deserved pray.

26 The royall Virgin, which beheld from farre,
   In pensive plight, and sad perplexitie,
   The whole atchievement of this doubtfull warre,
   Came running fast to greet his victorie,
   With sober gladnesse, and myld modestie,
   And with sweet joyous cheare him thus bespake;
   Faire braunch of noblesse, flowre of chevalrie,
   That with your worth the world amazed make,
How shall I quite the paines, ye suffer for my sake?

27 And you fresh bud of vertue springing fast,
   Whom these sad eyes saw nigh unto deaths dore,
   What hath poore Virgin for such perill past,
   Wherewith you to reward? Accept therefore
   My simple selfe, and service evermore;
   And he that high does sit, and all things see
   With equall eyes, their merites to restore,
   Behold what ye this day have done for mee,
And what I cannot quite, requite with usuree.

28 But sith the heavens, and your faire handeling
   Have made you maister of the field this day,
   Your fortune maister eke with governing,
   And well begun end all so well, I pray,
   Ne let that wicked woman scape away;
   For she it is, that did my Lord bethrall,
   My dearest Lord, and deepe in dongeon lay,
   Where he his better dayes hath wasted all.
O heare, how piteous he to you for ayd does call.

26. *quite*: repay (for).   27. *equall*: impartial.   *quite*: repay.
28. *scape*: escape.

29   Forthwith he gave in charge unto his Squire,
     That scarlot whore to keepen carefully;
     Whiles he himselfe with greedie great desire
     Into the Castle entred forcibly,
     Where living creature none he did espye;
     Then gan he lowdly through the house to call:
     But no man car'd to answere to his crye.
     There raignd a solemne silence over all,
  Nor voice was heard, nor wight was seene in bowre or hall.

30   At last with creeping crooked pace forth came
     An old old man, with beard as white as snow,
     That on a staffe his feeble steps did frame,
     And guide his wearie gate both too and fro:
     For his eye sight him failed long ygo,
     And on his arme a bounch of keyes he bore,
     The which unused rust did overgrow:
     Those were the keyes of every inner dore,
  But he could not them use, but kept them still in store.

31   But very uncouth sight was to behold,
     How he did fashion his untoward pace,
     For as he forward moov'd his footing old,
     So backward still was turnd his wrincled face,
     Unlike to men, who ever as they trace,
     Both feet and face one way are wont to lead.
     This was the auncient keeper of that place,
     And foster father of the Gyant dead;
  His name *Ignaro* did his nature right aread.

---

30. *frame*: support, steady.
31. *trace*: go, walk.   *aread*: indicate, explain.

32   His reverend haires and holy gravitie
         The knight much honord, as beseemed well,
         And gently askt, where all the people bee,
         Which in that stately building wont to dwell.
         Who answerd him full soft, he could not tell.
         Againe he askt, where that same knight was layd,
         Whom great *Orgoglio* with his puissaunce fell
         Had made his caytive thrall; againe he sayde,
     He could not tell: ne ever other answere made.

33   Then asked he, which way he in might pas:
         He could not tell, againe he answered.
         Thereat the curteous knight displeased was,
         And said, Old sire, it seemes thou hast not red
         How ill it sits with that same silver hed
         In vaine to mocke, or mockt in vaine to bee:
         But if thou be, as thou art pourtrahed
         With natures pen, in ages grave degree,
     Aread in graver wise, what I demaund of thee.

34   His answere likewise was, he could not tell.
         Whose sencelesse speach, and doted ignorance
         When as the noble Prince had marked well,
         He ghest his nature by his countenance,
         And calmd his wrath with goodly temperance.
         Then to him stepping, from his arme did reach
         Those keyes, and made himselfe free enterance.
         Each dore he opened without any breach;
     There was no barre to stop, nor foe him to empeach.

32. *as beseemed well*: as was most fitting.
33. *red*: (here) understood.   *sits with*: befits.   *pourtrahed*: portrayed.   *Aread*: tell.
34. *doted*: foolish, stupid.   *empeach*: hinder.

35 There all within full rich arayd he found,
  With royall arras and resplendent gold.
  And did with store of every thing abound,
  That greatest Princes presence might behold.
  But all the floore (too filthy to be told)
  With bloud of guiltlesse babes, and innocents trew,
  Which there were slaine, as sheepe out of the fold,
  Defiled was, that dreadfull was to vew,
And sacred ashes over it was strowed new.

36 And there beside of marble stone was built
  An Altare, carv'd with cunning imagery,
  On which true Christians bloud was often spilt,
  And holy Martyrs often doen to dye,
  With cruell malice and strong tyranny:
  Whose blessed sprites from underneath the stone
  To God for vengeance cryde continually,
  And with great griefe were often heard to grone,
That hardest heart would bleede, to heare their piteous
    mone.

37 Through every rowme he sought, and every bowr,
  But no where could he find that wofull thrall:
  At last he came unto an yron doore,
  That fast was lockt, but key found not at all
  Emongst that bounch, to open it withall;
  But in the same a little grate was pight,
  Through which he sent his voyce, and lowd did call
  With all his powre, to weet, if living wight
Were housed therewithin, whom he enlargen might.

35. *arras*: tapestry. *sacred*: (here) accursed.
36. *doen to dye*: put to death.
37. *grate*: grating. *pight*: placed. *enlargen*: set free.

38   Therewith an hollow, dreary, murmuring voyce
       These piteous plaints and dolours did resound;
       O who is that, which brings me happy choyce
       Of death, that here lye dying every stound,
       Yet live perforce in balefull darkenesse bound?
       For now three Moones have changed thrice their hew,
       And have beene thrice hid underneath the ground,
       Since I the heavens chearefull face did vew,
  O welcome thou, that doest of death bring tydings trew.

39   Which when that Champion heard, with percing point
       Of pitty deare his hart was thrilled sore,
       And trembling horrour ran through every joynt,
       For ruth of gentle knight so fowle forlore:
       Which shaking off, he rent that yron dore,
       With furious force, and indignation fell;
       Where entred in, his foot could find no flore,
       But all a deepe descent, as darke as hell,
  That breathed ever forth a filthie banefull smell.

40   But neither darkenesse fowle, nor filthy bands,
       Nor noyous smell his purpose could withhold,
       (Entire affection hateth nicer hands)
       But that with constant zeale, and courage bold,
       After long paines and labours manifold,
       He found the meanes that Prisoner up to reare;
       Whose feeble thighes, unhable to uphold
       His pined corse, him scarse to light could beare,
  A ruefull spectacle of death and ghastly drere.

---

40. *noyous*: noxious.   *nicer*: too fastidious.   *pined*: wasted away.   *drere*: gloom.

41 His sad dull eyes deepe sunck in hollow pits,
      Could not endure th'unwonted sunne to view;
      His bare thin cheekes for want of better bits,
      And empty sides deceived of their dew,
      Could make a stony hart his hap to rew;
      His rawbone armes, whose mighty brawned bowrs
      Were wont to rive steele plates, and helmets hew,
      Were cleane consum'd, and all his vitall powres
Decayd, and all his flesh shronk up like withered flowres.

42 Whom when his Lady saw, to him she ran
      With hasty joy: to see him made her glad,
      And sad to view his visage pale and wan,
      Who earst in flowres of freshest youth was clad.
      Tho when her well of teares she wasted had,
      She said, Ah dearest Lord, what evill starre
      On you hath fround, and pourd his influence bad,
      That of your selfe ye thus berobbed arre,
And this misseeming hew your manly looks doth marre?

43 But welcome now my Lord, in wele or woe,
      Whose presence I have lackt too long a day;
      And fie on Fortune mine avowed foe,
      Whose wrathfull wreakes them selves do now alay.
      And for these wrongs shall treble penaunce pay
      Of treble good: good growes of evils priefe.
      The chearelesse man, whom sorrow did dismay,
      Had no delight to treaten of his griefe;
His long endured famine needed more reliefe.

41. *bits*: i.e. of food. *deceived of*: denied. *bowrs*: muscles.
42. *misseeming*: unseemly.
43. *wreakes*: acts of vengeance. *priefe*: testing.

44 Faire Lady, then said that victorious knight,
      The things, that grievous were to do, or beare,
      Them to renew, I wote, breeds no delight;
      Best musicke breeds delight in loathing eare:
      But th'onely good, that growes of passed feare,
      Is to be wise, and ware of like agein.
      This dayes ensample hath this lesson deare
      Deepe written in my heart with yron pen,
  That blisse may not abide in state of mortall men.

45 Henceforth sir knight, take to you wonted strength,
      And maister these mishaps with patient might;
      Loe where your foe lyes stretcht in monstrous length,
      And loe that wicked woman in your sight,
      The roote of all your care, and wretched plight,
      Now in your powre, to let her live, or dye.
      To do her dye (quoth *Una*) were despight,
      And shame t'avenge so weake an enimy;
  But spoile her of her scarlot robe, and let her fly.

46 So as she bad, that witch they disaraid,
      And robd of royall robes, and purple pall,
      And ornaments that richly were displaid;
      Ne spared they to strip her naked all.
      Then when they had despoild her tire and call,
      Such as she was, their eyes might her behold,
      That her misshaped parts did them appall,
      A loathly, wrinckled hag, ill favoured, old,
  Whose secret filth good manners biddeth not be told.

44. *wote*: know.   *delight* (l. 4): see note.
45. *To do her dye*: to put her to death.
46. *pall*: cloak, robe.   *tire and call*: headdress and netted cap.   *ill favoured*: ugly
(but see glossary).

47 Her craftie head was altogether bald,
        And as in hate of honorable eld,
        Was overgrowne with scurfe and filthy scald;
        Her teeth out of her rotten gummes were feld,
        And her sowre breath abhominably smeld;
        Her dried dugs, like bladders lacking wind,
        Hong downe, and filthy matter from them weld;
        Her wrizled skin as rough, as maple rind,
    So scabby was, that would have loathd all womankind.

48 Her neather parts, the shame of all her kind,
        My chaster Muse for shame doth blush to write;
        But at her rompe she growing had behind
        A foxes taile, with dong all fowly dight;
        And eke her feete most monstrous were in sight;
        For one of them was like an Eagles claw,
        With griping talaunts armd to greedy fight,
        The other like a Beares uneven paw:
    More ugly shape yet never living creature saw.

49 Which when the knights beheld, amazd they were,
        And wondred at so fowle deformed wight.
        Such then (said *Una*) as she seemeth here,
        Such is the face of falshood, such the sight
        Of fowle *Duessa*, when her borrowed light
        Is laid away, and counterfesaunce knowne.
        Thus when they had the witch disrobed quight,
        And all her filthy feature open showne,
    They let her goe at will, and wander wayes unknowne.

---

47. *eld*: old age. *scald*: scabby disease. *feld*: ?fallen. *dugs*: breasts. *wrizled*:
wrinkled, shrivelled.
48. *talaunts*: talons.   49. *counterfesaunce*: deceit.

50   She flying fast from heavens hated face,
        And from the world that her discovered wide,
        Fled to the wastfull wildernesse apace,
        From living eyes her open shame to hide,
        And lurkt in rocks and caves long unespide.
        But that faire crew of knights, and *Una* faire
        Did in that castle afterwards abide,
        To rest them selves, and weary powres repaire,
    Where store they found of all, that dainty was and rare.

Canto 9

His loves and lignage Arthur tells:
  The knights knit friendly bands:
  Sir Trevisan flies from Despayre,
    Whom Redcrosse knight withstands.

1   O goodly golden chaine, wherewith yfere
        The vertues linked are in lovely wize:
        And noble minds of yore allyed were,
        In brave poursuit of chevalrous emprize,
        That none did others safety despize,
        Nor aid envy to him, in need that stands,
        But friendly each did others prayse devize
        How to advaunce with favourable hands,
    As this good Prince redeemd the *Redcrosse* knight from
        bands.

Argument. *lignage*: lineage.
1. *yfere*: together. *emprize*: undertaking, enterprise. *envy*: grudge.

2 Who when their powres, empaird through labour long,
     With dew repast they had recured well,
     And that weake captive wight now wexed strong,
     Them list no lenger there at leasure dwell,
     But forward fare, as their adventures fell,
     But ere they parted, *Una* faire besought
     That straunger knight his name and nation tell;
     Least so great good, as he for her had wrought,
   Should die unknown, and buried be in thanklesse thought.

3 Faire virgin (said the Prince) ye me require
     A thing without the compas of my wit:
     For both the lignage and the certain Sire,
     From which I sprong, from me are hidden yit.
     For all so soone as life did me admit
     Into this world, and shewed heavens light,
     From mothers pap I taken was unfit:
     And streight delivered to a Faery knight,
   To be upbrought in gentle thewes and martiall might.

4 Unto old *Timon* he me brought bylive,
     Old *Timon*, who in youthly yeares hath beene
     In warlike feates th'expertest man alive,
     And is the wisest now on earth I weene;
     His dwelling is low in a valley greene,
     Under the foot of *Rauran* mossy hore,
     From whence the river *Dee* as silver cleene
     His tombling billowes rolls with gentle rore:
   There all my dayes he traind me up in vertuous lore.

---

2. *empaird*: weakened. *recured*: recovered. *Them list*: they wished.
3. *without*: outside, beyond. *pap*: nipple, breast. *gentle thewes*: noble qualities.
4. *bylive*: forthwith. *mossy hore*: hoary with moss (see note).

5 Thither the great Magicien *Merlin* came,
  As was his use, ofttimes to visit me:
  For he had charge my discipline to frame,
  And Tutours nouriture to oversee.
  Him oft and oft I askt in privitie,
  Of what loines and what lignage I did spring:
  Whose aunswere bad me still assured bee,
  That I was sonne and heire unto a king,
  As time in her just terme the truth to light should bring.

6 Well worthy impe, said then the Lady gent,
  And Pupill fit for such a Tutours hand.
  But what adventure, or what high intent
  Hath brought you hither into Faery land,
  Aread Prince *Arthur*, crowne of Martiall band?
  Full hard it is (quoth he) to read aright
  The course of heavenly cause, or understand
  The secret meaning of th'eternall might,
  That rules mens wayes, and rules the thoughts of living
   wight.

7 For whither he through fatall deepe foresight
  Me hither sent, for cause to me unghest,
  Or that fresh bleeding wound, which day and night
  Whilome doth rancle in my riven brest,
  With forced fury following his behest,
  Me hither brought by wayes yet never found,
  You to have helpt I hold my selfe yet blest.
  Ah curteous knight (quoth she) what secret wound
  Could ever find, to grieve the gentlest hart on ground?

5. *nouriture*: training, education. *in privitie*: in private.
6. *gent*: gracious. *Aread*: tell.
7. *fatall*: ordained by fate. *Whilome*: (here) continuously. *on ground*: in the world, anywhere.

8 Deare Dame (quoth he) you sleeping sparkes awake,
      Which troubled once, into huge flames will grow,
      Ne ever will their fervent fury slake,
      Till living moysture into smoke do flow,
      And wasted life do lye in ashes low.
      Yet sithens silence lesseneth not my fire,
      But told it flames, and hidden it does glow,
      I will revele, what ye so much desire:
   Ah Love, lay downe thy bow, the whiles I may respire.

9 It was in freshest flowre of youthly yeares,
      When courage first does creepe in manly chest,
      Then first the coale of kindly heat appeares
      To kindle love in every living brest;
      But me had warnd old *Timons* wise behest,
      Those creeping flames by reason to subdew,
      Before their rage grew to so great unrest,
      As miserable lovers use to rew,
   Which still wex old in woe, whiles woe still wexeth new.

10 That idle name of love, and lovers life,
      As losse of time, and vertues enimy
      I ever scornd, and joyd to stirre up strife,
      In middest of their mournfull Tragedy,
      Ay wont to laugh, when them I heard to cry,
      And blow the fire, which them to ashes brent:
      Their God himselfe, griev'd at my libertie,
      Shot many a dart at me with fiers intent,
   But I them warded all with wary government.

8. *sithens*: since, seeing that.   *respire*: rest
9. *kindly*: natural.   *use to rew*: are used to lamenting.
10. *brent*: burnt.

11   But all in vaine: no fort can be so strong,
          Ne fleshly brest can armed be so sound,
          But will at last be wonne with battrie long,
          Or unawares at disavantage found;
          Nothing is sure, that growes on earthly ground:
          And who most trustes in arme of fleshly might,
          And boasts, in beauties chaine not to be bound,
          Doth soonest fall in disaventrous fight,
   And yeeldes his caytive neck to victours most despight.

12   Ensample make of him your haplesse joy,
          And of my selfe now mated, as ye see;
          Whose prouder vaunt that proud avenging boy
          Did soone pluck downe, and curbd my libertie.
          For on a day prickt forth with jollitie
          Of looser life, and heat of hardiment,
          Raunging the forest wide on courser free,
          The fields, the floods, the heavens with one consent
   Did seeme to laugh on me, and favour mine intent.

13   For-wearied with my sports, I did alight
          From loftie steed, and downe to sleepe me layd;
          The verdant gras my couch did goodly dight,
          And pillow was my helmet faire displayd:
          Whiles every sence the humour sweet embayd,
          And slombring soft my hart did steale away,
          Me seemed, by my side a royall Mayd
          Her daintie limbes full softly down did lay:
   So faire a creature yet saw never sunny day.

11. *disaventrous*: unfortunate, disastrous.
12. *mated*: overcome, defeated. *prickt forth*: urged forth. *hardiment*: boldness, courage.
13. *For-wearied*: exhausted. *dight*: adorn. *humour*: moisture. *embayd*: bathed.

14 Most goodly glee and lovely blandishment
    She to me made, and bad me love her deare,
    For dearely sure her love was to me bent,
    As when just time expired should appeare.
    But whether dreames delude, or true it were,
    Was never hart so ravisht with delight,
    Ne living man like words did ever heare,
    As she to me delivered all that night;
And at her parting said, She Queene of Faeries hight.

15 When I awoke, and found her place devoyd,
    And nought but pressed gras, where she had lyen,
    I sorrowed all so much, as earst I joyd,
    And washed all her place with watry eyen.
    From that day forth I lov'd that face divine;
    From that day forth I cast in carefull mind,
    To seeke her out with labour, and long tyne,
    And never vow to rest, till her I find,
Nine monethes I seeke in vaine yet ni'll that vow unbind.

16 Thus as he spake, his visage wexed pale,
    And chaunge of hew great passion did bewray;
    Yet still he strove to cloke his inward bale,
    And hide the smoke, that did his fire display,
    Till gentle *Una* thus to him gan say;
    O happy Queene of Faeries, that hast found
    Mongst many, one that with his prowesse may
    Defend thine honour, and thy foes confound:
True Loves are often sown, but seldom grow on ground.

---

14. *glee*: joy.   *hight*: was called.
15. *devoyd*: empty.   *tyne*: toil.   *ni'll*: will not.   16. *bale*: sorrow.
N<small>FQ</small>

17   Thine, O then, said the gentle *Redcrosse* knight,
        Next to that Ladies love, shalbe the place,
        O fairest virgin, full of heavenly light,
        Whose wondrous faith, exceeding earthly race,
        Was firmest fixt in mine extremest case.
        And you, my Lord, the Patrone of my life,
        Of that great Queene may well gaine worthy grace:
        For onely worthy you through prowes priefe
    Yf living man mote worthy be, to be her liefe.

18   So diversly discoursing of their loves,
        The golden Sunne his glistring head gan shew,
        And sad remembraunce now the Prince amoves,
        With fresh desire his voyage to pursew:
        Als *Una* earnd her traveill to renew.
        Then those two knights, fast friendship for to bynd,
        And love establish each to other trew,
        Gave goodly gifts, the signes of gratefull mynd,
    And eke as pledges firme, right hands together joynd.

19   Prince *Arthur* gave a boxe of Diamond sure,
        Embowd with gold and gorgeous ornament,
        Wherein were closd few drops of liquor pure,
        Of wondrous worth, and vertue excellent,
        That any wound could heale incontinent:
        Which to requite, the *Redcrosse* knight him gave
        A booke, wherein his Saveours testament
        Was writ with golden letters rich and brave;
    A worke of wondrous grace, and able soules to save.

17. *prowes priefe*: valour's proof, test of valour.   *liefe*: beloved.
18. *voyage*: journey.   *Als*: also.   *earnd*: yearned.
19. *Embowd* ?encircled.   *incontinent*: immediately, forthwith.

20 Thus beene they parted, *Arthur* on his way
      To seeke his love, and th'other for to fight
      With *Unaes* foe, that all her realme did pray.
      But she now weighing the decayed plight,
      And shrunken synewes of her chosen knight,
      Would not a while her forward course pursew,
      Ne bring him forth in face of dreadfull fight,
      Till he recovered had his former hew:
  For him to be yet weake and wearie well she knew.

21 So as they traveild, lo they gan espy
      An armed knight towards them gallop fast,
      That seemed from some feared foe to fly,
      Or other griesly thing, that him agast.
      Still as he fled, his eye was backward cast,
      As if his feare still followed him behind;
      Als flew his steed, as he his bands had brast,
      And with his winged heeles did tread the wind,
  As he had beene a fole of *Pegasus* his kind.

22 Nigh as he drew, they might perceive his head
      To be unarmd, and curld uncombed heares
      Upstaring stiffe, dismayd with uncouth dread;
      Nor drop of bloud in all his face appeares
      Nor life in limbe: and to increase his feares,
      In fowle reproch of knighthoods faire degree,
      About his neck an hempen rope he weares,
      That with his glistring armes does ill agree;
  But he of rope or armes has now no memoree.

20. *pray*: prey on.
21. *Als . . . as*: as . . . as if; i.e. his steed flew as fast as if . . . *brast*: burst, broken. *of Pegasus his kind*: like Pegasus (see note).
22. *Upstaring*: bristling, standing on end.

23 The *Redcrosse* knight toward him crossed fast,
   To weet, what mister wight was so dismayd:
   There him he finds all sencelesse and aghast,
   That of him selfe he seemd to be afrayd;
   Whom hardly he from flying forward stayd,
   Till he these wordes to him deliver might;
   Sir knight, aread who hath ye thus arayd,
   And eke from whom make ye this hasty flight:
For never knight I saw in such misseeming plight.

24 He answerd nought at all, but adding new
   Feare to his first amazment, staring wide
   With stony eyes, and hartlesse hollow hew,
   Astonisht stood, as one that had aspide
   Infernall furies, with their chaines untide.
   Him yet againe, and yet againe bespake
   The gentle knight; who nought to him replide,
   But trembling every joynt did inly quake,
And foltring tongue at last these words seemd forth to shake.

25 For Gods deare love, Sir knight, do me not stay;
   For loe he comes, he comes fast after mee.
   Eft looking backe would faine have runne away;
   But he him forst to stay, and tellen free
   The secret cause of his perplexitie:
   Yet nathemore by his bold hartie speach,
   Could his bloud-frosen hart emboldned bee,
   But through his boldnesse rather feare did reach,
Yet forst, at last he made through silence suddein breach.

---

23. *what mister wight*: what kind of person (see note).
24. *hartlesse*: disheartened. *foltring*: faltering, stammering.
25. *do me not stay*: force me not to stay. *Eft*: again. *nathemore*: none the more.

26 And am I now in safetie sure (quoth he)
       From him, that would have forced me to dye?
       And is the point of death now turnd fro mee,
       That I may tell this haplesse history?
       Feare nought: (quoth he) no daunger now is nye.
       Then shall I you recount a ruefull cace,
       (Said he) the which with this unlucky eye
       I late beheld, and had not greater grace
    Me reft from it, had bene partaker of the place.

27 I lately chaunst (Would I had never chaunst)
       With a faire knight to keepen companee,
       Sir *Terwin* hight, that well himselfe advaunst
       In all affaires, and was both bold and free,
       But not so happie as mote happie bee:
       He lov'd, as was his lot, a Ladie gent,
       That him againe lov'd in the least degree:
       For she was proud, and of too high intent,
    And joyd to see her lover languish and lament.

28 From whom returning sad and comfortlesse,
       As on the way together we did fare,
       We met that villen (God from him me blesse)
       That cursed wight, from whom I scapt whyleare,
       A man of hell, that cals himselfe *Despaire*:
       Who first us greets, and after faire areedes
       Of tydings strange, and of adventures rare:
       So creeping close, as Snake in hidden weedes,
    Inquireth of our states, and of our knightly deedes.

27. *gent*: gracious.
28. *blesse*: protect, deliver. *whyleare*: a while ago. *areedes*: tells.

29 Which when he knew, and felt our feeble harts
      Embost with bale, and bitter byting griefe,
      Which love had launched with his deadly darts,
      With wounding words and termes of foule repriefe
      He pluckt from us all hope of due reliefe,
      That earst us held in love of lingring life;
      Then hopelesse hartlesse, gan the cunning thiefe
      Perswade us die, to stint all further strife:
  To me he lent this rope, to him a rustie knife.

30 With which sad instrument of hastie death,
      That wofull lover, loathing lenger light,
      A wide way made to let forth living breath.
      But I more fearefull, or more luckie wight,
      Dismayd with that deformed dismall sight,
      Fled fast away, halfe dead with dying feare:
      Ne yet assur'd of life by you, Sir knight,
      Whose like infirmitie like chaunce may beare:
  But God you never let his charmed speeches heare.

31 How may a man (said he) with idle speach
      Be wonne, to spoyle the Castle of his health?
      I wote (quoth he) whom triall late did teach,
      That like would not for all this worldes wealth:
      His subtill tongue, like dropping honny, mealt'th
      Into the hart, and searcheth every vaine,
      That ere one be aware, by secret stealth
      His powre is reft, and weaknesse doth remaine.
  O never Sir desire to try his guilefull traine.

29. *Embost with bale*: ? enveloped in, sunk in, sorrow.   *repriefe*: reproof.
30. *deformed*: hateful, terrible.
31. *idle*: empty.   *spoyle*: despoil, ravage.

32   Certes (said he) hence shall I never rest,
      Till I that treachours art have heard and tride;
      And you Sir knight, whose name mote I request,
      Of grace do me unto his cabin guide.
      I that hight *Trevisan* (quoth he) will ride
      Against my liking backe, to doe you grace:
      But nor for gold nor glee will I abide
      By you, when ye arrive in that same place;
   For lever had I die, then see his deadly face.

33   Ere long they come, where that same wicked wight
      His dwelling has, low in an hollow cave,
      Farre underneath a craggie clift ypight,
      Darke, dolefull, drearie, like a greedie grave,
      That still for carrion carcases doth crave:
      On top whereof aye dwelt the ghastly Owle,
      Shrieking his balefull note, which ever drave
      Farre from that haunt all other chearefull fowle;
   And all about it wandring ghostes did waile and howle.

34   And all about old stockes and stubs of trees,
      Whereon nor fruit, nor leafe was ever seene,
      Did hang upon the ragged rocky knees;
      On which had many wretches hanged beene,
      Whose carcases were scattered on the greene,
      And throwne about the cliffs. Arrived there,
      That bare-head knight for dread and dolefull teene,
      Would faine have fled, ne durst approchen neare,
   But th'other forst him stay, and comforted in feare.

32. *Certes*: indeed, certainly. *treachours*: deceiver's, traitor's. *for gold nor glee*: ?(literally) for gold nor beauty. *lever had I die*: I would rather die.
  33. *clift*: cliff. *ypight*: placed, set.
  34. *knees*: (rocky) projections. *teene*: grief.

35   That darkesome cave they enter, where they find
     That cursed man, low sitting on the ground,
     Musing full sadly in his sullein mind;
     His griesie lockes, long growen, and unbound,
     Disordred hong about his shoulders round,
     And hid his face; through which his hollow eyne
     Lookt deadly dull, and stared as astound;
     His raw-bone cheekes through penurie and pine,
  Were shronke into his jawes, as he did never dine.

36   His garment nought but many ragged clouts,
     With thornes together pind and patched was,
     The which his naked sides he wrapt abouts;
     And him beside there lay upon the gras
     A drearie corse, whose life away did pas,
     All wallowd in his owne yet luke-warme blood,
     That from his wound yet welled fresh alas;
     In which a rustie knife fast fixed stood,
  And made an open passage for the gushing flood.

37   Which piteous spectacle, approving trew
     The wofull tale that *Trevisan* had told,
     When as the gentle *Redcrosse* knight did vew,
     With firie zeale he burnt in courage bold,
     Him to avenge, before his bloud were cold,
     And to the villein said, Thou damned wight,
     The author of this fact, we here behold,
     What justice can but judge against thee right,
  With thine owne bloud to price his bloud, here shed in
      sight?

35. *sullein*: gloomy.   *griesie*: ? grizzled (see glossary).   *pine*: starvation.
37. *approving*: proving.   *fact*: wicked deed.   *price*: pay for.

38 What franticke fit (quoth he) hath thus distraught
    Thee, foolish man, so rash a doome to give?
    What justice ever other judgement taught,
    But he should die, who merites not to live?
    None else to death this man despayring drive,
    But his owne guiltie mind deserving death.
    Is then unjust to each his due to give?
    Or let him die, that loatheth living breath?
Or let him die at ease, that liveth here uneath?

39 Who travels by the wearie wandring way,
    To come unto his wished home in haste,
    And meetes a flood, that doth his passage stay,
    Is not great grace to helpe him over past,
    Or free his feet, that in the myre sticke fast?
    Most envious man, that grieves at neighbours good,
    And fond, that joyest in the woe thou hast,
    Why wilt not let him passe, that long hath stood
Upon the banke, yet wilt thy selfe not passe the flood?

40 He there does now enjoy eternall rest
    And happie ease, which thou doest want and crave,
    And further from it daily wanderest:
    What if some litle paine the passage have,
    That makes fraile flesh to feare the bitter wave?
    Is not short paine well borne, that brings long ease,
    And layes the soule to sleepe in quiet grave?
    Sleepe after toyle, port after stormie seas,
Ease after warre, death after life does greatly please.

---

38. *uneath*: with difficulty, uneasily.   39. *fond*: foolish.

41 The knight much wondred at his suddeine wit,
        And said, The terme of life is limited,
        Ne may a man prolong, nor shorten it;
        The souldier may not move from watchfull sted,
        Nor leave his stand, untill his Captaine bed.
        Who life did limit by almightie doome,
        (Quoth he) knowes best the termes established;
        And he, that points the Centonell his roome,
    Doth license him depart at sound of morning droome.

42 Is not his deed, what ever thing is donne,
        In heaven and earth? did not he all create
        To die againe? all ends that was begonne.
        Their times in his eternall booke of fate
        Are written sure, and have their certaine date.
        Who then can strive with strong necessitie,
        That holds the world in his still chaunging state,
        Or shunne the death ordaynd by destinie?
    When houre of death is come, let none aske whence, nor why.

43 The lenger life, I wote the greater sin,
        The greater sin, the greater punishment:
        All those great battels, which thou boasts to win,
        Through strife, and bloud-shed, and avengement,
        Now praysd, hereafter deare thou shalt repent:
        For life must life, and bloud must bloud repay.
        Is not enough thy evill life forespent?
        For he, that once hath missed the right way,
    The further he doth goe, the further he doth stray.

41. *wit*: intelligence. *watchfull sted*: place of watch. *bed*: bid(s), commands.
he, that points the Centonell his roome: he who appoints the sentinel to his place.
droome: drum.
    42. *date*: assigned term of life.
    43. *avengement*: vengeance. *Is not enough . . . forespent?*: Has not your evil life
been wasted for long enough?

44 Then do no further goe, no further stray,
     But here lie downe, and to thy rest betake,
     Th'ill to prevent, that life ensewen may.
     For what hath life, that may it loved make,
     And gives not rather cause it to forsake?
     Feare, sicknesse, age, losse, labour, sorrow, strife,
     Paine, hunger, cold, that makes the hart to quake;
     And ever fickle fortune rageth rife,
All which, and thousands mo do make a loathsome life.

45 Thou wretched man, of death hast greatest need,
     If in true ballance thou wilt weigh thy state:
     For never knight, that dared warlike deede,
     More lucklesse disaventures did amate:
     Witnesse the dongeon deepe, wherein of late
     Thy life shut up, for death so oft did call;
     And though good lucke prolonged hath thy date,
     Yet death then, would the like mishaps forestall,
Into the which hereafter thou maiest happen fall.

46 Why then doest thou, O man of sin, desire
     To draw thy dayes forth to their last degree?
     Is not the measure of thy sinfull hire
     High heaped up with huge iniquitie,
     Against the day of wrath, to burden thee?
     Is not enough, that to this Ladie milde
     Thou falsed hast thy faith with perjurie,
     And sold thy selfe to serve *Duessa* vilde,
With whom in all abuse thou hast thy selfe defilde?

---

45. *disaventures*: misfortunes.   *amate*: daunt, subdue.
46. *sinfull hire*: wages of sin.   *falsed hast*: hast been false to.

47   Is not he just, that all this doth behold
      From highest heaven, and beares an equall eye?
      Shall he thy sins up in his knowledge fold,
      And guiltie be of thine impietie?
      Is not his law, Let every sinner die:
      Die shall all flesh? what then must needs be donne,
      Is it not better to doe willinglie,
      Then linger, till the glasse be all out ronne?
  Death is the end of woes: die soone, O faeries sonne.

48   The knight was much enmoved with his speach,
      That as a swords point through his hart did perse,
      And in his conscience made a secret breach,
      Well knowing true all, that he did reherse
      And to his fresh remembrance did reverse
      The ugly vew of his deformed crimes,
      That all his manly powres it did disperse,
      As he were charmed with inchaunted rimes,
  That oftentimes he quakt, and fainted oftentimes.

49   In which amazement, when the Miscreant
      Perceived him to waver weake and fraile,
      Whiles trembling horror did his conscience dant,
      And hellish anguish did his soule assaile,
      To drive him to despaire, and quite to quaile,
      He shew'd him painted in a table plaine,
      The damned ghosts, that doe in torments waile,
      And thousand feends that doe them endlesse paine
  With fire and brimstone, which for ever shall remaine.

47. *equall*: impartial.
48. *enmoved*: disturbed.   *reherse*: relate, tell.   *reverse*: bring back.
49. *dant*: daunt, overwhelm.   *table*: picture (see note).

50   The sight whereof so throughly him dismaid,
      That nought but death before his eyes he saw,
      And ever burning wrath before him laid,
      By righteous sentence of th'Almighties law:
      Then gan the villein him to overcraw,
      And brought unto him swords, ropes, poison, fire,
      And all that might him to perdition draw;
      And bad him choose, what death he would desire:
  For death was due to him, that had provokt Gods ire.

51   But when as none of them he saw him take,
      He to him raught a dagger sharpe and keene,
      And gave it him in hand: his hand did quake,
      And tremble like a leafe of Aspin greene,
      And troubled bloud through his pale face was seene
      To come, and goe with tydings from the hart,
      As it a running messenger had beene.
      At last resolv'd to worke his finall smart,
  He lifted up his hand, that backe again did start.

52   Which when as *Una* saw, through every vaine
      The crudled cold ran to her well of life,
      As in a swowne: but soone reliv'd againe,
      Out of his hand she snatcht the cursed knife,
      And threw it to the ground, enraged rife,
      And to him said, Fie, fie, faint harted knight,
      What meanest thou by this reprochfull strife?
      Is this the battell, which thou vauntst to fight
  With that fire-mouthed Dragon, horrible and bright?

50. *overcraw*: exult over.   51. *raught*: handed (to him).
52. *crudled*: curdled, frozen.

53 Come, come away, fraile, feeble, fleshly wight,
    Ne let vaine words bewitch thy manly hart,
    Ne divelish thoughts dismay thy constant spright.
    In heavenly mercies hast thou not a part?
    Why shouldst thou then despeire, that chosen art?
    Where justice growes, there grows eke greater grace,
    The which doth quench the brond of hellish smart,
    And that accurst hand-writing doth deface.
  Arise, Sir knight arise, and leave this cursed place.

54 So up he rose, and thence amounted streight.
    Which when the carle beheld, and saw his guest
    Would safe depart, for all his subtill sleight,
    He chose an halter from among the rest,
    And with it hung himselfe, unbid unblest.
    But death he could not worke himselfe thereby;
    For thousand times he so himselfe had drest,
    Yet nathelesse it could not doe him die,
  Till he should die his last, that is eternally.

Canto 10

Her faithfull knight faire Una brings
to house of Holinesse,
Where he is taught repentance, and
the way to heavenly blesse.

---

54. *amounted*: rose up. *carle*: churl, base fellow. *unbid*: unprayed-for. *drest*:
prepared. *nathelesse*: nevertheless.
  Argument. *blesse*: bliss.

1   What man is he, that boasts of fleshly might,
     And vaine assurance of mortality,
     Which all so soone, as it doth come to fight,
     Against spirituall foes, yeelds by and by,
     Or from the field most cowardly doth fly?
     Ne let the man ascribe it to his skill,
     That thorough grace hath gained victory.
     If any strength we have, it is to ill,
But all the good is Gods, both power and eke will.

2   By that, which lately hapned, *Una* saw,
     That this her knight was feeble, and too faint;
     And all his sinews woxen weake and raw,
     Through long enprisonment, and hard constraint,
     Which he endured in his late restraint,
     That yet he was unfit for bloudie fight:
     Therefore to cherish him with diets daint,
     She cast to bring him, where he chearen might,
Till he recovered had his late decayed plight.

3   There was an auntient house not farre away,
     Renowmd throughout the world for sacred lore,
     And pure unspotted life: so well they say
     It governed was, and guided evermore,
     Through wisedome of a matrone grave and hore;
     Whose onely joy was to relieve the needes
     Of wretched soules, and helpe the helpelesse pore:
     All night she spent in bidding of her bedes,
And all the day in doing good and godly deedes.

1. *thorough*: through.
2. *woxen*: grown.   *daint*: dainty.   *chearen*: be made cheerful, restored to health and spirits.   *Till . . . . his late decayed plight*: i.e. *from* his late decayed plight.
3. *Renowmd*: famous, renowned.   *bidding of her bedes*: saying her prayers.

4   Dame *Cælia* men did her call, as thought
        From heaven to come, or thither to arise,
        The mother of three daughters, well upbrought
        In goodly thewes, and godly exercise:
        The eldest two most sober, chast, and wise,
        Fidelia and *Speranza* virgins were,
        Though spousd, yet wanting wedlocks solemnize;
        But faire *Charissa* to a lovely fere
    Was lincked, and by him had many pledges dere.

5   Arrived there, the dore they find fast lockt;
        For it was warely watched night and day,
        For feare of many foes: but when they knockt,
        The Porter opened unto them streight way:
        He was an aged syre, all hory gray,
        With lookes full lowly cast, and gate full slow,
        Wont on a staffe his feeble steps to stay,
        Hight *Humiltá*. They passe in stouping low;
    For streight and narrow was the way, which he did show.

6   Each goodly thing is hardest to begin,
        But entred in a spacious court they see,
        Both plaine, and pleasant to be walked in,
        Where them does meete a francklin faire and free,
        And entertaines with comely courteous glee,
        His name was *Zele*, that him right well became,
        For in his speeches and behaviour hee
        Did labour lively to expresse the same,
    And gladly did them guide, till to the Hall they came.

4. *thewes*: qualities.   *solemnize*: solemnization.   *fere*: companion, husband.
pledges: (here) children.
    5. *stay*: support.   6. *francklin*: freeholder (see note).   *glee*: joy.

7　There fairely them receives a gentle Squire,
　　　Of milde demeanure, and rare courtesie,
　　　Right cleanly clad in comely sad attire;
　　　In word and deede that shew'd great modestie,
　　　And knew his good to all of each degree,
　　　Hight *Reverence*. He them with speeches meet
　　　Does faire entreat; no courting nicetie,
　　　But simple true, and eke unfained sweet,
　As might become a Squire so great persons to greet.

8　And afterwards them to his Dame he leades,
　　　That aged Dame, the Ladie of the place:
　　　Who all this while was busie at her beades:
　　　Which doen, she up arose with seemely grace,
　　　And toward them full matronely did pace.
　　　Where when that fairest *Una* she beheld,
　　　Whom well she knew to spring from heavenly race,
　　　Her hart with joy unwonted inly sweld,
　As feeling wondrous comfort in her weaker eld.

9　And her embracing said, O happie earth,
　　　Whereon thy innocent feet doe ever tread,
　　　Most vertuous virgin borne of heavenly berth,
　　　That to redeeme thy woefull parents head,
　　　From tyrans rage, and ever-dying dread,
　　　Hast wandred through the world now long a day;
　　　Yet ceasest not thy wearie soles to lead,
　　　What grace hath thee now hither brought this way?
　Or doen thy feeble feet unweeting hither stray?

8. *inly*: inwardly.　*eld*: old age.　　　　9. *tyrans*: tyrant's.

OFQ

10   Strange thing it is an errant knight to see
      Here in this place, or any other wight,
      That hither turnes his steps. So few there bee,
      That chose the narrow path, or seeke the right:
      All keepe the broad high way, and take delight
      With many rather for to go astray,
      And be partakers of their evill plight,
      Then with a few to walke the rightest way;
  O foolish men, why haste ye to your owne decay?

11   Thy selfe to see, and tyred limbs to rest,
      O matrone sage (quoth she) I hither came,
      And this good knight his way with me addrest,
      Led with thy prayses and broad-blazed fame,
      That up to heaven is blowne. The auncient Dame
      Him goodly greeted in her modest guise,
      And entertaynd them both, as best became,
      With all the court'sies, that she could devise,
  Ne wanted ought, to shew her bounteous or wise.

12   Thus as they gan of sundry things devise,
      Loe two most goodly virgins came in place,
      Ylinked arme in arme in lovely wise,
      With countenance demure, and modest grace,
      They numbred even steps and equall pace:
      Of which the eldest, that *Fidelia* hight,
      Like sunny beames threw from her Christall face,
      That could have dazd the rash beholders sight,
  And round about her head did shine like heavens light.

10. *chose*: choose.   11. *addrest*: directed.
12. *devise*: talk, converse.

13   She was araied all in lilly white,
      And in her right hand bore a cup of gold,
      With wine and water fild up to the hight,
      In which a Serpent did himselfe enfold,
      That horrour made to all, that did behold;
      But she no whit did chaunge her constant mood:
      And in her other hand she fast did hold
      A booke, that was both signd and seald with blood,
Wherein darke things were writ, hard to be understood.

14   Her younger sister, that *Speranza* hight,
      Was clad in blew, that her beseemed well;
      Not all so chearefull seemed she of sight,
      As was her sister; whether dread did dwell,
      Or anguish in her hart, is hard to tell:
      Upon her arme a silver anchor lay,
      Whereon she leaned ever, as befell:
      And ever up to heaven, as she did pray,
Her stedfast eyes were bent, ne swarved other way.

15   They seeing *Una*, towards her gan wend,
      Who them encounters with like courtesie;
      Many kind speeches they betwene them spend,
      And greatly joy each other well to see:
      Then to the knight with shamefast modestie
      They turne themselves, at *Unaes* meeke request,
      And him salute with well beseeming glee;
      Who faire them quites, as him beseemed best,
And goodly gan discourse of many a noble gest.

14. *swarved*: swerved, turned.
15. *shamefast*: bashful.   *gest*: exploit, deed of arms.

16   Then *Una* thus; But she your sister deare;
          The deare *Charissa* where is she become?
          Or wants she health, or busie is elsewhere?
          Ah no, said they, but forth she may not come:
          For she of late is lightned of her wombe,
          And hath encreast the world with one sonne more,
          That her to see should be but troublesome.
          Indeede (quoth she) that should her trouble sore,
     But thankt be God, and her encrease so evermore.

17   Then said the aged *Cælia*, Deare dame,
          And you good Sir, I wote that of your toyle,
          And labours long, through which ye hither came,
          Ye both forwearied be: therefore a whyle
          I read you rest, and to your bowres recoyle.
          Then called she a Groome, that forth him led
          Into a goodly lodge, and gan despoile
          Of puissant armes, and laid in easie bed;
     His name was meeke *Obedience* rightfully ared.

18   Now when their wearie limbes with kindly rest,
          And bodies were refresht with due repast,
          Faire *Una* gan *Fidelia* faire request,
          To have her knight into her schoolehouse plaste,
          That of her heavenly learning he might taste,
          And heare the wisedome of her words divine.
          She graunted, and that knight so much agraste,
          That she him taught celestiall discipline,
     And opened his dull eyes, that light mote in them shine.

16. *where is she become?*: what has become of her?
17. *read*: advise.   *recoyle*: return.   *ared*: ?interpreted, ?told.
18. *agraste*: favoured, was gracious to.

19   And that her sacred Booke, with bloud ywrit,
      That none could read, except she did them teach,
      She unto him disclosed every whit,
      And heavenly documents thereout did preach,
      That weaker wit of man could never reach,
      Of God, of grace, of justice, of free will,
      That wonder was to heare her goodly speach:
      For she was able, with her words to kill,
And raise againe to life the hart, that she did thrill.

20   And when she list poure out her larger spright,
      She would commaund the hastie Sunne to stay,
      Or backward turne his course from heavens hight;
      Sometimes great hostes of men she could dismay,
      Dry-shod to passe, she parts the flouds in tway;
      And eke huge mountaines from their native seat
      She would commaund, themselves to beare away,
      And throw in raging sea with roaring threat.
Almightie God her gave such powre, and puissance great.

21   The faithfull knight now grew in litle space,
      By hearing her, and by her sisters lore,
      To such perfection of all heavenly grace,
      That wretched world he gan for to abhore,
      And mortall life gan loath, as thing forlore,
      Greev'd with remembrance of his wicked wayes,
      And prickt with anguish of his sinnes so sore,
      That he desirde to end his wretched dayes:
So much the dart of sinfull guilt the soule dismayes.

---

20. *in tway*: in two.   21. *forlore*: (here) worthless.

22 But wise *Speranza* gave him comfort sweet,
    And taught him how to take assured hold
    Upon her silver anchor, as was meet;
    Else had his sinnes so great, and manifold
    Made him forget all that *Fidelia* told.
    In this distressed doubtfull agonie,
    When him his dearest *Una* did behold,
    Disdeining life, desiring leave to die,
She found her selfe assayld with great perplexitie.

23 And came to *Cælia* to declare her smart,
    Who well acquainted with that commune plight,
    Which sinfull horror workes in wounded hart,
    Her wisely comforted all that she might,
    With goodly counsell and advisement right;
    And streightway sent with carefull diligence,
    To fetch a Leach, the which had great insight
    In that disease of grieved conscience,
And well could cure the same; His name was *Patience*.

24 Who comming to that soule-diseased knight,
    Could hardly him intreat, to tell his griefe:
    Which knowne, and all that noyd his heavie spright
    Well searcht, eftsoones he gan apply reliefe
    Of salves and med'cines, which had passing priefe,
    And thereto added words of wondrous might:
    By which to ease he him recured briefe,
    And much asswag'd the passion of his plight,
That he his paine endur'd, as seeming now more light.

24. *noyd*: harmed. *priefe*: efficacy. *recured*: cured, restored to health.

25 But yet the cause and root of all his ill,
    Inward corruption, and infected sin,
    Not purg'd nor heald, behind remained still,
    And festring sore did rankle yet within,
    Close creeping twixt the marrow and the skin,
    Which to extirpe, he laid him privily
    Downe in a darkesome lowly place farre in,
    Whereas he meant his corrosives to apply,
And with streight diet tame his stubborne malady.

26 In ashes and sackcloth he did array
    His daintie corse, proud humors to abate,
    And dieted with fasting every day,
    The swelling of his wounds to mitigate,
    And made him pray both earely and eke late:
    And ever as superfluous flesh did rot
    Amendment readie still at hand did wayt,
    To pluck it out with pincers firie whot,
That soone in him was left no one corrupted jot.

27 And bitter *Penance* with an yron whip,
    Was wont him once to disple every day:
    And sharpe *Remorse* his hart did pricke and nip,
    That drops of bloud thence like a well did play;
    And sad *Repentance* used to embay
    His bodie in salt water smarting sore,
    The filthy blots of sinne to wash away.
    So in short space they did to health restore
The man that would not live, but carst lay at deathes dore.

25. *extirpe*: destroy. *streight*: strict.   26. *whot*: hot.
27. *disple*: discipline, (here) scourge. *embay*: bathe.

28 In which his torment often was so great,
    That like a Lyon he would cry and rore,
    And rend his flesh, and his owne synewes eat.
    His owne dear *Una* hearing evermore
    His ruefull shriekes and gronings, often tore
    Her guiltlesse garments, and her golden heare,
    For pitty of his paine and anguish sore;
    Yet all with patience wisely she did beare;
For well she wist, his crime could else be never cleare.

29 Whom thus recover'd by wise Patience,
    And trew *Repentance* they to *Una* brought:
    Who joyous of his cured conscience,
    Him dearely kist, and fairely eke besought
    Himselfe to chearish, and consuming thought
    To put away out of his carefull brest.
    By this *Charissa*, late in child-bed brought,
    Was woxen strong, and left her fruitfull nest;
To her faire *Una* brought this unacquainted guest.

30 She was a woman in her freshest age,
    Of wondrous beauty, and of bountie rare,
    With goodly grace and comely personage,
    That was on earth not easie to compare;
    Full of great love, but *Cupids* wanton snare
    As hell she hated, chast in worke and will;
    Her necke and breasts were ever open bare,
    That ay thereof her babes might sucke their fill;
The rest was all in yellow robes arayed still.

29. *unacquainted*: unfamiliar.

31 A multitude of babes about her hong,
    Playing their sports, that joyd her to behold,
    Whom still she fed, whiles they were weake and young,
    But thrust them forth still, as they wexed old:
    And on her head she wore a tyre of gold,
    Adornd with gemmes and owches wondrous faire,
    Whose passing price uneath was to be told;
    And by her side there sate a gentle paire
Of turtle doves, she sitting in an yvorie chaire.

32 The knight and *Una* entring, faire her greet,
    And bid her joy of that her happie brood;
    Who them requites with court'sies seeming meet,
    And entertaines with friendly chearefull mood.
    Then *Una* her besought, to be so good,
    As in her vertuous rules to schoole her knight,
    Now after all his torment well withstood,
    In that sad house of *Penaunce*, where his spright
Had past the paines of hell, and long enduring night.

33 She was right joyous of her just request,
    And taking by the hand that Faeries sonne,
    Gan him instruct in every good behest,
    Of love, and righteousnesse, and well to donne,
    And wrath, and hatred warely to shonne,
    That drew on men Gods hatred, and his wrath,
    And many soules in dolours had fordonne:
    In which when him she well instructed hath,
From thence to heaven she teacheth him the ready path.

---

31. *tyre*: headdress.   *owches*: ornaments, jewels.
33. *to donne*: to do.   *shonne*: shun.   *fordonne*: ruined utterly.

34   Wherein his weaker wandring steps to guide,
         An auncient matrone she to her does call,
         Whose sober lookes her wisedome well descride:
         Her name was *Mercie*, well knowne over all,
         To be both gratious, and eke liberall:
         To whom the carefull charge of him she gave,
         To lead aright, that he should never fall
         In all his wayes through this wide worldes wave,
      That Mercy in the end his righteous soule might save.

35   The godly Matrone by the hand him beares
         Forth from her presence, by a narrow way,
         Scattred with bushy thornes, and ragged breares,
         Which still before him she remov'd away,
         That nothing might his ready passage stay:
         And ever when his feet encombred were,
         Or gan to shrinke, or from the right to stray,
         She held him fast, and firmely did upbeare,
      As carefull Nourse her child from falling oft does reare.

36   Eftsoones unto an holy Hospitall,
         That was fore by the way, she did him bring,
         In which seven Bead-men that had vowed all
         Their life to service of high heavens king
         Did spend their dayes in doing godly thing:
         Their gates to all were open evermore,
         That by the wearie way were traveiling,
         And one sate wayting ever them before,
      To call in commers-by, that needy were and pore.

35. *breares*: briars.
36. *fore by*: close by.   *Bead-men*: men of prayer (see note).

37　The first of them that eldest was, and best,
　　　Of all the house had charge and governement,
　　　As Guardian and Steward of the rest:
　　　His office was to give entertainement
　　　And lodging, unto all that came, and went:
　　　Not unto such, as could him feast againe,
　　　And double quite, for that he on them spent,
　　　But such, as want of harbour did constraine:
　　Those for Gods sake his dewty was to entertaine.

38　The second was as Almner of the place,
　　　His office was, the hungry for to feed,
　　　And thristy give to drinke, a worke of grace:
　　　He feard not once him selfe to be in need,
　　　Ne car'd to hoord for those, whom he did breede:
　　　The grace of God he layd up still in store,
　　　Which as a stocke he left unto his seede;
　　　He had enough, what need him care for more?
　　And had he lesse, yet some he would give to the pore.

39　The third had of their wardrobe custodie,
　　　In which were not rich tyres, nor garments gay,
　　　The plumes of pride, and wings of vanitie,
　　　But clothes meet to keepe keene could away,
　　　And naked nature seemely to aray;
　　　With which bare wretched wights he dayly clad,
　　　The images of God in earthly clay;
　　　And if that no spare cloths to give he had,
　　His owne coate he would cut, and it distribute glad.

---

38. *Almner*: almoner.　　　　　　39. *tyres*: headdresses.　*could*: cold.

40　The fourth appointed by his office was,
　　　　Poore prisoners to relieve with gratious ayd,
　　　　And captives to redeeme with price of bras,
　　　　From Turkes and Sarazins, which them had stayd;
　　　　And though they faultie were, yet well he wayd,
　　　　That God to us forgiveth every howre
　　　　Much more then that, why they in bands were layd,
　　　　And he that harrowd hell with heavie stowre,
　　　The faultie soules from thence brought to his heavenly
　　　　　bowre.

41　The fift had charge sicke persons to attend,
　　　　And comfort those, in point of death which lay;
　　　　For them most needeth comfort in the end,
　　　　When sin, and hell, and death do most dismay
　　　　The feeble soule departing hence away.
　　　　All is but lost, that living we bestow,
　　　　If not well ended at our dying day.
　　　　O man have mind of that last bitter throw;
　　　For as the tree does fall, so lyes it ever low.

42　The sixt had charge of them now being dead,
　　　　In seemely sort their corses to engrave,
　　　　And deck with dainty flowres their bridall bed,
　　　　That to their heavenly spouse both sweet and brave
　　　　They might appeare, when he their soules shall save.
　　　　The wondrous workemanship of Gods owne mould,
　　　　Whose face he made, all beasts to feare, and gave
　　　　All in his hand, even dead we honour should.
　　　Ah dearest God me graunt, I dead be not defould.

　　40. *bras*: money. *stayd*: (here) imprisoned. *harrowd*: robbed, despoiled (see note).
　　41. *throw*: throe, pang.　　　　42. *engrave*: bury, entomb.

43 The seventh now after death and buriall done,
   Had charge the tender Orphans of the dead
   And widowes ayd, least they should be undone:
   In face of judgement he their right would plead,
   Ne ought the powre of mighty men did dread
   In their defence, nor would for gold or fee
   Be wonne their rightfull causes downe to tread:
   And when they stood in most necessitee,
He did supply their want, and gave them ever free.

44 There when the Elfin knight arrived was,
   The first and chiefest of the seven, whose care
   Was guests to welcome, towardes him did pas:
   Where seeing *Mercie*, that his steps up bare,
   And always led, to her with reverence rare
   He humbly louted in meeke lowlinesse,
   And seemely welcome for her did prepare:
   For of their order she was Patronesse,
Albe *Charissa* were their chiefest founderesse.

45 There she awhile him stayes, him selfe to rest,
   That to the rest more able he might bee:
   During which time, in every good behest
   And godly worke of Almes and charitee
   She him instructed with great industree;
   Shortly therein so perfect he became,
   That from the first unto the last degree,
   His mortall life he learned had to frame
In holy righteousnesse, without rebuke or blame.

44. *up bare*: upbore, supported. *louted*: bowed. *Albe*: although.

46   Thence forward by that painfull way they pas,
          Forth to an hill, that was both steepe and hy;
          On top whereof a sacred chappell was,
          And eke a litle Hermitage thereby,
          Wherein an aged holy man did lye,
          That day and night said his devotion,
          Ne other worldly busines did apply;
          His name was heavenly *Contemplation*;
      Of God and goodnesse was his meditation.

47   Great grace that old man to him given had;
          For God he often saw from heavens hight,
          All were his earthly eyen both blunt and bad,
          And through great age had lost their kindly sight,
          Yet wondrous quick and persant was his spright,
          As Eagles eye, that can behold the Sunne:
          That hill they scale with all their powre and might,
          That his frayle thighes nigh wearie and fordonne
      Gan faile, but by her helpe the top at last he wonne.

48   There they do finde that godly aged Sire,
          With snowy lockes adowne his shoulders shed,
          As hoarie frost with spangles doth attire
          The mossy braunches of an Oke halfe ded.
          Each bone might through his body well be red,
          And every sinew seene through his long fast:
          For nought he car'd his carcas long unfed;
          His mind was full of spirituall repast,
      And pyn'd his flesh, to keepe his body low and chast.

46. *apply*: attend to.
47. *All were* . . .: Although . . . were.   *blunt*: dim.   *persant*: piercing.   *fordonne*: exhausted.
48. *pyn'd*: wasted away (with hunger).

49   Who when these two approching he aspide,
       At their first presence grew agrieved sore,
       That forst him lay his heavenly thoughts aside;
       And had he not that Dame respected more,
       Whom highly he did reverence and adore,
       He would not once have moved for the knight.
       They him saluted standing far afore;
       Who well them greeting, humbly did requight,
  And asked, to what end they clomb that tedious height.

50   What end (quoth she) should cause us take such paine,
       But that same end, which every living wight
       Should make his marke, high heaven to attaine?
       Is not from hence the way, that leadeth right
       To that most glorious house, that glistreth bright
       With burning starres, and everliving fire,
       Whereof the keyes are to thy hand behight
       By wise *Fidelia*? she doth thee require,
  To shew it to this knight, according his desire.

51   Thrise happy man, said then the father grave,
       Whose staggering steps thy steady hand doth lead,
       And shewes the way, his sinfull soule to save.
       Who better can the way to heaven aread,
       Then thou thy selfe, that was both borne and bred
       In heavenly throne, where thousand Angels shine?
       Thou doest the prayers of the righteous sead
       Present before the majestie divine,
  And his avenging wrath to clemencie incline.

49. *afore*: in front.   *clomb*: climbed.   **50.** *behight*: entrusted.
51. *aread*: (here) direct.

52   Yet since thou bidst, thy pleasure shalbe donne.
         Then come thou man of earth, and see the way,
         That never yet was seene of Faeries sonne,
         That never leads the traveiler astray,
         But after labours long, and sad delay,
         Brings them to joyous rest and endlesse blis.
         But first thou must a season fast and pray,
         Till from her bands the spright assoiled is,
And have her strength recur'd from fraile infirmitis.

53   That done, he leads him to the highest Mount;
         Such one, as that same mighty man of God,
         That bloud-red billowes like a walled front
         On either side disparted with his rod,
         Till that his army dry-foot through them yod,
         Dwelt fortie dayes upon; where writ in stone
         With bloudy letters by the hand of God,
         The bitter doome of death and balefull mone
He did receive, whiles flashing fire about him shone.

54   Or like that sacred hill, whose head full hie,
         Adornd with fruitfull Olives all arownd,
         Is, as it were for endlesse memory
         Of that deare Lord, who oft thereon was fownd,
         For ever with a flowring girlond crownd:
         Or like that pleasaunt Mount, that is for ay
         Through famous Poets verse each where renownd,
         On which the thrise three learned Ladies play
Their heavenly notes, and make full many a lovely lay.

---

52. *assoiled*: absolved.   53. *yod*: went.
54. *each where*: everywhere.

55 From thence, far off he unto him did shew
    A litle path, that was both steepe and long,
    Which to a goodly Citie led his vew;
    Whose wals and towres were builded high and strong
    Of perle and precious stone, that earthly tong
    Cannot describe, nor wit of man can tell;
    Too high a ditty for my simple song;
    The Citie of the great king hight it well,
Wherein eternall peace and happinesse doth dwell.

56 As he thereon stood gazing, he might see
    The blessed Angels to and fro descend
    From highest heaven, in gladsome companee,
    And with great joy into that Citie wend,
    As commonly as friend does with his frend.
    Whereat he wondred much, and gan enquere,
    What stately building durst so high extend
    Her loftie towres unto the starry sphere,
And what unknowen nation there empeopled were.

57 Faire knight (quoth he) *Jerusalem* that is,
    The new *Jerusalem*, that God has built
    For those to dwell in, that are chosen his,
    His chosen people purg'd from sinfull guilt,
    With pretious bloud, which cruelly was spilt
    On cursed tree, of that unspotted lam,
    That for the sinnes of all the world was kilt:
    Now are they Saints all in that Citie sam,
More deare unto their God, then younglings to their dam.

57. *lam*: lamb.   *kilt*: killed.   *sam*: together.

PFQ

58 Till now, said then the knight, I weened well,
        That great *Cleopolis*, where I have beene,
        In which that fairest *Faerie Queene* doth dwell,
        The fairest Citie was, that might be seene;
        And that bright towre all built of christall cleene,
        Panthea, seemd the brightest thing, that was:
        But now by proofe all otherwise I weene;
        For this great Citie that does far surpas,
    And this bright Angels towre quite dims that towre of glas.

59 Most trew, then said the holy aged man;
        Yet is *Cleopolis* for earthly frame,
        The fairest peece, that eye beholden can:
        And well beseemes all knights of noble name,
        That covet in th'immortall booke of fame
        To be eternized, that same to haunt,
        And doen their service to that soveraigne Dame,
        That glorie does to them for guerdon graunt:
    For she is heavenly borne, and heaven may justly vaunt.

60 And thou faire ymp, sprong out from English race,
        How ever now accompted Elfins sonne,
        Well worthy doest thy service for her grace,
        To aide a virgin desolate foredonne.
        But when thou famous victorie hast wonne,
        And high emongst all knights hast hong thy shield,
        Thenceforth the suit of earthly conquest shonne,
        And wash thy hands from guilt of bloudy field:
    For bloud can nought but sin, and wars but sorrowes yield.

59. *peece*: work of art, structure.   *covet*: desire.   *doen*: do.
60. *accompted*: accounted, considered to be.   *suit*: pursuit.   *shonne*: shun.

61   Then seeke this path, that I to thee presage,
          Which after all to heaven shall thee send;
          Then peaceably thy painefull pilgrimage
          To yonder same *Jerusalem* do bend,
          Where is for thee ordaind a blessed end:
          For thou emongst those Saints, whom thou doest see,
          Shalt be a Saint, and thine owne nations frend
          And Patrone: thou Saint *George* shalt called bee,
      Saint *George* of mery England, the signe of victoree.

62   Unworthy wretch (quoth he) of so great grace,
          How dare I thinke such glory to attaine?
          These that have it attaind, were in like cace
          (Quoth he) as wretched, and liv'd in like paine.
          But deeds of armes must I at last be faine,
          And Ladies love to leave so dearely bought?
          What need of armes, where peace doth ay remaine,
          (Said he) and battailes none are to be fought?
      As for loose loves are vaine, and vanish into nought.

63   O let me not (quoth he) then turne againe
          Backe to the world, whose joyes so fruitlesse are;
          But let me here for aye in peace remaine,
          Or streight way on that last long voyage fare,
          That nothing may my present hope empare.
          That may not be (said he) ne maist thou yit
          Forgo that royall maides bequeathed care,
          Who did her cause into thy hand commit,
      Till from her cursed foe thou have her freely quit.

61. *presage*: point out.   *mery*: pleasant, agreeable.
62. *faine . . . to*: glad to.   *As for . . . vaine*: as for loose loves, they are vain.
63. *empare*: impair.   *bequeathed*: entrusted.

64   Then shall I soone, (quoth he) so God me grace,
        Abet that virgins cause disconsolate,
        And shortly backe returne unto this place,
        To walke this way in Pilgrims poore estate.
        But now aread, old father, why of late
        Didst thou behight me borne of English blood,
        Whom all a Faeries sonne doen nominate?
        That word shall I (said he) avouchen good,
     Sith to thee is unknowne the cradle of thy brood.

65   For well I wote, thou springst from ancient race
        Of *Saxon* kings, that have with mightie hand
        And many bloudie battailes fought in place
        High reard their royall throne in *Britane* land,
        And vanquisht them, unable to withstand:
        From thence a Faerie thee unweeting reft,
        There as thou slepst in tender swadling band,
        And her base Elfin brood there for thee left.
     Such men do Chaungelings call, so chaungd by Faeries theft.

66   Thence she thee brought into this Faerie lond,
        And in an heaped furrow did thee hyde,
        Where thee a Ploughman all unweeting fond,
        As he his toylesome teme that way did guyde,
        And brought thee up in ploughmans state to byde,
        Whereof *Georgos* he thee gave to name;
        Till prickt with courage, and thy forces pryde,
        To Faery court thou cam'st to seeke for fame,
     And prove thy puissaunt armes, as seemes thee best became.

---

64. *behight*: pronounce.   *avouchen*: prove, establish.
66. *to name*: as a name.

67 O holy Sire (quoth he) how shall I quight
      The many favours I with thee have found,
      That hast my name and nation red aright,
      And taught the way that does to heaven bound?
      This said, adowne he looked to the ground,
      To have returnd, but dazed were his eyne,
      Through passing brightnesse, which did quite confound
      His feeble sence, and too exceeding shyne.
    So darke are earthly things compard to things divine.

68 At last whenas himselfe he gan to find,
      To *Una* back he cast him to retire;
      Who him awaited still with pensive mind.
      Great thankes and goodly meed to that good syre,
      He thence departing gave for his paines hyre.
      So came to *Una*, who him joyd to see,
      And after litle rest, gan him desire,
      Of her adventure mindfull for to bee.
    So leave they take of *Cælia*, and her daughters three.

67. *bound*: lead.   68. *hyre*: payment (see note).

Canto 11

The knight with that old Dragon fights
two dayes incessantly:
The third him overthrowes, and gayns
most glorious victory.

1 High time now gan it wex for *Una* faire,
To thinke of those her captive Parents deare,
And their forwasted kingdome to repaire:
Whereto whenas they now approched neare,
With hartie words her knight she gan to cheare,
And in her modest manner thus bespake;
Deare knight, as deare, as ever knight was deare,
That all these sorrowes suffer for my sake,
High heaven behold the tedious toyle, ye for me take.

2 Now are we come unto my native soyle,
And to the place, where all our perils dwell;
Here haunts that feend, and does his dayly spoyle,
Therefore henceforth be at your keeping well,
And ever ready for your foeman fell.
The sparke of noble courage now awake,
And strive your excellent selfe to excell;
That shall ye evermore renowmed make,
Above all knights on earth, that batteill undertake.

1. *forwasted*: completely ravaged.   2. *keeping*: watch, guard.

3   And pointing forth, lo yonder is (said she)
        The brasen towre in which my parents deare
        For dread of that huge feend emprisond be,
        Whom I from far see on the walles appeare,
        Whose sight my feeble soule doth greatly cheare:
        And on the top of all I do espye
        The watchman wayting tydings glad to heare,
        That O my parents might I happily
    Unto you bring, to ease you of your misery.

4   With that they heard a roaring hideous sound,
        That all the ayre with terrour filled wide,
        And seemd uneath to shake the stedfast ground.
        Eftsoones that dreadfull Dragon they espide,
        Where stretcht he lay upon the sunny side
        Of a great hill, himselfe like a great hill.
        But all so soone, as he from far descride
        Those glistring armes, that heaven with light did fill,
    He rousd himselfe full blith, and hastned them untill.

5   Then bad the knight his Lady yede aloofe,
        And to an hill her selfe with draw aside,
        From whence she might behold that battailles proof
        And eke be safe from daunger far descryde:
        She him obayd, and turnd a little wyde.
        Now O thou sacred Muse, most learned Dame,
        Faire ympe of *Phœbus*, and his aged bride,
        The Nourse of time, and everlasting fame,
    That warlike hands ennoblest with immortall name;

---

4. *uneath*: ?underneath, ?almost; or, with difficulty.   *blith*: blithely, joyfully.
them untill: towards them.
    5. *yede aloofe*: move away.

6   O gently come into my feeble brest,
       Come gently, but not with that mighty rage,
       Wherewith the martiall troupes thou doest infest,
       And harts of great Heroës doest enrage,
       That nought their kindled courage may aswage,
       Soone as thy dreadfull trompe begins to sownd;
       The God of warre with his fiers equipage
       Thou doest awake, sleepe never he so sownd,
   And scared nations doest with horrour sterne astownd.

7   Faire Goddesse lay that furious fit aside,
       Till I of warres and bloudy *Mars* do sing,
       And Briton fields with Sarazin bloud bedyde,
       Twixt that great faery Queene and Paynim king,
       That with their horrour heaven and earth did ring,
       A worke of labour long, and endlesse prayse:
       But now a while let downe that haughtie string,
       And to my tunes thy second tenor rayse,
   That I this man of God his godly armes may blaze.

8   By this the dreadfull Beast drew nigh to hand,
       Halfe flying, and halfe footing in his hast,
       That with his largenesse measured much land,
       And made wide shadow under his huge wast;
       As mountaine doth the valley overcast.
       Approching nigh, he reared high afore
       His body monstrous, horrible, and vast,
       Which to increase his wondrous greatnesse more,
   Was swolne with wrath, and poyson, and with bloudy gore.

6. *sterne*: terrible.
7. *fit*: strain (of music).   *bedyde*: dyed.   *haughtie*: (here) high-pitched.

9   And over, all with brasen scales was armd,
      Like plated coate of steele, so couched neare,
      That nought mote perce, ne might his corse be harmd
      With dint of sword, nor push of pointed speare;
      Which as an Eagle, seeing pray appeare,
      His aery plumes doth rouze, full rudely dight,
      So shaked he, that horrour was to heare,
      For as the clashing of an Armour bright,
    Such noyse his rouzed scales did send unto the knight.

10 His flaggy wings when forth he did display,
      Were like two sayles, in which the hollow wynd
      Is gathered full, and worketh speedy way:
      And eke the pennes, that did his pineons bynd,
      Were like mayne-yards, with flying canvas lynd,
      With which whenas him list the ayre to beat,
      And there by force unwonted passage find,
      The cloudes before him fled for terrour great,
    And all the heavens stood still amazed with his threat.

11 His huge long tayle wound up in hundred foldes,
      Does overspred his long bras-scaly backe,
      Whose wreathed boughts when ever he unfoldes,
      And thicke entangled knots adown does slacke,
      Bespotted as with shields of red and blacke,
      It sweepeth all the land behind him farre,
      And of three furlongs does but litle lacke;
      And at the point two stings in-fixed arre,
    Both deadly sharpe, that sharpest steele exceeden farre.

9. *couched neare*: closely set.
10. *flaggy*: drooping.   *pennes*: quills.   11. *boughts*: folds.

12　But stings and sharpest steele did far exceed
　　　　The sharpnesse of his cruell rending clawes;
　　　　Dead was it sure, as sure as death in deed,
　　　　What ever thing does touch his ravenous pawes,
　　　　Or what within his reach he ever drawes.
　　　　But his most hideous head my toung to tell
　　　　Does tremble: for his deepe devouring jawes
　　　　Wide gaped, like the griesly mouth of hell,
　　Through which into his darke abisse all ravin fell.

13　And that more wondrous was, in either jaw
　　　　Three ranckes of yron teeth enraunged were,
　　　　In which yet trickling bloud and gobbets raw
　　　　Of late devoured bodies did appeare,
　　　　That sight thereof bred cold congealed feare:
　　　　Which to increase, and all atonce to kill,
　　　　A cloud of smoothering smoke and sulphur seare
　　　　Out of his stinking gorge forth steemed still,
　　That all the ayre about with smoke and stench did fill.

14　His blazing eyes, like two bright shining shields,
　　　　Did burne with wrath, and sparkled living fyre;
　　　　As two broad Beacons, set in open fields,
　　　　Send forth their flames farre off to every shyre,
　　　　And warning give, that enemies conspyre,
　　　　With fire and sword the region to invade;
　　　　So flam'd his eyne with rage and rancorous yre:
　　　　But farre within, as in a hollow glade,
　　Those glaring lampes were set, that made a dreadfull shade.

13. *gobbets*: lumps of flesh.

15 So dreadfully he towards him did pas,
  Forelifting up aloft his speckled brest,
  And often bounding on the brused gras,
  As for great joyance of his newcome guest.
  Eftsoones he gan advance his haughtie crest,
  As chauffed Bore his bristles doth upreare,
  And shoke his scales to battell readie drest;
  That made the *Redcrosse* knight nigh quake for feare,
As bidding bold defiance to his foeman neare.

16 The knight gan fairely couch his steadie speare,
  And fiercely ran at him with rigorous might:
  The pointed steele arriving rudely theare,
  His harder hide would neither perce, nor bight,
  But glauncing by forth passed forward right;
  Yet sore amoved with so puissant push,
  The wrathfull beast about him turned light,
  And him so rudely passing by, did brush
With his long tayle, that horse and man to ground did rush.

17 Both horse and man up lightly rose againe,
  And fresh encounter towards him addrest:
  But th'idle stroke yet backe recoyld in vaine,
  And found no place his deadly point to rest.
  Exceeding rage enflam'd the furious beast,
  To be avenged of so great despight;
  For never felt his imperceable brest
  So wondrous force, from hand of living wight;
Yet had he prov'd the powre of many a puissant knight.

15. *Forelifting*: lifting up in front.
17. *imperceable*: un-pierceable. *prov'd*: tested.

18   Then with his waving wings displayed wyde,
      Himselfe up high he lifted from the ground,
      And with strong flight did forcibly divide
      The yielding aire, which nigh too feeble found
      Her flitting partes, and element unsound,
      To beare so great a weight: he cutting way
      With his broad sayles, about him soared round:
      At last low stouping with unweldie sway,
  Snatcht up both horse and man, to beare them quite away.

19   Long he them bore above the subject plaine,
      So farre as Ewghen bow a shaft may send,
      Till struggling strong did him at last constraine,
      To let them downe before his flightes end:
      As hagard hauke presuming to contend
      With hardie fowle, above his hable might,
      His wearie pounces all in vaine doth spend,
      To trusse the pray too heavie for his flight;
  Which comming downe to ground, does free it selfe by
      fight.

20 He so disseized of his gryping grosse,
      The knight his thrillant speare againe assayd
      In his bras-plated body to embosse,
      And three mens strength unto the stroke he layd;
      Wherewith the stiffe beame quaked, as affrayd,
      And glauncing from his scaly necke, did glyde
      Close under his left wing, then broad displayd.
      The percing steele there wrought a wound full wyde,
  That with the uncouth smart the Monster lowdly cryde.

---

19. *subject*: situated beneath.   *Ewghen*: made of yew.   *hagard*: wild, untrained.
hable: able.   *pounces*: claws.   *trusse*: clutch firmly (see note).
   20. *thrillant*: piercing.   *embosse*: plunge in, thrust in.   *beame*: shaft.

21 He cryde, as raging seas are wont to rore,
        When wintry storme his wrathfull wreck does threat,
        The rolling billowes beat the ragged shore,
        As they the earth would shoulder from her seat,
        And greedie gulfe does gape, as he would eat
        His neighbour element in his revenge:
        Then gin the blustring brethren boldly threat,
        To move the world from off his stedfast henge,
    And boystrous battell make, each other to avenge.

22 The steely head stucke fast still in his flesh,
        Till with his cruell clawes he snatcht the wood,
        And quite a sunder broke. Forth flowed fresh
        A gushing river of blacke goarie blood,
        That drowned all the land, whereon he stood;
        The streame thereof would drive a water-mill.
        Trebly augmented was his furious mood
        With bitter sense of his deepe rooted ill,
    That flames of fire he threw forth from his large nosethrill.

23 His hideous tayle then hurled he about,
        And therewith all enwrapt the nimble thyes
        Of his froth-fomy steed, whose courage stout
        Striving to loose the knot, that fast him tyes,
        Himselfe in streighter bandes too rash implyes,
        That to the ground he is perforce constraynd
        To throw his rider: who can quickly ryse
        From off the earth, with durty bloud distaynd,
    For that reprochfull fall right fowly he disdaynd.

21. *wreck*: destruction.   *henge*: hinge (see note).
22. *nosethrill*: nostril.
23. *thyes*: thighs, flanks.   *streighter*: narrower.   *implyes*: entangles.   *can quickly ryse*: quickly rose.   *distaynd*: stained.

24 And fiercely tooke his trenchand blade in hand,
     With which he stroke so furious and so fell,
     That nothing seemd the puissance could withstand:
     Upon his crest the hardned yron fell,
     But his more hardned crest was armd so well,
     That deeper dint therein it would not make;
     Yet so extremely did the buffe him quell,
     That from thenceforth he shund the like to take,
But when he saw them come, he did them still forsake.

25 The knight was wrath to see his stroke beguyld,
     And smote againe with more outrageous might;
     But backe againe the sparckling steele recoyld,
     And left not any marke, where it did light;
     As if in Adamant rocke it had bene pight.
     The beast impatient of his smarting wound,
     And of so fierce and forcible despight,
     Thought with his wings to stye above the ground;
But his late wounded wing unserviceable found.

26 Then full of griefe and anguish vehement,
     He lowdly brayd, that like was never heard,
     And from his wide devouring oven sent
     A flake of fire, that flashing in his beard,
     Him all amazd, and almost made affeard:
     The scorching flame sore swinged all his face,
     And through his armour all his bodie seard,
     That he could not endure so cruell cace,
But thought his armes to leave, and helmet to unlace.

24. *trenchand*: trenchant, sharp.
25. *impatient of*: suffering with difficulty.   *stye*: mount.
26. *swinged*: singed, scorched.

27 Not that great Champion of the antique world,
     Whom famous Poetes verse so much doth vaunt,
     And hath for twelve huge labours high extold,
     So many furies and sharpe fits did haunt,
     When him the poysoned garment did enchaunt
     With *Centaures* bloud, and bloudie verses charm'd,
     As did this knight twelve thousand dolours daunt,
     Whom fyrie steele now burnt, that earst him arm'd,
That erst him goodly arm'd, now most of all him harm'd.

28 Faint, wearie, sore, emboyled, grieved, brent
     With heat, toyle, wounds, armes, smart, and inward fire
     That never man such mischiefes did torment;
     Death better were, death did he oft desire,
     But death will never come, when needes require.
     Whom so dismayd when that his foe beheld,
     He cast to suffer him no more respire,
     But gan his sturdie sterne about to weld,
And him so strongly stroke, that to the ground him feld.

29 It fortuned (as faire it then befell)
     Behind his backe unweeting, where he stood,
     Of auncient time there was a springing well,
     From which fast trickled forth a silver flood,
     Full of great vertues, and for med'cine good.
     Whylome, before that cursed Dragon got
     That happie land, and all with innocent blood
     Defyld those sacred waves, it rightly hot
The well of life, ne yet his vertues had forgot.

28. *emboyled*: ?panting, ?agitated. *grieved*: injured. *brent*: burnt. *respire*: rest.
29. *hot*: was called.

30 For unto life the dead it could restore,
    And guilt of sinfull crimes cleane wash away,
    Those that with sicknesse were infected sore,
    It could recure, and aged long decay
    Renew, as one were borne that very day.
    Both *Silo* this, and *Jordan* did excell,
    And th'English *Bath*, and eke the german *Spau*,
    Ne can *Cephise*, nor *Hebrus* match this well:
Into the same the knight backe overthrowen, fell.

31 Now gan the golden *Phœbus* for to steepe
    His fierie face in billowes of the west,
    And his faint steedes watred in Ocean deepe,
    Whiles from their journall labours they did rest,
    When that infernall Monster, having kest
    His wearie foe into that living well,
    Can high advance his broad discoloured brest,
    Above his wonted pitch, with countenance fell,
And clapt his yron wings, as victor he did dwell.

32 Which when his pensive Ladie saw from farre,
    Great woe and sorrow did her soule assay,
    As weening that the sad end of the warre,
    And gan to highest God entirely pray,
    That feared chance from her to turne away;
    With folded hands and knees full lowly bent
    All night she watcht, ne once adowne would lay
    Her daintie limbs in her sad dreriment,
But praying still did wake, and waking did lament.

31. *journall*: daily.   *kest*: cast.
32. *entirely*: earnestly.   *dreriment*: sorrow.

33 The morrow next gan early to appeare,
     That *Titan* rose to runne his daily race;
     But early ere the morrow next gan reare
     Out of the sea faire *Titans* deawy face,
     Up rose the gentle virgin from her place,
     And looked all about, if she might spy
     Her loved knight to move his manly pace:
     For she had great doubt of his safety,
Since late she saw him fall before his enemy.

34 At last she saw, where he upstarted brave
     Out of the well, wherein he drenched lay;
     As Eagle fresh out of the Ocean wave,
     Where he hath left his plumes all hoary gray,
     And deckt himselfe with feathers youthly gay,
     Like Eyas hauke up mounts unto the skies,
     His newly budded pineons to assay,
     And marveiles at himselfe, still as he flies:
So new this new-borne knight to battell new did rise.

35 Whom when the damned feend so fresh did spy,
     No wonder if he wondred at the sight,
     And doubted, whether his late enemy
     It were, or other new supplied knight.
     He, now to prove his late renewed might,
     High brandishing his bright deaw-burning blade,
     Upon his crested scalpe so sore did smite,
     That to the scull a yawning wound it made:
The deadly dint his dulled senses all dismaid.

34. *Eyas hauke*: young hawk.
35. *deaw-burning*: glittering with dew.

36 I wote not, whether the revenging steele
    Were hardned with that holy water dew,
    Wherein he fell, or sharper edge did feele,
    Or his baptized hands now greater grew;
    Or other secret vertue did ensew;
    Else never could the force of fleshly arme,
    Ne molten mettall in his bloud embrew:
    For till that stownd could never wight him harme,
By subtilty, nor slight, nor might, nor mighty charme.

37 The cruell wound enraged him so sore,
    That loud he yelled for exceeding paine;
    As hundred ramping Lyons seem'd to rore,
    Whom ravenous hunger did thereto constraine:
    Then gan he tosse aloft his stretched traine,
    And therewith scourge the buxome aire so sore,
    That to his force to yeelden it was faine;
    Ne ought his sturdie strokes might stand afore,
That high trees overthrew, and rocks in peeces tore.

38 The same advauncing high above his head,
    With sharpe intended sting so rude him smot,
    That to the earth him drove, as stricken dead,
    Ne living wight would have him life behot:
    The mortall sting his angry needle shot
    Quite through his shield, and in his shoulder seasd,
    Where fast it stucke, ne would there out be got:
    The griefe thereof him wondrous sore diseasd,
Ne might his ranckling paine with patience be appeasd.

---

36. *embrew*: plunge, be steeped. *stownd*: time, occasion.
37. *buxome*: yielding.
38. *intended*: stretched out. *behot*: promised. *griefe*: pain. *diseasd*: distressed.

39 But yet more mindfull of his honour deare,
    Then of the grievous smart, which him did wring,
    From loathed soile he can him lightly reare,
    And strove to loose the farre infixed sting:
    Which when in vaine he tryde with struggeling,
    Inflam'd with wrath, his raging blade he heft,
    And strooke so strongly, that the knotty string
    Of his huge taile he quite a sunder cleft,
Five joynts thereof he hewd, and but the stump him left.

40 Hart cannot thinke, what outrage, and what cryes,
    With foule enfouldred smoake and flashing fire,
    The hell-bred beast threw forth unto the skyes,
    That all was covered with darknesse dire:
    Then fraught with rancour, and engorged ire,
    He cast at once him to avenge for all,
    And gathering up himselfe out of the mire,
    With his uneven wings did fiercely fall
Upon his sunne-bright shield, and gript it fast withall.

41 Much was the man encombred with his hold,
    In feare to lose his weapon in his paw,
    Ne wist yet, how his talants to unfold;
    Nor harder was from *Cerberus* greedie jaw
    To plucke a bone, then from his cruell claw
    To reave by strength the griped gage away:
    Thrise he assayd it from his foot to draw,
    And thrise in vaine to draw it did assay,
It booted nought to thinke, to robbe him of his pray.

39. *heft*: heaved.
40. *outrage*: (here) ?furious clamour. *enfouldred*: ?black as a thunder-cloud.
engorged: swallowed.
41. *talants*: talons. *reave*: wrench. *gage*: pledge.

42 Tho when he saw no power might prevaile,
    His trustie sword he cald to his last aid,
    Wherewith he fiercely did his foe assaile,
    And double blowes about him stoutly laid,
    That glauncing fire out of the yron plaid;
    As sparckles from the Andvile use to fly,
    When heavie hammers on the wedge are swaid;
    Therewith at last he forst him to unty
One of his grasping feete, him to defend thereby.

43 The other foot, fast fixed on his shield,
    Whenas no strength, nor stroks mote him constraine
    To loose, ne yet the warlike pledge to yield,
    He smot thereat with all his might and maine,
    That nought so wondrous puissance might sustaine;
    Upon the joynt the lucky steele did light,
    And made such way, that hewd it quite in twaine;
    The paw yet missed not his minisht might,
But hong still on the shield, as it at first was pight.

44 For griefe thereof, and divelish despight,
    From his infernall fournace forth he threw
    Huge flames, that dimmed all the heavens light,
    Enrold in duskish smoke and brimstone blew;
    As burning *Aetna* from his boyling stew
    Doth belch out flames, and rockes in peeces broke,
    And ragged ribs of mountaines molten new,
    Enwrapt in coleblacke clouds and filthy smoke,
That all the land with stench, and heaven with horror choke.

---

42. *Andvile*: anvil.   *use to fly*: are wont to fly.   *swaid*: swung.
43. *minisht*: diminished.   44. *griefe*: pain.   *stew*: cauldron.

45 The heate whereof, and harmefull pestilence
      So sore him noyd, that forst him to retire
      A little backward for his best defence,
      To save his bodie from the scorching fire,
      Which he from hellish entrailes did expire.
      It chaunst (eternall God that chaunce did guide)
      As he recoyled backward, in the mire
      His nigh forwearied feeble feet did slide,
And downe he fell, with dread of shame sore terrifide.

46 There grew a goodly tree him faire beside,
      Loaden with fruit and apples rosie red,
      As they in pure vermilion had beene dide,
      Whereof great vertues over all were red:
      For happie life to all, which thereon fed,
      And life eke everlasting did befall:
      Great God it planted in that blessed sted
      With his almightie hand, and did it call
The tree of life, the crime of our first fathers fall.

47 In all the world like was not to be found,
      Save in that soile, where all good things did grow,
      And freely sprong out of the fruitfull ground,
      As incorrupted Nature did them sow,
      Till that dread Dragon all did overthrow.
      Another like faire tree eke grew thereby,
      Whereof who so did eat, eftsoones did know
      Both good and ill: O mornefull memory:
That tree through one mans fault hath doen us all to dy.

45. *noyd*: hurt.   *expire*: breathe out.
46. *red*: declared.   *sted*: place.

48   From that first tree forth flowd, as from a well,
        A trickling streame of Balme, most soveraine
        And daintie deare, which on the ground still fell,
        And overflowed all the fertill plaine,
        As it had deawed bene with timely raine:
        Life and long health that gratious ointment gave,
        And deadly woundes could heale, and reare againe
        The senselesse corse appointed for the grave.
    Into that same he fell: which did from death him save.

49   For nigh thereto the ever damned beast
        Durst not approch, for he was deadly made,
        And all that life preserved, did detest:
        Yet he it oft adventur'd to invade.
        By this the drouping day-light gan to fade,
        And yeeld his roome to sad succeeding night,
        Who with her sable mantle gan to shade
        The face of earth, and wayes of living wight,
    And high her burning torch set up in heaven bright.

50   When gentle *Una* saw the second fall
        Of her deare knight, who wearie of long fight,
        And faint through losse of bloud, mov'd not at all,
        But lay as in a dreame of deepe delight,
        Besmeard with pretious Balme, whose vertuous might
        Did heale his wounds, and scorching heat alay,
        Againe she stricken was with sore affright,
        And for his safetie gan devoutly pray;
    And watch the noyous night, and wait for joyous day.

---

49. *deadly made*: see note.   50. *noyous*: irksome.

51 The joyous day gan early to appeare,
      And faire *Aurora* from the deawy bed
      Of aged *Tithone* gan her selfe to reare,
      With rosie cheekes, for shame as blushing red;
      Her golden lockes for haste were loosely shed
      About her eares, when *Una* her did marke
      Clymbe to her charet, all with flowers spred,
      From heaven high to chase the chearelesse darke;
    With merry note her loud salutes the mounting larke.

52 Then freshly up arose the doughtie knight,
      All healed of his hurts and woundes wide,
      And did himselfe to battell readie dight;
      Whose early foe awaiting him beside
      To have devourd, so soone as day he spyde,
      When now he saw himselfe so freshly reare,
      As if late fight had nought him damnifyde,
      He woxe dismayd, and gan his fate to feare;
    Nathlesse with wonted rage he him advaunced neare.

53 And in his first encounter, gaping wide,
      He thought attonce him to have swallowd quight,
      And rusht upon him with outragious pride;
      Who him r'encountring fierce, as hauke in flight,
      Perforce rebutted backe. The weapon bright
      Taking advantage of his open jaw,
      Ran through his mouth with so importune might,
      That deepe emperst his darksome hollow maw,
    And back retyrd, his life bloud forth with all did draw.

51. *for shame . . . red*: blushing red as if for shame.
52. *dight*: prepare.   *damnifyde*: damaged.   *woxe*: grew.   *Nathlesse*: nevertheless.
53. *rebutted*: made (him) recoil.   *emperst*: pierced.

54   So downe he fell, and forth his life did breath,
        That vanisht into smoke and cloudes swift;
        So downe he fell, that th'earth him underneath
        Did grone, as feeble so great load to lift;
        So downe he fell, as an huge rockie clift,
        Whose false foundation waves have washt away,
        With dreadfull poyse is from the mayneland rift,
        And rolling downe, great *Neptune* doth dismay;
    So downe he fell, and like an heaped mountaine lay.

55   The knight himselfe even trembled at his fall,
        So huge and horrible a masse it seem'd;
        And his deare Ladie, that beheld it all,
        Durst not approch for dread, which she misdeem'd,
        But yet at last, when as the direfull feend
        She saw not stirre, off-shaking vaine affright,
        She nigher drew, and saw that joyous end:
        Then God she praysd, and thankt her faithfull knight,
    That had atchiev'd so great a conquest by his might.

54. *clift*: cliff.   *poyse*: weight, heavy fall.
55. *misdeem'd*: misjudged.

Canto 12

Faire Una to the Redcrosse knight
betrouthed is with joy:
Though false Duessa it to barre
her false sleights doe imploy.

1 Behold I see the haven nigh at hand,
     To which I meane my wearie course to bend;
     Vere the maine shete, and beare up with the land,
     The which afore is fairely to be kend,
     And seemeth safe from stormes, that may offend;
     There this faire virgin wearie of her way
     Must landed be, now at her journeyes end:
     There eke my feeble barke a while may stay,
   Till merry wind and weather call her thence away.

2 Scarsely had *Phœbus* in the glooming East
     Yet harnessed his firie-footed teeme,
     Ne reard above the earth his flaming creast,
     When the last deadly smoke aloft did steeme,
     That signe of last outbreathed life did seeme
     Unto the watchman on the castle wall;
     Who thereby dead that balefull Beast did deeme,
     And to his Lord and Ladie lowd gan call,
   To tell, how he had seene the Dragons fatall fall.

1. *Vere*: let out.   *beare up with*: put the helm up towards.   *afore*: ahead.   *kend*:
(here) seen.

3   Uprose with hastie joy, and feeble speed
        That aged Sire, the Lord of all that land,
        And looked forth, to weet, if true indeede
        Those tydings were, as he did understand,
        Which whenas true by tryall he out fond,
        He bad to open wyde his brazen gate,
        Which long time had bene shut, and out of hond
        Proclaymed joy and peace through all his state;
    For dead now was their foe, which them forrayed late.

4   Then gan triumphant Trompets sound on hie,
        That sent to heaven the ecchoed report
        Of their new joy, and happie victorie
        Gainst him, that had them long opprest with tort,
        And fast imprisoned in sieged fort.
        Then all the people, as in solemne feast,
        To him assembled with one full consort,
        Rejoycing at the fall of that great beast,
    From whose eternall bondage now they were releast.

5   Forth came that auncient Lord and aged Queene,
        Arayd in antique robes downe to the ground,
        And sad habiliments right well beseene;
        A noble crew about them waited round
        Of sage and sober Peres, all gravely gownd;
        Whom farre before did march a goodly band
        Of tall young men, all hable armes to sownd,
        But now they laurell braunches bore in hand;
    Glad signe of victorie and peace in all their land.

3. *out of hond*: immediately.   *forrayed*: ravaged, harrassed.
4. *tort*: wrong.   *consort*: accord.
5. *sad*: sober.   *habiliments*: attire.   *well beseene*: appropriate.   *sownd*: ?wield.

6 Unto that doughtie Conquerour they came,
    And him before themselves prostrating low,
    Their Lord and Patrone loud did him proclame,
    And at his feet their laurell boughes did throw.
    Soone after them all dauncing on a row
    The comely virgins came, with girlands dight,
    As fresh as flowres in medow greene do grow,
    When morning deaw upon their leaves doth light:
And in their hands sweet Timbrels all upheld on hight.

7 And them before, the fry of children young
    Their wanton sports and childish mirth did play,
    And to the Maydens sounding tymbrels sung
    In well attuned notes, a joyous lay,
    And made delightfull musicke all the way,
    Until they came, where that faire virgin stood;
    As faire *Diana* in fresh sommers day
    Beholds her Nymphes, enraung'd in shadie wood,
Some wrestle, some do run, some bathe in christall flood.

8 So she beheld those maydens meriment
    With chearefull vew; who when to her they came,
    Themselves to ground with gratious humblesse bent,
    And her ador'd by honorable name,
    Lifting to heaven her everlasting fame:
    Then on her head they set a girland greene,
    And crowned her twixt earnest and twixt game;
    Who in her selfe-resemblance well beseene,
Did seeme such, as she was, a goodly maiden Queene.

6. *on hight*: on high.
7. *fry*: swarms, troops (of children). *enraung'd*: at large.
8. *well beseene*: (most) appropriate-looking.

9   And after, all the raskall many ran,
        Heaped together in rude rablement,
        To see the face of that victorious man:
        Whom all admired, as from heaven sent,
        And gazd upon with gaping wonderment.
        But when they came, where that dead Dragon lay,
        Stretcht on the ground in monstrous large extent,
        The sight with idle feare did them dismay,
    Ne durst approch him nigh, to touch, or once assay.

10   Some feard, and fled; some feard and well it faynd;
        One that would wiser seeme, then all the rest,
        Warnd him not touch, for yet perhaps remaynd
        Some lingring life within his hollow brest,
        Or in his wombe might lurke some hidden nest
        Of many Dragonets, his fruitfull seed;
        Another said, that in his eyes did rest
        Yet sparckling fire, and bad thereof take heed;
    Another said, he saw him move his eyes indeed.

11   One mother, when as her foolehardie chyld
        Did come too neare, and with his talants play,
        Halfe dead through feare, her litle babe revyld,
        And to her gossips gan in counsell say;
        How can I tell, but that his talents may
        Yet scratch my sonne, or rend his tender hand?
        So diversly themselves in vaine they fray;
        Whiles some more bold, to measure him nigh stand,
    To prove how many acres he did spread of land.

        9. *raskall many*: the mob (see note).   *rablement*: rabble.
        10. *Dragonets*: young dragons.
        11. *talants*: talons.   *fray*: frighten.

12   Thus flocked all the folke him round about,
        The whiles that hoarie king, with all his traine,
        Being arrived, where that champion stout
        After his foes defeasance did remaine,
        Him goodly greetes, and faire does entertaine,
        With princely gifts of yvorie and gold,
        And thousand thankes him yeelds for all his paine.
        Then when his daughter deare he does behold,
     Her dearely doth imbrace, and kisseth manifold.

13   And after to his Pallace he them brings,
        With shaumes, and trompets, and with Clarions sweet;
        And all the way the joyous people sings,
        And with their garments strowes the paved street:
        Whence mounting up, they find purveyance meet
        Of all, that royall Princes court became,
        And all the floore was underneath their feet
        Bespred with costly scarlot of great name,
     On which they lowly sit, and fitting purpose frame.

14   What needs me tell their feast and goodly guize,
        In which was nothing riotous nor vaine?
        What needs of daintie dishes to devize,
        Of comely services, or courtly traync?
        My narrow leaves cannot in them containe
        The large discourse of royall Princes state.
        Yet was their manner then but bare and plaine:
        For th'antique world excesse and pride did hate;
     Such proud luxurious pompe is swollen up but late.

    12. *defeasance*: defeat.
    13. *shaumes*: instruments similar to the clarinet. *purveyance*: provision. *scarlot*:
a rich cloth. *name*: reputation. *purpose*: conversation.
    14. *devize*: talk.

15   Then when with meates and drinkes of every kinde
         Their fervent appetites they quenched had,
         That auncient Lord gan fit occasion finde,
         Of straunge adventures, and of perils sad,
         Which in his travell him befallen had,
         For to demaund of his renowmed guest:
         Who then with utt'rance grave, and count'nance sad,
         From point to point, as is before exprest,
     Discourst his voyage long, according his request.

16   Great pleasure mixt with pittifull regard,
         That godly King and Queene did passionate,
         Whiles they his pittifull adventures heard,
         That oft they did lament his lucklesse state,
         And often blame the too importune fate,
         That heapd on him so many wrathfull wreakes:
         For never gentle knight, as he of late,
         So tossed was in fortunes cruell freakes;
     And all the while salt teares bedeawd the hearers cheaks.

17   Then said that royall Pere in sober wise;
         Deare Sonne, great beene the evils, which ye bore
         From first to last in your late enterprise,
         That I note, whether prayse, or pitty more:
         For never living man, I weene, so sore
         In sea of deadly daungers was distrest;
         But since now safe ye seised have the shore,
         And well arrived are, (high God be blest)
     Let us devize of ease and everlasting rest.

15. *sad*: sober, grave.
16. *pittifull* (l. 1): full of pity.   *passionate*: express with feeling.   *pittifull* (l. 3): to be pitied.   *bedeawd*: bedewed.
17. *note*: know not.   *devize*: talk.

18   Ah dearest Lord, said then that doughty knight,
          Of ease or rest I may not yet devize;
          For by the faith, which I to armes have plight,
          I bounden am streight after this emprize,
          As that your daughter can ye well advize,
          Backe to returne to that great Faerie Queene,
          And her to serve six yeares in warlike wize,
          Gainst that proud Paynim king, that workes her teene:
      Therefore I ought crave pardon, till I there have beene.

19   Unhappie falles that hard necessitie,
          (Quoth he) the troubler of my happie peace,
          And vowed foe of my felicitie;
          Ne I against the same can justly preace:
          But since that band ye cannot now release,
          Nor doen undo; (for vowes may not be vaine)
          Soone as the terme of those six yeares shall cease,
          Ye then shall hither backe returne againe,
      The marriage to accomplish vowd betwixt you twain.

20   Which for my part I covet to performe,
          In sort as through the world I did proclame,
          That who so kild that monster most deforme,
          And him in hardy battaile overcame,
          Should have mine onely daughter to his Dame,
          And of my kingdome heire apparaunt bee:
          Therefore since now to thee perteines the same,
          By dew desert of noble chevalree,
      Both daughter and eke kingdome, lo I yield to thee.

18. *emprize*: undertaking, adventure.   *teene*: grief, harm.
19. *preace*: press.
20. *covet*: desire.   *In sort as*: since, even as.

21 Then forth he called that his daughter faire,
  The fairest *Un'* his onely daughter deare,
  His onely daughter, and his onely heyre;
  Who forth proceeding with sad sober cheare,
  As bright as doth the morning starre appeare
  Out of the East, with flaming lockes bedight,
  To tell that dawning day is drawing neare,
  And to the world does bring long wished light;
So faire and fresh that Lady shewd her selfe in sight.

22 So faire and fresh, as freshest flowre in May;
  For she had layd her mournefull stole aside,
  And widow-like sad wimple throwne away,
  Wherewith her heavenly beautie she did hide,
  Whiles on her wearie journey she did ride;
  And on her now a garment she did weare,
  All lilly white, withoutten spot, or pride,
  That seemd like silke and silver woven neare,
But neither silke nor silver therein did appeare.

23 The blazing brightnesse of her beauties beame,
  And glorious light of her sunshyny face
  To tell, were as to strive against the streame.
  My ragged rimes are all too rude and bace,
  Her heavenly lineaments for to enchace.
  Ne wonder; for her owne deare loved knight,
  All were she dayly with himselfe in place,
  Did wonder much at her celestiall sight:
Oft had he seene her faire, but never so faire dight.

---

22. *woven neare*: closely woven.
23. *enchace*: adorn, embellish. *All were she*: although she had been.

24 So fairely dight, when she in presence came,
  She to her Sire made humble reverence,
  And bowed low, that her right well became,
  And added grace unto her excellence:
  Who with great wisedome, and grave eloquence
  Thus gan to say. But eare he thus had said,
  With flying speede, and seeming great pretence,
  Came running in, much like a man dismaid,
A Messenger with letters, which his message said.

25 All in the open hall amazed stood,
  At suddeinnesse of that unwarie sight,
  And wondred at his breathlesse hastie mood.
  But he for nought would stay his passage right
  Till fast before the king he did alight;
  Where falling flat, great humblesse he did make,
  And kist the ground, whereon his foot was pight;
  Then to his hands that writ he did betake,
Which he disclosing, red thus, as the paper spake.

26 To thee, most mighty king of *Eden* faire,
  Her greeting sends in these sad lines addrest,
  The wofull daughter, and forsaken heire
  Of that great Emperour of all the West;
  And bids thee be advized for the best,
  Ere thou thy daughter linck in holy band
  Of wedlocke to that new unknowen guest;
  For he already plighted his right hand
Unto another love, and to another land.

24. *pretence*: (here) concern, show.
25. *unwarie*: unexpected. *did alight*: stopped, halted.

R<small>FQ</small>

27 To me sad mayd, or rather widow sad,
    He was affiaunced long time before,
    And sacred pledges he both gave, and had,
    False erraunt knight, infamous, and forswore:
    Witnesse the burning Altars, which he swore,
    And guiltie heavens of his bold perjury,
    Which though he hath polluted oft of yore,
    Yet I to them for judgement just do fly,
And them conjure t'avenge this shamefull injury.

28 Therefore since mine he is, or free or bond,
    Or false or trew, or living or else dead,
    Withhold, O soveraine Prince, your hasty hond
    From knitting league with him, I you aread;
    Ne weene my right with strength adowne to tread,
    Through weakenesse of my widowhed, or woe:
    For truth is strong, her rightfull cause to plead,
    And shall find friends, if need requireth soe,
So bids thee well to fare, Thy neither friend, nor foe,
    Fidessa.

29 When he these bitter byting words had red,
    The tydings straunge did him abashed make,
    That still he sate long time astonished
    As in great muse, ne word to creature spake.
    At last his solemne silence thus he brake,
    With doubtfull eyes fast fixed on his guest;
    Redoubted knight, that for mine onely sake
    Thy life and honour late adventurest,
Let nought be hid from me, that ought to be exprest.

---

28. *bond*: bound. *aread*: advise.

30   What meane these bloudy vowes, and idle threats,
      Throwne out from womanish impatient mind?
      What heavens? what altars? what enraged heates
      Here heaped up with termes of love unkind,
      My conscience cleare with guilty bands would bind?
      High God be witnesse, that I guiltlesse ame.
      But if your selfe, Sir knight, ye faultie find,
      Or wrapped be in loves of former Dame,
  With crime do not it cover, but disclose the same.

31   To whom the *Redcrosse* knight this answere sent,
      My Lord, my King, be nought hereat dismayd,
      Till well ye wote by grave intendiment,
      What woman, and wherefore doth me upbrayd
      With breach of love, and loyalty betrayd.
      It was in my mishaps, as hitherward
      I lately traveild, that unwares I strayd
      Out of my way, through perils straunge and hard;
  That day should faile me, ere I had them all declard.

32   There did I find, or rather I was found
      Of this false woman, that *Fidessa* hight,
      Fidessa hight the falsest Dame on ground,
      Most false *Duessa*, royall richly dight,
      That easie was t' invegle weaker sight:
      Who by her wicked arts, and wylie skill,
      Too false and strong for earthly skill or might,
      Unwares me wrought unto her wicked will,
  And to my foe betrayd, when least I feared ill.

          30. *unkind*: unnatural.
          31. *intendiment*: careful consideration.

33 Then stepped forth the goodly royall Mayd,
   And on the ground her selfe prostrating low,
   With sober countenaunce thus to him sayd;
   O pardon me, my soveraigne Lord, to show
   The secret treasons, which of late I know
   To have bene wroght by that false sorceresse.
   She onely she it is, that earst did throw
   This gentle knight into so great distresse,
That death him did awaite in dayly wretchednesse.

34 And now it seemes, that she suborned hath
   This craftie messenger with letters vaine,
   To worke new woe and improvided scath,
   By breaking of the band betwixt us twaine;
   Wherein she used hath the practicke paine
   Of this false footman, clokt with simplenesse,
   Whom if ye please for to discover plaine,
   Ye shall him *Archimago* find, I ghesse,
The falsest man alive; who tries shall find no lesse.

35 The king was greatly moved at her speach,
   And all with suddein indignation fraight,
   Bad on that Messenger rude hands to reach.
   Eftsoones the Gard, which on his state did wait,
   Attacht that faitor false, and bound him strait:
   Who seeming sorely chauffed at his band,
   As chained Beare, whom cruell dogs do bait,
   With idle force did faine them to withstand,
And often semblaunce made to scape out of their hand.

34. *improvided scath*: unforseen harm.   *practicke paine*: cunning pains, efforts.
35. *fraight*: fraught.   *Attacht*: arrested.   *faitor*: villain.   *faine*: feign.

36   But they him layd full low in dungeon deepe,
       And bound him hand and foote with yron chains.
       And with continuall watch did warely keepe;
       Who then would thinke, that by his subtile trains
       He could escape fowle death or deadly paines?
       Thus when that Princes wrath was pacifide,
       He gan renew the late forbidden banes,
       And to the knight his daughter deare he tyde,
    With sacred rites and vowes for ever to abyde.

37   His owne two hands the holy knots did knit,
       That none but death for ever can devide;
       His owne two hands, for such a turne most fit,
       The housling fire did kindle and provide,
       And holy water thereon sprinckled wide;
       At which the bushy Teade a groome did light,
       And sacred lampe in secret chamber hide,
       Where it should not be quenched day nor night,
    For feare of evill fates, but burnen ever bright.

38   Then gan they sprinckle all the posts with wine,
       And made great feast to solemnize that day;
       They all perfumde with frankencense divine,
       And precious odours fetcht from far away,
       That all the house did sweat with great aray:
       And all the while sweete Musicke did apply
       Her curious skill, the warbling notes to play,
       To drive away the dull Melancholy;
    The whiles one sung a song of love and jollity.

         36. *banes*: banns (of marriage).
         37. *housling*: (here) sacramental.   *Teade*: torch.
         38. *curious*: ingenious, elaborate.

39 During the which there was an heavenly noise
        Heard sound through all the Pallace pleasantly,
        Like as it had bene many an Angels voice,
        Singing before th'eternall majesty,
        In their trinall triplicities on hye;
        Yet wist no creature, whence that heavenly sweet
        Proceeded, yet each one felt secretly
        Himselfe thereby reft of his sences meet,
    And ravished with rare impression in his sprite.

40 Great joy was made that day of young and old,
        And solemne feast proclaimd throughout the land,
        That their exceeding merth may not be told:
        Suffice it heare by signes to understand
        The usuall joyes at knitting of loves band.
        Thrise happy man the knight himselfe did hold,
        Possessed of his Ladies hart and hand,
        And ever, when his eye did her behold,
    His heart did seeme to melt in pleasures manifold.

41 Her joyous presence and sweet company
        In full content he there did long enjoy,
        Ne wicked envie, ne vile gealosy
        His deare delights were able to annoy:
        Yet swimming in that sea of blisfull joy,
        He nought forgot, how he whilome had sworne,
        In case he could that monstrous beast destroy,
        Unto his Farie Queene backe to returne:
    The which he shortly did, and *Una* left to mourne.

---

39. *trinall triplicities*: threefold groups of three (see note).

42 Now strike your sailes ye jolly Mariners,
      For we be come unto a quiet rode,
      Where we must land some of our passengers,
      And light this wearie vessell of her lode.
      Here she a while may make her safe abode,
      Till she repaired have her tackles spent,
      And wants supplide. And then againe abroad
      On the long voyage whereto she is bent:
Well may she speede and fairely finish her intent.

42. *strike . . . sailes*: lower sails.   *rode*: sheltered near-shore anchorage.

NOTES

Proem

1. *Lo I the man*: One manuscript of Virgil's *Aeneid* bears in the margin a proem of four lines beginning *Ille ego, qui quondam . . ., etc.* It is thought to be authentic, although since the days of antiquity the words *Arma virumque cano* (Arms and the man I sing) have been regarded as the opening words.

maske . . . in lowly Shepheards weeds: as the poet of *The Shepheardes Calender*, published in 1579.

Mine Oaten reeds: the primitive flute or pipes of a shepherd.

of Knights and Ladies gentle deeds: imitated from the opening lines of Ariosto's *Orlando Furioso*:

> Le donne, i cavalier, l'arme, gli amori
> Le cortesie, l'audaci imprese io canto.

Whose prayses having slept . . ., etc.: 'And now that their praises have slept in long silence, the Muse areeds (commands) me (though I be altogether too mean) to blazon (them) abroad amongst her learned throng (of poets, sages, etc.).'

2. *O holy virgin, chiefe of nine*: Clio, the Muse of History, is first of the Nine Muses (in Hesiod's *Theogony* 77). Spenser presumably should have invoked Calliope, the Muse of Epic Poetry. But he may intend, by invoking the Muse of History, to imply that his story is not mere fabling. In the Proem to Book II he announces that he presents 'antique history' of the 'happy land of Faerie', not 'th'aboundance of an idle braine' or 'painted forgery'. Chaucer invokes Clio at the beginning of Book II, and Calliope at the beginning of Book III of *Troilus and Criseyde*; and Spenser invokes Clio again before the fight between the Red Cross Knight and the Dragon in Canto 11.

weaker Novice: a Latinism for 'too weak'.

Tanaquill: Caia Tanaquil, an Etruscan, the wife of Tarquinius Priscus, the first of the Tarquin (Etruscan) kings of Rome. Vives in *De instructione*

feminae christianae names her as type of a noble queen, and Spenser
here, and in II.10.76, applies the name and the idea to Gloriana, the
Queen of his Faerie Land.

Briton Prince: Arthur. One of the background situations of *The Faerie
Queene* is Arthur's long searching for Gloriana.

3. *impe*: child (Latin, *impotus*, a graft or young shoot).

impe of highest Jove: Cupid, the son of Jupiter (Jove) and Venus.

Mart: Mars, God of War. (So in Chaucer, *Troilus and Criseyde*,
2.988.)

in loves and gentle jollities arrayd: Spenser is thinking of Mars's adultery
with Venus, as in Ovid *Metamorphoses*, IV.170ff. Spenser has promised
the reader wars and loves, and accordingly calls on Mars, as both war-
god and lover, as well as Venus and Cupid, to help him.

4. *Goddesse heavenly bright*: Gloriana, that is Queen Elizabeth.

Mirrour of grace: a reference to the Platonic notion that all beautiful
things on earth are mirrors of the divine beauty.

Phoebus lampe: the light of the sun.

that true glorious type . . . the argument of mine afflicted style: Una, the
heroine of Book I, who represents Truth, is a 'type' of Elizabeth, says
Spenser, with the characteristic honorific and laudatory hyperbole of
the time. She is the subject of his pen, which he declares is overwhelmed
by a sense of its inadequacy to deal with so noble a subject.

O dearest dred: 'beloved and revered'.

Canto 1

[Una or Truth accompanies the Red Cross Knight, an untried knight
who has taken on the quest to overthrow a dragon which has occupied
her parents' land. They lose their way in the Wandering Wood, the
Red Cross Knight overcomes the monster Error, they meet the enchanter
Archimago, and, unsuspecting, go to his 'hermitage' to spend the night.
He calls up infernal spirits, sending one to Morpheus to get idle and
lustful dreams for the Knight, and making the other into the likeness
of Una. The latter comes to the Red Cross Knight's bed. He is perplexed
at the apparent change in virtuous Una, but treats 'her' gently and sends
her away.]

1. *A gentle Knight*: the Knight of the Red Cross, 'St. *George* of mery

England' in I.10.61, wears the armour of Christ, with the red cross on it to signify the cross and the blood of Christ. Yet he is himself an untried knight at the beginning of the book ('yet armes till that time did he never wield'), and he yearns

> To prove his puissance in battell brave
> . . . and his new force to learne.
>
> (I.1.3.)

So, the Christian man goes forth to do battle against error, falsehood, and temptation in the world, armed with the armour of Christ it is true, but vulnerable and often led astray and into danger.

silver shielde: in Hardyng's *Chronicle*, Joseph of Arimathea, having converted Arviragus,

> gave hym then a shield of silver white,
> A crosse endlong and overthwart full perfecte:
> These armes were used through all Britain
> For a common signe eche manne to know his nacioun
> From enemies: which now we call certain
> Saint Georges armes.

The shield of Sir Galahad, who is of the kindred of Joseph of Arimathea, is white as any snow, and with a red cross in the middle. (Malory, *Works*, ed. Vinaver, Oxford, 1947, p. 877.) In the Prefatory Letter to Sir Walter Raleigh, Spenser, giving an account of the opening of the poem (which in fact does not tally with the opening we have), presents the Red Cross Knight as a clownish young man who takes on the quest of a fair lady and is given the armour she had brought with her to Gloriana's court ('that is the armour of a Christian man specified by Saint Paul v. Ephes'—*Ephesians* vi.11–17). In earlier English doctrinal allegories by Stephen Hawes, *The Passetyme of Pleasure* (1509) and *The Exemple of Vertu* (1512), the heroes Graund Amour and Youth, who journey to achieve respectively worldly glory and moral purity, wear the same armour, the Christian soldier's panoply described by St. Paul.

2. *And dead as living ever him ador'd*: adored Him who was dead and is ever living; cf. *Revelation* i.18: 'I am he that liveth, and was dead; and, behold, I am alive for evermore, Amen.'

For soveraine hope, which in his helpe he had: he had great hope, and the cross scored on the shield was a sign of it, in the help he would receive as a Christian from the strength of Christian belief.

3. *greatest Gloriana*: Queen Elizabeth. In the Prefatory Letter Spenser wrote: 'In that Faery Queene I mean *Glory* in my generall intention, but in my particular I conceive the most excellent and glorious person of our soveraine the Queene.' It was court fashion to address the Virgin Queen under such symbolic names as Gloriana, Oriana, Diana, Cynthia.

a Dragon: the Devil, Satan.

4. *A lovely ladie*: Una, or Truth. Also the one true faith—by which Spenser meant the Anglican faith. Una, *one* and true, is contrasted with Duessa, deceitful, false, and full of *duplicity*. Una is a proper name which Spenser would very probably have come across in Ireland.

This is the first of the countless running emblems that appear in *The Faerie Queene*. The lovely lady, clad in white but veiled under a black stole, on the lowly white ass moves slowly and sadly into our field of vision, leading a milk-white lamb (innocence). It is an effective emblem of sorrowful virtue, but we must not try to see it too realistically. Fortunately, having made his point, Spenser allows the lamb quietly to disappear, and the ass, too, soon ceases to figure at all significantly, except when it reappears in I.6.19, re-emphasizing that it symbolizes the true Church (to Spenser the Church of England) which is the servant and the supporter of Truth. (See note to I.6.19.)

5. *from East to Westerne shore*: Spenser means, in declaring that Una's parents descend from kings and queens not of the West only, that the true Church derives not from the Church of Rome alone.

infernall feend: Satan, who, coming into the world, has exiled man from his true inheritance of God's world. A fuller account of the plight of Una's parents is given in I.7.43ff.

6. *a Dwarfe*: the laggard dwarf has been interpreted as common sense or prudence, contrasted with divine truth.

his lemans lap: Spenser is characteristically cavalier with classical mythology, and makes Earth the paramour of Jupiter. Heaven and Earth are lovers, and there is a concealed sexual image here in his picture of the storm sent by Jove.

7. *A shadie grove, etc.*: Notice that the grove *promises* shelter, *seems* to

afford them good cover, and is so dense that it *hides* the light of heaven. The implication, which is indeed accurate, is that it will not really give them sound shelter; and that it is a bad place, for the good light of heaven cannot be seen from within it. It is so, for this is the Wandering Wood, the Wood of Error. This is the first example in the poem of Spenser's characteristic care to warn the alert reader subtly of what his attitude to a given character, scene, or episode ought to be.

8. *the trees*: Spenser incorporates in *The Faerie Queene* the characteristic devices, features, and conventions of classical poetry and particularly of epic. The grove with its listed trees descends from Ovid (*Metamorphoses*, X. 90ff.), and there are parallels in Lucan (*Pharsalia*, III. 440), Statius (*Thebaid*, VI. 98), Claudian (*De raptu Proserpinae*, II. 107), *The Romaunt of the Rose*, Boccaccio (*Teseide*, XI. 22–24), Chaucer (*The Parlement of Foules*, 176ff.—to which Spenser was closely indebted), and Tasso (*Gerusalemme Liberata*, III. 75, 76). Spenser mentions ten of the thirteen his master Chaucer lists in *The Parlement*, making similar comments about their usefulness or characteristics, and adds another seven. But notice that he takes the opportunity of pointing out the melancholy, mournful, grievous, or unsound: the funeral Cypress, the weeping Fir, the Willow 'worne of forlorne Paramours', the bleeding Myrrh, the Maple 'seeldom inward sound'. Again he is warning the reader.

sayling Pine: because used in ship-building, the trunk serving for masts. There may also be some suggestion of the movement of a pine in a high wind, and of the sound of the wind through its branches, like the wind in rigging and sails. Chaucer writes of the sailing *Fir*.

vine-prop Elme: the elm used for supports for vines. Ovid has *Amictae vitibus ulni*, the elms clothed with vines (*Metamorphoses*, X. 100).

poplar never dry: the poplar (black or white Italian poplar) especially flourishes in damp places, along river banks, for example.

builder Oake: the oak, used in building, as in Chaucer. In medieva England, and for long afterwards, oak was the chief building timber.

Cypresse funerall: Pliny, *Natural History*, XVI. 33, writes of cypress hung on a house as a sign of death. Chaucer in *The Parlement* writes of the cypress 'deth to pleyne' (lamenter of death, or for lamenting), Sidney in *Arcadia* of 'Cypress branches wherewith in old time they were wont to dress graves', and Feste in *Twelfth Night* sings a song which looks forward to death, when the body will be laid in sad cypress: either a coffin made of cypress wood, or in a coffin in which fronds of cypress have been laid, presumably because it is aromatic. Spenser, at the end of Canto 1, Book II, of *The Faerie Queene*, shows Sir Guyon and the Palmer decorating the grave they have prepared for the bodies of Mordant and Amavia with 'sad Cypresse'. (The cypress is often planted in cemeteries in Italy and France, and indeed in England: there, presumably, for its shade, here because it is evergreen. But see the story of Cyparissus, who died of grief, having accidentally killed a beloved stag (Ovid, *Met*. X. 120) and was turned into a cypress, Apollo, who loved him decreeing that cypress should for ever be a symbol of sorrow and grief; Spenser tells it in Canto 6. (See note to I.6.17.)

9. *the Laurell*: the laurel wreath was the sign of triumph for the victorious conqueror, emperor, and poet.

the Firre that weepeth still: because it exudes resin.

the Willow: badge of deserted lovers. Desdemona, in *Othello*, IV. iii, speaks of her mother's maid, Barbary, who was forsaken by her lover:

> . . . she had a song of 'willow',
> An odd thing 'twas, but it express'd her fortune
> And she died singing it . . .

and herself sings a song of a false love, with the 'willow' refrain taken from John Heywood's 'Song of the Green Willow'.

the Eugh: bows were made of yew.

The Sallow for the mill: this is perplexing. Willow is not a useful wood, being stringy and soft, and the tree grows to no great size.

the Mirrhe sweete bleeding in the bitter wound: the word 'myrrh' is used both of a gum resin used in perfumery and medicine, and of an aromatic plant, sweet cicely. Spenser is thinking of Ovid's account (*Metamorphoses*, X) of Myrrha. She had indulged her incestuous desire for her own father, Cinyras, with the complicity of her nurse. When Cinyras discovered that his young bedfellow was his daughter, he at once determined to kill her, but she escaped, and, penitent before the gods, was freed from human life and penalty by being transformed into a myrrh-tree. Ovid vividly describes Myrrha's weeping, and the agony and the wound by which Adonis, her child by her father, was born, slowly struggling from the tear in the bark. Notice the density of Spenser's writing: the myrrh is sweet-scented; bleeding because of the resinous gum; the wound from which the sweet gum comes is bitter because it painfully tore to bring forth in grief and pain the incestuous child of Myrrha. All this meaning is conveyed in one line.

The warlike Beech: warlike because the war-chariots of the ancients were reputedly made of beech.

The carver Holme: used for carving.

12. *Oft fire is without smoke*: the first instance of Spenser's use of proverbs and proverbial expressions, of which there are innumerable examples throughout the poem. It is one of the ways by which he keeps his romance world in touch with ordinary everyday and contemporary life.

Shame were to revoke . . .: 'it would be shameful to turn back for fear of some imagined evil'.

13. *the wandring wood*: the wood which causes wandering, that is moral wandering, error.

14. *his glistring armour*: an unusual imagination has prompted this subtle picture of the fearsome den slightly lit by the mere presence of the knight's goodly armour. Kitchin found this 'a passage worthy of Rembrandt's most gloomy pencil'.

Halfe like a serpent: the monster Error is imitated from Hesiod's picture of Echidna (*Theogony*, V. 301), with possibly some suggestions from Dante's Geryon (Fraud) in *Inferno* (XVII. 10–27). Milton's Sin (*Paradise Lost*, II. 650–9), is clearly related to Spenser's Error.

15. *A thousand yong ones*: if Una is one, the one true faith, Error and her thousand hideous young represent the multiplicity of false belief.

Of sundry shapes: the children of error and falsehood take a thousand different forms in life.

Into her mouth they crept: it was popularly supposed that, when disturbed or pursued, the adder took its young into its mouth.

17. *Elfe*: from Old English *aelf*, an elf or fairy. In *The Faerie Queene* an elf is always a knight of Faerie land, as opposed to Briton knights or Sarazin knights. The fairy world of medieval literature was by no means

inhabited only by tiny sprites, but by beings of normal size and human appearance. Indeed, Oberon in *Huon of Bordeaux* is probably the first small literary fairy, the size of a 3-year-old child. It was not until Elizabethan times, perhaps not until Shakespeare, that the fairy regularly became the tiny being we now imagine, who had long existed in folklore. Spenser is truer to the literature of fairy, Shakespeare closer to the spoken tales of the countryside. (See K. M. Briggs, *The Anatomy of Puck*, Routledge & Kegan Paul, 1959.)

18. This stanza is the first in the poem to exhibit one of Spenser's characteristic methods of getting his effects: heavy alliteration. The thudding 'd's at the beginning, and the looping 'wr's and 'w's at the end, effectively combine sound and sense to convey the knight's fierce blows and the serpent's wreathing coils. Alliteration and onomatopoeia always go hand in hand in Spenser, to such an extent that many critics have complained of excess. The emphasis is, I feel, entirely justified, for we can think of nothing but what he is determined we shall think of, while the consonants alliterate and chime.

So wrapt in Errour's endlesse traine: Spenser makes sure we don't miss the moral significance. Error is half-serpent; God help us when imprisoned in the endless coils of falseness or sin.

19. *His gall did grate*: the gall was thought to be the seat of anger. The Greek χόλος and χολή, from which we draw the word choleric, and the Latin *bilis*, from which we get the word bile, both mean anger as well as gall.

20. An example of Spenser's characteristically strong emphasis, condemned by some as excessive, in order to arouse a strong emotional reaction in the reader. The repetition and piling-up of the emotive words *spewd, filthy, maw, poyson, horrible, lumpes, gobbets, stunck, vildly, vomit, loathly, weedy, filthy, parbreake, defiled*, which not only connote disgusting or repulsive objects or sensations but are expressively ugly in sound, in fact make such passages irresistibly effective.

full of bookes and papers was: but Spenser weakens his achieved imaginative effect in order to point a moral. The monster is but an allegorical representation, this line reminds us, and the vomit of Error consists of the polemical books and pamphlets of the Catholic propagandists and erroneous theological writing, and probably also of the scurrilous propaganda and attacks upon the Queen. There was a great outbreak of pamphleteering during Elizabeth's reign, and it was also an age of great public defamation and denigration.

loathly frogs and toades: as in *Revelation* xvi. 13.

which eyes did lacke . . . in the weedy gras: a vividly conveyed idea. Spenser constantly astonishes the reader by the detail he can afford time and space to devise in the course of this long poem.

21. *Old father Nilus*: it was commonly believed, from ancient times, that after the flooding of the Nile the sun burning on the slime generated creatures. Probably, as so often, Ovid was Spenser's source: in *Metamorphoses*, I. 411ff. he writes of labourers finding many animals, some still imperfectly or incompletely formed, in the mud heated by the aethereal sun.

23. This stanza gives us the first example of another Spenserian literary virtue, his ready and effective use of contrast. After stanzas 18, 20, and 22, with their powerful presentation of evil, ugliness, and horror, he gives us the relief of the opening of stanza 23, with its pastoral pleasantness, before going on to develop the effective image of the cloud of gnats. Spenser was a knowledgeable and vivid describer of nature. This is, too, the first of many images prompted by his life in Ireland.

26. *unkindly Impes*: unkindly meaning primarily unnatural here, but, as with Hamlet's 'A little more than kin and less than kind', there is probably an element of double meaning.

bowels gushing forth: possibly Spenser thought of the end of Judas, in *Acts* i. 18: 'falling headlong, he burst asunder in the midst, and all his bowels gushed out'.

27. *borne under happy starre*: Your fortune throughout life depended on the aspect of the heavens and the relationship of the star rising at that moment to the other stars, some benign, some malignant.

that Armorie: the armour of a Christian. (See notes to I.1.)

28. *which beaten was most plaine*: it is surprisingly easy to get out of the Wandering Wood. The implication is that it is easy to break away from Error if you just set your back to it.

29. *an aged Sire*: Archimago, the chief enchanter (arch-magus). He represents Evil, the evil of falseness, deceit, and hypocrisy. That is why

> Sober he *seemde*, and very sagely sad,
>
> .   .   .   .
>
> And often knockt his brest, *as one that did repent.*

It is a powerful presentation, and the Red Cross Knight and Una are completely deceived. In Ariosto's *Orlando Furioso*, II. 15 and VIII. 27, Angelica encounters an aged devout hermit, an enchanter who conjures up false sprites to mislead her lover Rinaldo, and who later drugs and attempts to ravish her.

34. *His holy things*: among the evil and falseness that Archimago stands for, on one level of the allegory, the falseness and evil of Catholicism is clearly meant. The hermitage, the sacred well, the holy 'things'—his offices and devotions—and, in the next stanza, the tales of saints and Popes and the slighting reference to his strewing of 'Ave-Marys' after and before, point this clearly.

Ave-Mary: 'Hail, Mary', repeated at intervals during Catholic services and private devotions.

36. Night, as messenger of Morpheus the god of sleep, sprinkles 'slumbering deaw' on them. In Virgil (*Aeneid*, V. 854ff.) Morpheus shakes on Palinurus a bough dripping with Lethe water and steeped in the Styx; perhaps Spenser remembered the Lethean and Stygian reference when he wrote of the 'sad humour'.

37. *Plutoes griesly Dame*: Persephone or Proserpina, Queen of Hell after being seized by Pluto and carried down to his realm of Hell.

Great Gorgon: not the Gorgon or Medusa but the medieval Demogorgon, regarded by some as the author of creation, by others, including Spenser, as a great magician who commanded the spirits of the lower world. His name was thought to have great power in incantations. The name may come from Plato's Demiourgos. In Boccaccio, *De Genealogia Deorum* (1.1), he is the grandfather of all the gods and heroes, the creator of all things; he lives in the bowels of the earth, and people are afraid to utter his name. Boccaccio derived the name from the Greek words meaning daemon of the earth. Lucan (*Pharsalia*, VI. 744–6) derived it from the Latin words meaning daemon of the Gorgons. In Tasso, *Gerusalemme Liberata* (XII. 10), the enchanter Ismen threatens the spirits with what Milton (*Paradise Lost*, II. 964) calls 'the dreaded name of

Demogorgon'. In Marlowe's *Dr. Faustus* (Revels series, Methuen, 1962, Scene 3, ll. 18ff.) he makes the third of an infernal trinity, Lucifer, Beelzebub and Demogorgon. (In Shelley's *Prometheus Unbound* Demogorgon stands for a beneficent eternal principle or power which ousts the gods of a false theology.)

Cocytus: from the Greek word meaning lamentation: Cocytus, one of the four rivers of the underworld, is the river of wailing and lamentation.

Styx: the river of hate. Even these terrible rivers quake and flee at sight of Demogorgon. (The other two are Acheron, of grief, and Phlegethon, of burning.) Spenser gives more details of them in his account of Mammon's dwelling in the underworld in Book II, Canto 7.

38. *like little flyes*: flies are often thought to be evil spirits. Beelzebub, one of the great fallen angels in Milton, is god of flies.

39. *Tethys*: wife of Oceanus, and daughter of Uranus (heaven) and Ge (earth), and the mother of the chief rivers of the world.

Cynthia: the moon. It is one of the names (others being Artemis and Diana) of the moon-goddess, from Mount Cynthus in Delos, her birthplace.

40. *double gates*: in Homer (*Odyssey*, XIX. 562ff.) and Virgil (*Aeneid*, VI. 893f.), there are two gates of Sleep, one of horn, from which true dreams proceed, and one of ivory, which sends forth false dreams. Spenser imagines the horn one to be cased in silver: he *may* mean by this to emphazise showiness and meretriciousness.

wakefull dogges: Spenser's invention, a characteristically subtle and complex addition.

41. Spenser also seems indebted to Chaucer's description of Morpheus's cave in *The Book of the Duchess* (ll. 155ff.).

43. *Hecate*: a powerful and mysterious goddess of the underworld, especially associated with night and darkness and the fell deeds that can take place under cover of darkness. Virgil (*Aeneid*, VI. 247) calls her supreme in Heaven and in Hell. The Renaissance mythographer Natale Conti (Natalis Comes) in his *Mythologiae* (III. 15) describes her as the daughter of Night, patron of magic and the black arts of potions and poisons, goddess of dreams. She was regarded, by Spenser as by Shakespeare (*Macbeth*, II. i. 51; *King Lear*, I. i. 112), as Queen of Night; in

Macbeth she appears in Act III, Scene 5, and in Act IV, Scene 1, as mistress and president of the witches.

44. *a diverse dream*: a dream to divert or distract. The false manufactured spirit appears in Homer (*Iliad*, V, a false Aeneas) and in Virgil (*Aeneid*, X, a false Turnus), and is fairly common in another of the literary forms which Spenser imitated and was indebted to, Romance. In *Morte Darthur* Sir Percivale is tempted by a 'gentlewoman of great beauty', in fact 'the master fiend of hell', who vanishes when he luckily gains control of himself enough to make the sign of the cross. (Malory, *Works*, ed. Vinaver, O.U.P., 1947, vol. ii, pp. 916ff.) In Tasso, *Gerusalemme Liberata*, VII. 99, a spirit in the shape of the lady-knight Clorinda is forged by Satan. Perhaps the closest parallels to this deception of Archimago's are the hermit in *Orlando Furioso*, II and VII, and the magician Atlante's method of luring people to his castle by showing them, as Sir John Harington renders it in his version of Ariosto's *Orlando Furioso* (XIII. 42ff.),

> by strange illusion distrest,
> Each one of the party whom he loveth best.

> Each one doth deeme he sees in great distresse,
> His love, his friend, his fellow or his page,
> According as mens reasons more or lesse,
> Are weake or strong such passion to asswage:
> Thus do they follow this their foolish guesse,
> Vntill they come like birds into a cage . . .

But Spenser is more detailed, circumstantial and convincing. Archimago, Falseness itself, is a great and successful falsifier and deceiver. He is not just a Romance magician, but a powerful necromancer who does the work of Evil. The allegorist in Spenser is well served here by the possibilities he finds in the epic and romantic material.

48. The knight, his senses already aroused by the amorous dream Archimago has sent him, finds Una, as he thinks, brought to his bed by Venus herself, while the Graces seem to sing a hymeneal chant and Flora crowns her with ivy. Ivy is 'wanton' in Book II.5.29 and elsewhere because it clings and embraces, and is also sacred to Bacchus. Flora, as the Gloss to the March eclogue of Spenser's *The Shepheardes*

Calender points out, is not only goddess of flowers 'but indede (as saith Tacitus) a famous harlot, which with the abuse of her body having gotten great riches, made the people of Rome her heyre'. So in addition to all the suggestions of the illicit, the wanton, the erotic, and the unrestrained, there is added a suggestion of the vileness and deceit of Romishness. A good example of Spenser's care to provide elaborate allusive detail.

Canto 2

[Archimago, angered at the failure of his deceits, makes one of the evil spirits into the image of a young squire, puts 'him' to bed with 'Una' and calls the Red Cross Knight to witness their 'wanton lust and lewd embracement'. The Red Cross Knight cannot sleep after seeing this tormenting sight, and leaves the hermitage at dawn. Una is grieved by his departure and sets out in search of him, and Archimago disguises himself as the Red Cross Knight with the idea of working her 'further smarts'. The Red Cross Knight encounters a Saracen knight, Sansfoy, whose companion is the lavishly and wantonly beautiful Duessa. Sansfoy attacks the Knight and is killed by him, whereupon Duessa changes sides, denigrates the dead Saracen, and, saying her name is Fidessa, craves the Red Cross Knight's mercy. He responds and quickly surrenders to her deceiving but palpable charms. They lie in dalliance in the shade of two mossy trees. The Red Cross Knight plucks a bough of one of the trees to make a garland for 'Fidessa', and the tree speaks, saying it is a knight Fradubio who had abandoned his beloved, Fraelissa, for Duessa. But one day by chance he saw Duessa 'in her proper hew'; the beautiful-seeming girl was in fact a 'filthy foule old woman'. He began to keep away from her, looking for an opportunity to escape, but she perceived his thought and imprisoned him and Fraelissa in the two trees. He warns the Red Cross Knight of the peril he is in with Duessa, but he is completely enchanted by her and disregards the warning.]

1. *The Northerne wagoner*: Boötes, from the Greek word meaning wagoner, or ploughman; a northern constellation, sometimes called 'The Wagoner', at the tail of the Great Bear, which itself is often called The Plough or 'Charles's Wain'. It contains the bright star Arcturus.

his sevenfold teme: the seven stars of the constellation.

the stedfast starre: The Pole Star. In our latitude it is stedfast because it never sets.

Chaunticlere: the 'clear-singing' cock. Spenser took him no doubt from his favourite Chaucer, who took him from the medieval cycle of animal stories that bears the name of *Reynard the Fox*, its principal character. In this introductory stanza, setting the scene, Spenser uses classical (*Phoebus* fiery carre), astronomical, and popular reference, a deliberate eclecticism characteristic of him. After a little reading of Spenser, I think this ceases to seem odd or indecorous. In any case, it helps to keep his great poem poised, as it is and as he intended, between the grandeurs of classical epic, the fancy of romance, and the proverbial, English, and everyday.

Phoebus fiery carre: the sun. The sun-god Phoebus Apollo was supposed to drive his chariot daily across the sky.

2. *sad Proserpines wrath*: see note to I.1.37.

3. *that miscreated faire*: the spirit in the likeness of Una (I.1.45). Falsely created by Archimago, and falsely fair.

4. *Venus shamefull chaine*: locked together in copulation, subjects of the goddess of love.

6. *Hesperus*: the evening star. This is the planet Venus, which is both the morning and the evening star.

7. Another example of Spenser's deliberate providing of relief and contrast.

rosy-fingred Morning: Homer's phrase.

aged Tithones saffron bed: Tithonus was loved by Eos (Aurora) the goddess of the dawn, who procured for him the gift of immortality, but not, unfortunately, that of eternal youth. In the end he came to long for death, and was ultimately changed into a grasshopper. Tennyson wrote a short lament as if by him, called *Tithonus*. The saffron bed is probably a memory of Homer's 'saffron-mantled Dawn', but the dawn is often yellow or golden, and there *may* also be a hint of age, the sere and yellow leaf.

her purple robe: from Ovid's *purpureae Aurorae* (*Met*. III. 184).

the high hills Titan discovered: the sun had touched the high hills and revealed them by its light.

10. *Proteus*: a god of the sea who could change himself into any shape,

animal, vegetable, or mineral, in order to avoid seizure, as in Homer (*Od.* IV. 384ff.) and Virgil (*Georgics*, IV. 387ff.).

11. *Saint George himself*: the very pattern of the good and noble knight.

12. *The true Saint George*: the Red Cross Knight. (See Canto 10, stanzas 60ff. and note.)

Will was his guide: he followed, at the moment, his will, not Truth, having been separated from Truth (Una) by the devices of Archimago.

A faithlesse Sarazin: in the Italian romantic epics the romantic adventures take place in the context of unending war between Frank and Saracen, Christian and Infidel. In this they were indebted to the great medieval epic 'matter of France', which dealt with the wars of Charlemagne and was much concerned with his struggles with the Moors. Ariosto's *Orlando Furioso* (1516) begins (in Harington's English version published in 1590):

> Of Dames, of Knights, of armes, of loves delight,
> Of courtesies, of high attempts I speake,
> Then when the *Moores* transported all their might
> On *Africke* seas, the force of France to break:
> Incited by the youthfull heate and spight
> Of *Agramant* their King, that vow'd to wreake
> The death of King *Trayano* (lately slaine)
> Upon the Romane Emperore *Charlemaine*.

Tasso's *Gerusalemme Liberata* (1581) takes place outside Jerusalem, which the Frankish (Christian) armies are attempting to recapture from the Turks. It looks as if at one time Spenser intended to have a similar conflict in the background of *The Faerie Queene*. In I.11.7 he writes of the time when he will sing of wars and of

> . . . Briton fields with Sarazin bloud bedyde,
> Twixt that great faery Queene and Paynim King.

In I.12.17 the Red Cross Knight tells how he must return to the Faerie Queene

> And her to serve six yeares in warlike wize,
> Gainst that proud Paynim king, that workes her teene.

In III.3.27 there is mention of the 'powre of forrein Paynims' which invade the land, and in III.3.52 reference to King Uther making 'Strong warre upon the Paynim brethren'. Spenser did not pursue the idea. It was presumably too much even for his copious invention and power of control over material, but in Book V the Souldan is one of the great adversaries that have to be overcome. The three Paynim brothers, Sansloy, Sansjoy, and Sansfoy, whose names explain their significance, are the only important survivals from the poet's probable early intention. Clearly, in a book devoted to truth and true religion, infidel enemies who represent the lawlessness, the joylessness, and the faithlessness of Paganism and/or irreligion fitly ally themselves with the falseness and evil of Roman Catholicism, shown in Archimago and his subordinates and helpers. In the Italian romantic epics, the Saracen knights are enemy knights in a historical situation. Many of them are noble and virtuous, and many of them, falling in love with Christian damsels, come to accept the Christian faith. Characteristically, Spenser deepens the significances in his chosen source-material. The three pagan brothers here are not simply enemy knights but powerful symbols of evil and error, hateful agents of evil. See note to I.11.7.

13. *a goodly Lady clad in scarlot red*: this is Duessa, Falsehood. Her name points a contrast between her 'doubleness' and Una; duplicity is her nature. She represents also the falseness of Rome, the Roman Church, and, in the personal and historical allegory, Mary Queen of Scots. She is tried and found guilty in Book V, Canto 9 of *The Faerie Queene*, and in that book, the one most consistently concerned with Tudor and Elizabethan historical events, it is made very clear that the trial of Mary Queen of Scots is intended. (See especially V.9.48.)

a Persian mitre: a high mitre-like cap, in Herodotus the head-dress for religious observances of the Babylonians as the tiara was of the Persians. In Virgil (*Aen*. IV. 216) the *mitra* is referred to as worn by lascivious and effeminate people, and Levantines or Asiatics at that. Spenser means to imply this. There is probably also a suggestion of the papal head-dress, a high-raised cap, encircled with three crowns and ornamented with jewels.

14. *the red bloud trickling*: characteristically Spenserian; he will often suddenly introduce down-to-earth realism. The whole poem, imaginative

and unnaturalistic as it is, is soundly anchored in the realities of ordinary human living and experience.

16. *As when two rams*: Virgil (*Aen*. XII. 715ff.) has a similar fight, but between two bulls. Such an image has its element of grotesqueness for us who live in an almost completely urbanized society, but in any period before this the sight of such a fight would have been familiar, and not un-terrifying, to everyone.

17. *Each others equall puissaunce envies*: 'each admires or grudges the other's equal valour'.

through their iron sides with cruell spies Doth seek to pierce: 'tries to spot weak points in the other's armour', as, in Virgil, does Tarchon in *Aen*. XI. 746ff., Aeneas in XII. 919ff.

18. *that charme*: this is the first we have heard about any magical property in the Knight's Red Cross. Italian romance is full of magic shields, spears, and swords, and there are plenty in *The Faerie Queene*. But how different this is from mere magic. Indeed, it is not really magic: the cross arouses a supernatural awe in the pagan knight, as if he knew he was in contact with holy things. We are reminded (I.1.2) of

> the deare remembrance of his dying Lord
> For whose sweete sake that glorious badge he wore,

and that the cross is also scored on his shield 'For soveraine hope, which in his helpe he had'.

from blame him fairely blest: this literally means 'from injury delivered him completely'. The phrase has been variously but not satisfactorily elucidated. I wonder whether the subject is not the Knight himself, not Sansfoy, but the shield: if the comma after 'shield' were omitted, or moved to come after 'glauncing downe', this sense would be clear.

22. *an Emperour*: Duessa, falsely seeming innocent and virtuous as well as grief-stricken, and successfully deluding the Red Cross Knight, identifies herself as coming from Rome (and so representing both Roman Catholicism and the falseness of the Romish religion), and tells a false story of her unwilling subjection to Sansloy.

26. *Fidessa*: she calls herself not by her real name of Duessa, but falsely Fidessa, which suggests faithfulness.

27. *dainty they say maketh derth*: a proverb: "fastidiousness invites

deprivation; if you're fastidious about food you will come to hunger".
Here it means that a woman's coyness creates increased hunger or desire
for her.

28. Notice how clearly Spenser warns the reader. The trees are covered
with *grey* moss, their leaves *tremble* with every blast, the *fearful* shepherd
will never go there he is so frightened of the place, the ground is '*unlucky*'
or ill-omened.

29. *Phoebus*: the sun.

31. *out of whose rift there came*: Spenser shows himself a master of the
quietly horrific.

a piteous yelling voyce: such a scene has a long epic and romance
ancestry. In Virgil (*Aen.* III. 25ff.) Aeneas, tearing boughs to deck an
altar, hears the piteous cry of Polydorus from the wound; the wild
cherries and myrtles had grown from the javelin hafts left in the wounds
of the murdered man. Dante (*Inferno*, XIII. 22ff.) comes to a wood and
tears a branch from a great thorn-tree, from which a lamenting voice
issues. The wood consists of men who have committed suicide and been
turned into trees. In Ariosto (*Orl. Fur.* VI. 26ff.) there is a characteristically semi-comic arborification, of Astolfo, the English knight, who has
been turned into a myrtle-tree by the enchantress Alcina after she has
tired of him. But Harington, in the 'Morall' in his translation, notes
'how men, given over to sensuality, lose in the end the very forme of
man (which is reason) and so become beastes or stockes'. In Tasso
(*Ger. Lib.* XIII. 20ff.) Tancred comes to the wood outside Jerusalem
in the trees of which the pagan magician Ismen has set spirits (XIII. 8)
to frighten the Christians away should they come to the wood for
siege-timber. When Tancred strikes a particular tree, the spirit within
it cries out that it is Clorinda, his beloved. Spenser's scene is not as
grave as Virgil's or Dante's, or as light-hearted as Ariosto's, or as
supernatural as Tasso's, but it is not mere magic. The two trees are
two lovers deceived and punished by the very enchantress whom the
Red Cross Knight accompanies. Despite all the warnings, the Knight
is still bemused by Duessa's beauty and femininity: the ordinary Christian in the world, for whom the Red Cross Knight stands, is always in
danger from the deceivings and enchantments of the Devil, and often
incapable of distinguishing the true from the false, especially when he

is separated from his rightful companion and patroness, Truth. Spenser has very successfully elaborated and expanded from the classical and romance originals: he is remarkably apt at assimilating and transforming for his own purpose the literary stock of which he is master.

32. *the dreadfull passion*: the emotion of dread or fear.

Limbo lake: Limbo (from Latin *limbus*, a border or hem) was supposed to be an outer area fringing Hell, where dwelt, awaiting the Resurrection, the souls of those debarred from Heaven through no fault of their own—having been born before the time of Christ, or being unbaptized. In Dante (*Inferno*, IV) it is a lake, and is a quiet and not unpleasant retreat. Spenser, however, thinks of it as the abode of lost and damned souls.

33. *Fradubio*: the name suggests doubt. The man wavered between his true love and Duessa. He probably represents, in the theological allegory, the doubters who waver between the old faith (Catholicism) and the new (Anglicanism).

Boreas: the north wind.

34. *He oft finds med'cine . . ., etc.*: further proverbial sayings. 'Tell your pain and it will be eased'; 'He who conceals, doubles his grief'. One is reminded of *Romeo and Juliet* (I.i. and III.ii) both by the content and by the rhyming couplet.

37. *Fraelissa*: probably from Italian *fralezza*, of a weak, frail nature. Spenser's account of Duessa's devilry, though here only reported by a character (Fradubio), is extremely vivid and emotive. This is also true of many of his descriptions of pictures and tapestries: he 'brings to life' always and effortlessly. He refines and elaborates the episode by showing the devilish inventiveness of Duessa, who makes the beautiful Fraelissa appear foul to Fradubio in order to gain him herself. This is also premonitory, as Fradubio soon sees her (stanzas 40, 41) 'in her proper hew', and she is later shown to be unspeakably foul and ugly when stripped of her finery (II.8.46ff.). Ariosto's Alcina (*Orl. Fur.*, VII. 59ff.) is revealed as foul and filthy when Ruggiero wears the magic ring sent him by Bradamante. But apart from their common duplicity, and this episode, Alcina is really the progenitor not of Duessa so much as of Acrasia in Book II.

40. *origane and thyme*: origane is marjoram, and, in Gerard's *Herbal* (1597, p. 542) 'healeth scabs, itchings, and scurvinesse, being used in bathes'.

43. *Till we be bathed in a living well*: allegorically this must mean until they are regenerated by God's grace through the sacraments of baptism and eucharist, but in the story we do not hear of their redemption. In the Scriptures, 'living water' is the spirit and grace of God (*Jeremiah* II. 13, *John* IV. 10, *Revelation* XXII. 1). Later in this book, in Canto 11, the Red Cross Knight is twice saved, literally and figuratively, by living water.

44. *bough did thrust into the ground*: notice again Spenser's care to give circumstantial detail.

Canto 3

[Una, seeking the Red Cross Knight, meets a fierce Lion, which fawns upon her and accompanies her as her guard and companion. They spend the night at the cottage of blind Corceca and her daughter Abessa; the Lion kills and dismembers a robber, Kirkrapine, returning to the cottage with his loot stolen from churches; and the next morning the two go on their way. They are pursued unavailingly by Corceca and Abessa. Una now encounters Archimago as the Red Cross Knight, and is overjoyed. Riding along together, they encounter the Saracen Sansloy, who immediately attacks Archimago, thinking him to be the Red Cross Knight (who had slain his brother Sansfoy). Archimago is cowardly, but forced to fight. He is wounded, and is recognized when Sansloy 'rudely' takes off his helmet. Una is in great distress and perplexity; Sansloy, inflamed now with lust, plucks her from her palfrey, the Lion attacks him and is slain, and Sansloy bears her away.]

1. *lately through her brightnesse blind*: seems to mean 'recently blinded by beauty's brightness', and if so it is probably a reference to some recent favour received from Queen Elizabeth, or from some lady, possibly the Rosalind of *The Shepheardes Calender*.

4. A characteristic Spenserian contrast is provided by this picture of Una lying on the grass, which follows that of Duessa lying on the ground in her false swoon for 'feigned feare' at the end of the previous canto.

the great eye of heaven: the sun. There is a connexion in Spenser's mind between Una and the 'woman clothed with the sun' who fled into the wilderness from a dragon in Revelation XII.

5 and 6. *A ramping Lyon*: the lion was supposed to reverence true

virgins and royal personages. The belief can be traced back to Pliny, but there are many Tudor and Elizabethan examples. In the *Myrroure for Magistrates* (Tragedy of Lord Hastings, ll. 282–3): 'Lyons . . . feare the sacred lawes / Of prynces bloud'; in *1 Henry IV* (II. iv. 267) Falstaff cries: 'beware instinct—the lion will not touch the true prince . . .'; A. Munday's translation (1588) of *Palmerin d'Oliva* (Pt. II, Ch. 5): 'The Lyons comming about him, smelling on his clothes would not touch him; but (as it were knowing the bloud royall) lay downe at his feet and licked him.' But Spenser also knew the English romances. In *Guy of Warwick* Guy rescues a lion from a dragon and the lion licks his feet, leaps up playfully at his throat, 'wallows' on the ground, fawns on him like a puppy, and follows him faithfully (ll. 3891–920). In *The Seven Champions of Christendom*, in which, of course, St. George, the national patron saint is the champion of England, two lions fawn on Sabra, and St. George says: 'I have by this sufficiently proved thy true virginitie: for it is the nature of a lion . . . not to harm the unspotted virgin, but humbly to lay his bristled head upon a maiden's lap'. In *Sir Beves of Hampton*, Josian, the heroine, separated from her champion, is spared by lions and later revered by them:

	And the twoo lyons at hur feete,	
grinning	Grennand on hur with much grame	*wrath*
	But they ne myght do hur no shame.	
	For the kind of Lyouns, y-wys,	
	A Kynges doughter, that maid is,	
	Kynges doughter, quene and maide both,	
	The lyouns myght do hur noo wroth.	

(A text, 2387–94.)

Spenser also probably knew the episode in Malory (*Works*, pp. 912ff.) in which Sir Percivale went to the help of a lion battling with a serpent ('for he was the more naturall beste of the two'), and the lion fawned on him 'as a spanyell, and he stroked hym on the necke and on the sholdirs and thanked God of the feliship of that beste', and 'all that nyght the lyon and he slepte togydirs'; he is later told by an old priest that the lion 'betokenyth the new law of Holy Chirche, that is to undirstonde fayth, good hope, belyeve and baptyme'.

(It has recently been suggested also (A. D. S. Fowler, *Spenser and the Numbers of Time*, Routledge, Kegan Paul, 1964, pp. 67ff.) that Spenser 'utilises an antique emblem of *iustitia*, in which a lion's domestication at the hand of a woman represents the power of justice over ferocious passions', but it seems that Spenser is really thinking of the lion's instinctive reverence for Una's innate virtue, as in the medieval examples cited, and there are several other instances of wild animals and simple folk immediately recognizing her holiness.)

In 'A Learned and Comfortable Sermon' in *Of the Laws of Ecclesiastical Polity*, Books 1 to 4, p. 12, Hooker, thinking of Daniel in the lions' den, wrote: 'Lions, beasts ravenous by nature and keen with hunger, being set to devour, have as it were religiously adored the very flesh of faithful man.'

7. *But he my Lyon*: King of the beasts, noble protector and champion. Una fitly sees the Red Cross Knight in these terms, and draws a sad comparison between his desertion of her now and the real lion's humble devotion. This lament makes us see Una as not only an effective symbol, but, for the first time, as a real woman.

10. *She could not heare, nor speake, nor understand*: Abessa represents superstition, and, as the name, with its suggestion of 'abbess', implies, Spenser means particularly the ignorant superstition of Roman Catholicism.

12. *her mother blynd*: Corceca, from, it is thought, 'Cui caecum est cor' (whose heart is blind), and so the blind foolish devotion of superstitious Roman Catholicism. Probably Spenser remembers *Ephesians* iv. 18: 'Having the understanding darkened, being alienated from the life of God through the ignorance that is in them, because of the blindness of their heart'. Spenser gives a very vivid picture of the dumb girl running in fear (of Truth) to warn her old blind mother.

13. *her unruly Page*: the Lion.

Pater nosters: Spenser scorns the superstitious observances of Catholicism. 900 times a day did the old blind woman say the Lord's Prayer, and thrice 900 times 'Hail Mary'.

14. *thrise three times did fast*: went without three meals three days a week.

her beads she did forget: although she could say her 2700 'Hail Marys', when in real fear and real need she cannot pray at all. Another hit at superstitious practices and their superficiality and inefficacy.

16. *Aldebaran*: a star of the first magnitude, reddish in colour.

Cassiopeias chaire: a constellation in the northern hemisphere.

17. *sturdie thiefe*: Kirkrapine. When Spenser's allegory descends to the absolutely specific and local, as here (and as in the description of the books and pamphlets spewed forth by Error in I.1.20), it is usually unsuccessful as well as unpoetic. Both examples seem to belong to a possible early plan for Book I, in which the chief allegory was probably to have been the defence of the Church of England and the pillorying of Roman Catholicism. As he wrote, he enlarged, and Book I became also and chiefly concerned with Truth and Falseness in life as in religion, and, in addition, with the Christian man's journey through the errors and temptations of life.

21. *that long wandring Greeke*: Ulysses (Odysseus), who wandered for ten years after the fall of Troy before he succeeded in reaching Ithaca, his home.

refused deitie: Calypso offered him immortality if he would remain with her, but he refused, longing for his home and his wife Penelope. (Homer, *Od.* V.)

26. *that wilde Champion*: the Lion.

27. Spenser can write excellent *speech*: this of Una's reminds one of the early Shakespeare. The antithesis and the conceits are characteristically Shakespearian.

30. *A dram of sweet is worth a pound of sowre*: another proverbial expression. Notice how swiftly Una forgives her (supposed) lover's errancy.

31. *Tethys saltish teare*: the salt tears of Tethys, wife of Oceanus and so the sea-goddess: a characteristic epic inflation for 'the sea'.

31. *Orions hound*: Sirius, the hound of Orion, the mighty hunter of Boeotia. Sirius, the dog-star, when high in the heavens, supposedly brought great heat.

Nereus crownes with cups: drinks healths to Nereus, a sea-god of the Mediterranean.

35. *vainely crossed shield*: the feigned red cross on his shield had no power to defend him.

36. *Lethe lake*: the word Lethe signifies oblivion or forgetfulness, and the Lethean lake or river is a river in Hades which causes all who drink of it to forget their past lives. Milton (*P. L.* II. 75) writes of 'The sleepy drench of that forgetful lake'. Spenser seems to think of Lethe as the lake by the side of which the ghosts of the unburied dead wait helplessly for passage ('Cocytus and the Stygian marsh' in Virgil, *Aen.* VI. 323). He means that because Sansloy has now avenged the death of his brother Sansfoy at the hands of the Red Cross Knight (whom Sansloy, like Una, takes the disguised Archimago to be), Sansfoy's soul will no longer have to wait but may pass in peace.

infernall Furies: the avenging deities of Hell, Megaera, Allecto, and Tisiphone. They execute the curses pronounced upon criminals (and also torture the guilty with the stings of conscience).

39. *And on those guilefull dazed eyes, etc.*: Notice the economy and effectiveness of this.

41. *lust did now inflame*: Spenser lets the characters live in their own right, and widens the scope and reference of his allegory in so doing. Sansloy, the lawless Saracen, representative of paganism and irreligion, becomes a Saracen swash-buckler lusting after a beautiful Christian virgin.

Canto 4

[The Red Cross Knight is led by Duessa to the House of Pride, where he meets Lucifera (Pride) and the other deadly sins, Idleness, Gluttony, Lechery, Avarice, Envy, and Wrath, and Satan with them. The third Saracen brother, Sansjoy, attacks the Red Cross Knight, but Lucifera stops the fight and decrees a proper contest for the following day. In the night Duessa goes to Sansjoy's chamber, tells him of her love for his brother, and of her 'capture' by the Red Cross Knight, and puts herself under his protection.]

2. Spenser from time to time gives us a brief summary of preceding events, especially when we rejoin characters whom we parted from a canto or so before.

All bare through peoples feet: the implication is that many travel the broad highway to the House of Pride, but, as we see in the next stanza, few return from it. It is Pride's house, but it might more aptly have been called the House of Sin, for all the sins are there to be found, presided over by their chief, Pride.

4. *A stately Pallace*: it has resemblances both to Chaucer's House of Fame, and to the house of Alcina in *Orlando Furioso*. Chaucer's

> Al was of ston of beryle,
> Both the castel and the tour,
> And eke the halle and every bour,
> Wythouten peces or joynynges.
>   (*House of Fame*, 1184ff.);

it has

>   pynacles
> Ymageries and tabernacles,
> I say, and ful eke of wyndowes;

and, though not built on sand, it has 'feble fundament', being built on ice. Alcina's house (*Orl. Fur.* VI. 59) is stately, shining, seemingly all of gold; and an easy well-beaten track leads to it. Atlante's magic castle, too (*Orl. Fur.* II, 41, 42) has many towers and shines with exceeding brightness; it is not made of lime and stone, but of polished steel tempered in the Stygian Lake. Spenser makes it clear that Pride's house looks deceptively splendid but is not strongly made; it is only covered with gold foil, is weakly founded on sand, and, at the back,

> the hinder parts, that few could spie,
> Were ruinous and old, but painted cunningly.

The Faerie Queene is naturally much concerned with falseness, and with the difference between appearances and reality. The wandering wood in Canto 1 *seemed* to offer shelter; Pride's house *seems* to be stately and strong. There are descriptions of other deceptive places in the poem, and the poet always gives us due warning of their falseness or meretriciousness.

6. *Malvenù*: 'ill-come', the opposite of 'welcome', but with some suggestion of 'ill-advised', its modern meaning.

arras: tapestry hangings, named from the city famous for their manufacture.

T<small>FQ</small>

7. *Persia selfe*: Persia had been from early times a symbol of extravagant wealth and splendour. Aeschylus in the *Persae* (472 B.C.), the historian Herodotus (*c.* 450 B.C.), and Xenophon (*c.* 400 B.C.) had presented in their various ways accounts of the magnificence and power of the Persian Empire. Perhaps the Queen, Lucifera (Canto 8), derives something from Atossa, mother of Xerxes, in Aeschylus and Herodotus, and from Vashti in Esther i; as the splendour of her court owes something to the description of Ahasuerus's court in Esther and that of Artaxerxes in Ezra vii. In the last two the Persian monarch is reported to have 7 counsellors (Ezra vii. 14) or 7 chamberlains (Esther i. 10), as Lucifera has 7. Cambises, King of Persia, Atossa's brother, was in Elizabethan times, from the appearance of Thomas Preston's *Cambyses* (1569), proverbial for his magnificence and grandiloquence, and Marlowe in *Tamburlaine*, although he shows 'the state of Persia droop and languish' (I.i.155) and speedily brought into vassalage, takes it for granted that Persia symbolizes extravagant pride and glory. Spenser always uses Persia in this sense: see for example III.1.14, where Malecasta is

> . . . found sitting on a sumptuous bed,
> That glistred all with gold and precious shew,
> As the proud *Persian* Queenes accustomed.

8. Spenser runs some risk in describing her so clearly in terms of the sun, gold, and precious stones. He usually reserves such comparisons for his virtuous characters.

9. But in this stanza he corrects the fault, if it be one, by referring to the presumptuousness of Phaeton, son of Apollo, who tried to drive the chariot of the sun, and, failing to control the steeds and coming too near the earth, which threatened its destruction, was killed by a flash of lightning sent by Zeus (Jupiter or Jove).

the welkin way most beaten plaine: the established path of the sun through the heavens.

10. *A dreadfull Dragon*: a dragon is often a sign, or carries a suggestion, of Satan, from the enemy of God vividly portrayed in Revelation xii. 7–9.

a mirrhour bright: Pride is vain as well as proud, taking delight in regarding her own beauty.

11. Spenser has invented this mythological genealogy, making the Queen of the House of Pride fitly the daughter of the gods of the underworld. She herself, in her pride, is not content to be merely the daughter of Pluto, but claims to be the daughter of Jupiter himself.

thundring Jove: Jupiter Tonans, lord of the thunderbolt.

12. *Lucifera*: Spenser contrives the name from that of Lucifer. Early in Christian times a connexion became established between Lucifer the morning star and Lucifer the fallen angel through Isaiah xiv. 12: 'How art thou fallen from heaven, O Lucifer, son of the Morning!' The Hebrew word for the morning star, Hillel, comes from a verb which also means to be haughty, proud, arrogant, and the connexion has remained.

six wisards old: who with her made up the seven deadly sins.

14. A vivid picture of disdain, and an effective mockery of court behaviour.

16. *Aurora*: goddess of the dawn; appropriate because Lucifera's name derives from that of the morning star.

17. *Flora in her prime*: the goddess of flowers, in springtime. Spenser says that Lucifera *seemed* as fresh as Flora. Perhaps he also had in mind the association of Flora with lasciviousness. See note to 1. 48.

Junoes golden chaire: so in Homer (*Iliad*, V. 727), but there drawn by horses.

heavens bras-paved way: as in Homer (*Iliad*, XIV. 173).

full of Argus eyes: the mythical Argus, surnamed Panoptes (all-seeing), had a hundred eyes, some of which were always alert. When he died, Hera (Juno) placed his eyes as a memorial in the tail of the peacock, the bird sacred to her. The peacock is, of course, a symbol of worldly pride and vanity, presumably because of its gorgeous colouring, splendid spread of tail, and proud strutting.

18. *six unequall beasts*: the procession of the six counsellors of Lucifera, that is the 7 deadly sins of whom Pride is the chief, seems to owe a lot to Gower's *Mirour de l'Omme*. The parallels are many (see Spenser, *Variorum* edition, Book I, pp. 407ff.), the chief ones being the association of the sin, the beast it rides, the object it carries, and the malady from which it suffers; but the indebtedness is questioned on the ground that,

with only one copy of the *Mirour* extant, it may have been little known in Spenser's day. There is no proof that Spenser knew it (though other works of Gower he certainly knew, and he was extremely well read in medieval as in other literature). His details are rarely *identical* with Gower's.

with like conditions to their kinds applyde: the six beasts were taught to obey the 'bestiall beheasts' of the six deadly sins, and the sins, the counsellors, and the beasts they rode were of like disposition. So Idleness was on a slothful ass, Gluttony on a greedy swine, etc.

Idleness the nourse of sin: Idleness comes first, and is the nurse of sin, because idleness is the condition which most easily admits or inadvertently encourages the other sins. Chaucer writes in the Second Nun's Prologue (Chaucer, *Works*, ed. Robinson, new ed., Houghton, Mifflin, 1961):

> The ministre and the norice unto vices,
> Which that men clepe in Englissh ydelnesse.

Spenser presents him as dressed like a monk, carrying a breviary, much worn but not with reading, riding on an ass, heavy with sleep, and shaking with fever. Gower's Idleness rides on an ass but carries an owl and suffers from 'lethargy'.

21. *Gluttony*, riding on a swine, with gross belly, vomiting all the way, carrying a boozing-can, and suffering from dropsy: Gower's Gluttony rides a wolf, carries a kite and a wine-vessel, and suffers from 'loup royal'. Spenser's detail of the elongated crane's neck probably comes from Alciati's emblem of *Gula*, Emblem XC (Alciati, *Emblemata*, Frankfort, 1583, Antwerp, 1584), which itself comes from Aristotle's telling (*Nicomachaean Ethics* III. 13) of a glutton who wished his neck were as long as a crane's that he might the longer enjoy the taste of his food.

22. The picture is also like representations of drunken Silenus in painting, and in the emblem-books.

24. *Lechery*, riding on a goat, bearing a burning heart in his hand, and suffering (probably) from syphilis: Gower's Lechery also rides a goat, but carries a dove and suffers from leprosy.

25. *greene gowne*: green was the colour of virility and licentiousness.

In Shakespeare, *Love's Labour's Lost* (I. ii. 83) Don Adriano says 'Green, indeed, is the colour of lovers'; and Juliet's green-sickness (*Romeo and Juliet* III. v. 156) is lovesickness, desire for a man.

27. *Avarice*, on a camel laden with gold, starving, near to death, wretched, fearful, and suffering from gout: Gower's Avarice rides a horse, carries a hawk and purses, and suffers from dropsy.

30. *Envy*, on a wolf, chewing a toad, but inwardly chewing his own maw, with a snake secreted in his bosom, and suffering from leprosy: Gower's Envy rides a dog, carries a sparrowhawk, and suffers from fever. Spenser may remember that in Ovid, *Met.* II. 760, Envy is found eating the flesh of vipers; and in Alciati's Emblem LXXI Envy is a naked hag chewing vipers.

31. *full of eyes*: because Envy is always on the look-out for something to be envious about.

33. *Wrath*, on a Lion, bearing a burning brand and suffering from spleen, palsy, and frenzy: Gower's Wrath rides a boar, carries a cock, and suffers from heart trouble. Red, of course, is the colour of the choleric or wrathful humour.

35. In this account of the mischiefs of wrath Spenser borrows details from the account in Chaucer (*Knightes Tale*, 1995ff.) of the temple of Mars, the god of war.

swelling Splene: physicians believed that a swollen spleen was both a symptom and a cause of anger. A 'splenetic' man is still a hot-tempered one.

Saint Fraunces fire: erysipelas, a disease accompanied by inflamed and burning skin.

36. Satan himself is the waggoner.

Showting for joy: presumably at the spectacle of the procession of the seven deadly sins. I suppose Spenser means to point out the ignorant folly of people who sillily applaud any show and do not stop to consider what it may import.

38. *Sansjoy*: the third of the three Sarazin brothers.

39. *Faery champions page*: the dwarf who followed and attended the Red Cross Knight.

that same envious gage / Of victors glory: 'that pledge or sign of the glory of victory'.

which ought that warlike wage: 'to whom that reward of warlike prowess really belonged'.

41. *renverst*: the reversed shield was a sign of disgrace.

44. *Morpheus had with leaden mace*: the god of sleep, thought of as carrying a leaden mace. In *Julius Caesar* (IV. iii. 266) Brutus calls on 'murd'rous slumber' to lay 'its leaden mace' on the boy Lucius.

Arrested: Spenser continues effectively the image suggested by 'mace', for the sergeant or sheriff's officer in Elizabethan times, and later, carried a mace with which he touched the shoulder of the person to be arrested.

46. *launcht with lovely dart*: lanced or pierced by the dart of love, Cupid's dart.

48. *wandring Stygian shores*: the shore of the infernal river Styx, on which the ghosts wander until they obtain passage. (Cf. Virgil, *Aen.* VI. 312ff., and see note to III. 36 above.)

49. *helplesse hap it booteth not to mone*: 'it is no use lamenting that fortune which cannot be helped (avoided or remedied)'.

shall him pay his dewties last: 'shall perform his last obsequies', that is 'shall slay the Red Cross Knight as a propitiatory sacrifice to his ghost'.

50. *oddes of armes*: 'disparity of chances in war', or 'probability of mishaps in battle'.

51. *Sans-foyes dead dowry*: 'the dowry of dead Sansfoy'.

Canto 5

[The next day the Red Cross Knight and Sansjoy fight, and the latter is saved from death by a 'darkesome cloud' sent, presumably at Duessa's behest, by the 'infernall powres', under cover of which he vanishes. Duessa runs straight to the Red Cross Knight and is the first to acclaim him. At night Duessa goes to the secret chamber in which Sansjoy lies in woeful plight, and then to the abode of Night to call on her to avenge her descendants (the Saracen brothers). She returns with Night, binds up Sansjoy's wounds, and takes him to the underworld to Aesculapius to be cured. Duessa then returns to the House of Pride, to find that the Red Cross Knight has gone.]

2. The matter and imagery, as well as the jubilant movement of the verse, make a strong contrast with the previous canto. Spenser remembers

Psalm xix, in which the sun 'is as a bridegroom coming out of his chamber, and rejoiceth as a strong man to run a race'. Like the poet Henry Vaughan, Spenser seems to describe dawn and the reawakening of the world in all its splendour with special pleasure and power.

4. *woven maile*: mail (from Fr. *Maille*) is chain armour.

wines of Greece and Araby: wines of Greece were renowned in Spenser's day (Holinshed (I. 281) mentions 'Grecian' among his thirty kinds of wine 'of strength and value'), but wines of Araby, if there were such, were not. He probably means by Araby the exotic East generally, and may mean the Levantine wines of Antioch and the Lebanon.

5. *paled greene*: the field enclosed by a paling for the tournament lists.

Both those the lawrell girlonds: both Duessa and the shield are to be the prizes for the victor.

7. The knight fights for praise and honour, the Sarazin for blood and vengeance.

8. *Gryfon*: griffin, a fabulous beast with eagle's head, trunk, and wings, and lion's hind quarters and tail.

The wise Southsayer: would take such a fight (between a griffin making away with its victim and a dragon) for a portent, so great and terrible would it be. So, by implication, is the great conflict between the Red Cross Knight and Sansjoy.

10. Sansjoy, catching sight of the shield of his dead brother, Sansfoy, hung up, is stirred to greater anger and endeavour. So, in *Aeneid*, XII. 940ff., is Aeneas, who is about to give way to his stricken opponent's plea for mercy, when he sees that Turnus is wearing as a trophy the belt of young Pallas, whom he had slain, whereupon Aeneas swiftly dispatches Turnus.

wayling by black Stygian lake: another reference (and so in the next stanza) to the 'long wandring woe' of the dead awaiting passage on the shores of the Styx.

sluggish german: Sansjoy calls himself a sluggard brother; 'german' is in fact any blood relation.

13. *a darkesome clowd | Upon him fell*: the Red Cross Knight is about to give Sansjoy the mortal stroke when the 'infernall powres' (stanza 14) save him by sending a concealing cloud. Spenser makes use of famous incidents from earlier epics whenever he can. In Homer (*Il*. III. 380)

Aphrodite rescues Paris from Menelaus, carrying him off in a thick mist; Apollo picks up Aeneas and saves him in a black cloud (*Il*. V. 344); Neptune saves Aeneas by drawing a mist over the eyes of Achilles (*Il*. XX. 321). Virgil (*Aen*. V. 810) repeats the story of Neptune's rescue of Aeneas from Achilles by this means. In Tasso, *Ger. Lib*. VII. 43, the enchantress Armida rescues Rambaldo from Tancred by sending sudden darkness.

17. *In wine and oyle*: as the Samaritan did to the man who fell among thieves (Luke x. 34).

sweet musicke did divide: to 'divide', to 'play divisions', signified to 'play brilliant passages', to improvise brilliantly.

18. The idea of the crocodile's false tears used to beguile the unwary, from which we get the phrase 'crocodile tears', was not in the original bestiaries, but by the sixteenth century was well established and accepted. Othello says (IV. i. 240):

> If that the earth could teem with women's tears,
> Each drop she falls would prove a crocodile.

The idea of the crocodile falsely weeping to lull suspicion and arouse sympathy is found in Hakluyt (Sparke's narrative of Hawkins' second voyage) and in *2 Henry VI*, III. i. 226:

> . . . the mourning crocodile
> With sorrow snares relenting passengers.

19. *shyning lampes*: the stars.

20. A typical stanza, of the kind often criticized for excess and repetitiveness. Note how the accumulation of emotive words, *griesly, deadly sad, foule, blacke, pitchie, darkesome, hated, coleblacke, hellish, rustie,* builds up the irresistible effect.

Duessa summoning Night may owe something to Circe's summoning of Night and the Gods of Night from Erebus and Chaos in Ovid (*Met.* XIV. 403).

22. *most auncient Grandmother*: Spenser is here indebted to Natale Conti (*Mythologiae*, III. 12) who writes that Night is called 'most ancient' because she was born of Chaos and lived before the world was formed into order, that she is the mother of falsehood (as, in Spenser, of Duessa), and has the black mantle, the chariot, and the horses described

by Spenser. In the oldest cosmogonies Night is one of the very first of all created things, daughter of Chaos, sister of Erebus, mother of Aether (the sky) and Hemera (day).

Demogorgon: see note on I.1.37.

23. *old Aveugles sonnes*: Spenser here makes the three Sarazins sons of Aveugle, the Blind.

28. A vivid and sensitive picture of Night's four-horse team softly swimming away in the air.

30. *The wakefull dogs*: in Virgil (*Aen*. VI. 257) dogs howl as Hecate, goddess of Night, draws near.

the ghastly Owle: feared by the Romans as a messenger of death, though the Greeks admired it as the bird of wisdom. Chaucer (*Parlement of Fowles*, 343) calls it the bird 'that of dethe the bode bringeth'. In *Macbeth* it is 'the fatal bellman' that 'clamours' on the night of Duncan's murder.

31. *deepe Avernus hole*: Lacus Avernus in Campania was regarded by the Latins as the entrance to Hell; it lies in an ancient volcanic crater, and gives off mephitic vapours. Virgil describes it in *Aen*. VI. 237. Spenser seems to think of it, as did Homer and Aeschylus, not as a lake but as a cavern. With this journey to the underworld compare that in *The Faerie Queene*, II. 7.

dreadfull Furies: they rest in Erebus, a gloomy cavern underground on the way to Hades, until a curse pronounced on some earthly criminal calls them up. I do not know why Spenser refers to them as having been chained.

33. *Acheron*: river of lamentation, from Gk ἄχος, Milton's 'sad Acheron of sorrow' (*P. L.* II. 578).

Phlegeton: river of burning fire, from Gk φλέγειν, Milton's 'fierce Phlegeton/Whose waves of torrent fire inflame with rage' (*P.L.*, II. 580).

34. *dreadfull Cerberus*: the three-headed watch-dog of the infernal regions. Spenser draws on Virgil's description (*Aen*. VI. 417ff.).

35. *Ixion, etc.*: the tortures here described are derived from the accounts in Homer (*Od*. XI. 582ff.), Ovid (*Met*. IV. 458ff. and X. 41ff.), and Virgil (*Aen*. VI. 601ff.). Ixion was punished, for aspiring to the love of Hera, by being kept for ever rolling in the infernal air, chained to a fiery winged wheel. *Sisyphus* was condemned for ever to push a huge stone

up a hill until it nearly reached the top, when it rolled down again. *Tantalus* was not 'hong by the chin' but kept standing in water up to his chin, suffering agonies of thirst amid plenty, for the water sank as he lowered his face to drink it. The giant *Tityus*, having assaulted Leto, was killed by Zeus, and in the underworld vultures for ever fed upon his liver. *Typhoeus* is not anywhere else described as stretched on a rack or engine of torture, but as being buried under Etna. *Theseus*, for attempting to carry off Persephone from Hades, was condemned to endless imprisonment in the underworld. The *fifty sisters*, or Danaïdes, for slaying their husbands, were condemned to endless drawing of water into vessels full of holes. (One reputedly ignored her father's order to commit this crime, but it would have been absurd, as well as metrically difficult, for Spenser to have written precisely 'And forty-nine sisters . . .'.)

37. *Hippolytus*: Spenser's vivid account is substantially faithful to Euripides's *Hippolytus*, save that in the play Phaedra is pure and resists the passion for Hippolytus of which she is a victim, and in the end hangs herself. (The story has also been told by Racine (*Phèdre*), by the American poet Robinson Jeffers (*The Cretan Woman*), and by Mary Renault (*The Bull from the Sea*).)

Notice with what energy and economy Spenser brings to life a story in parenthesis as it were. In other parts of the poem he can often be seen vivifying a picture or a tapestry or a twice-told tale in the same way (e.g., the account of the willing rape of Leda in III.11).

39. The later events, involving Aesculapius, are not from Euripides.

And of course the whole macabre episode of Night bringing Sansjoy to the underworld to be healed by Aesculapius is Spenser's own splendid imagining.

47. The list of wretches in thrall to one or other of the seven deadly sins, but mostly prey to pride, comes chiefly from Chaucer's *Monkes Tale*, which was indebted to Boccaccio's *De Casibus Illustrium Virorum*.

King of Babylon: Nebuchadnezzar (in Chaucer). Spenser departs a little from Daniel iv and vi, where the King 'did eat grass as an ox' but was not turned into an ox, and from Boccaccio. But Gower (*Confessio Amantis*, I. 2786ff.) shows how 'lich an Ox . . . He graseth . . .' and 'thoghte him colde grases goode'.

Croesus: King of Lydia 5th century B.C. (in Chaucer). Herodotus tells of him in his *History* (I.26).

Antiochus: King of Syria, 2nd century B.C., who twice captured Jerusalem and constantly reviled and insulted the Jews (in Chaucer).

48. *Nimrod*: the 'mighty hunter' of Genesis X. 8, who founded a great empire between the Tigris and Euphrates.

Ninus: mythical founder of Nineveh.

that mightie Monarch: Alexander the Great, King of Macedon, who succeeded his father Philip in 336 B.C. Conqueror of Darius of Persia, he extended his great Empire into the Indian sub-continent. He is not elsewhere accused of dishonouring his father or his father's name, but he allowed himself, during his expedition to Egypt, to be saluted as Son of Ammon, Jupiter Ammon. He died of fever, not shamefully. Chaucer is more sympathetic to 'worthy, gentil Alisandre' and mourns with his death 'the death of gentillesse and of franchise' (generosity, noble bounty).

49. *Romulus*: mythical founder of Rome and so the 'grandsyre' of the Romans whose names follow in Spenser's list.

proud Tarquin: Tarquinius Superbus, seventh and last of the kings of Rome, named Superbus for his arrogant and tyrannical character.

too lordly Lentulus: the family of Lentulus was famous for its pride. It is not known if Spenser alludes to any particular member of it.

Stout Scipio: Scipio Africanus. His pride was shown in his struggles with the tribunes of the people, in rescuing his brother from prison in defiance of their authority, and, when brought to trial, in defying the laws and refusing to defend himself, relying on the power of his great name.

stubborne Hanniball: the great leader of the Carthaginians against Rome in the Second Punic War. He was 'stubborne', tenacious, rather, and remarkable for his powers of endurance, tenacity of purpose, and resolution; he is presumably shown a victim in the house of Pride because he was a great soldier and leader rather than as an exemplar of pride in himself, as are Tarquin, Lentulus, and Scipio.

49. *Ambitious Sylla*: Sulla, a poor boy whose ambition carried him to absolute power.

sterne Marius: Sulla's great rival, stern, ambitious, and cruel.

High Caesar, great Pompey, and fierce Antonius: Julius Caesar, Pompeius Magnus, and Marcus Antonius. It is interesting that Shakespeare presents a sick Caesar, brought low, a Pompey far from great, and an Antony by no means fierce, in *Julius Caesar* and *Antony and Cleopatra*.

50. *forgetfull of their yoke*: forgetting the subordination that Elizabethans (inheriting from the Middle Ages) thought was right for women.

Semiramis: the mythical joint-founder with Ninus of Nineveh, and, after his death, some say, the builder of Babylon. I do not know where Spenser got his story of her death.

Sthenoboea: who slew herself (by drinking hemlock, not by strangling herself) because of her unrequited love for Bellerophon.

53. Compare these features of the House of Pride with its appearance as the Red Cross Knight approaches in I.4.2–5.

Canto 6

[Una, continually pestered by the lustful Sansloy, is rescued from him by a troop of fauns and satyrs, who worship her. She stays long with them and teaches them truth. Sir Satyrane, born of a satyr father and a human girl, finds Una with the fauns and satyrs, helps her to leave them, and travels with her. They meet Archimago, now disguised as a pilgrim, and are told by him, falsely, that the Red Cross Knight is dead, killed by Sansloy. Satyrane rides off to find Sansloy, and fights with him.]

2. *Una*: whom we now rejoin, having last seen her in 3.43 and 44.

from one to other Ynd: meaning a very great distance, as if she had wandered from India to the West Indies.

3. Sansloy's attempt to seduce Una by wiles and then, that failing, to have her by force is reminiscent of Odorico's similar assault on Isabella in Ariosto (*Orl. Fur.* XIII. 26–28).

6. This extravagant idea of the interaction of human and cosmic is common in Elizabethan literature, is more than a *façon de parler*, and illustrates the accepted view of the relationship between macrocosm and microcosm. See E. M. W. Tillyard, *The Elizabethan World Picture* (Chatto and Windus, 1943 and later), and J. B. Bamborough, *The Little World of Man* (Longmans, 1952). Macbeth, for example, calls on the stars to hide their fires so that light may not see his 'black and deep desires' (I.iv.50). But in the Bible (see, for example, Isaiah xiii. 10,

Ezekiel xxxii. 7, Joel ii. 10, Matthew xxiv. 29) at times of distress, fear, or agony the stars melt and drop from the sky, or the sun or moon hides its light.

7. *Faunes and Satyres*: fauns, spirits of the countryside, are half goat, half man, horned, but with human face and upper parts, and goat's lower parts. Satyrs, attendants of Dionysus and spirits of the woods and hills, representing fertility, are mainly human, but with some animal parts. Natale Conti (*Myth.* 10) says the fauns and Sylvanus are tutelary deities who watch over those who work in field and forest.

Sylvanus: a Roman divinity of the woods.

8. Ariosto's Isabella is rescued by a band of savage outlaws, as Una by the troop of fauns and satyrs.

11. *backward bent knees*: Spenser is always astonishingly careful over details; the goat-legged fauns and satyrs cannot kneel, but they do their best to reverence Una.

14. *Cypresse stadle*: a staff of cypress wood. Why cypress is explained in stanza 17.

Yvie: because it is sacred to Bacchus, and suggests wine and festivity.

15. *Bacchus merry fruit they did invent*: 'they had discovered (invenio) some wine'.

Cybeles franticke rites: Cybele or Rhea, great mother of the gods, was worshipped by her priests, the Corybantes, with wild music and dancing.

that mirrhour rare: meaning Una, mirror of beauty and perfection.

Dryope: a daughter of King Dryops, who was stolen by hamadryads and carried off to the woods, becoming a nymph. In Virgil (*Aen.* X. 550) she is called the consort of Faunus, not Sylvanus, but the two were often confused, and indeed it is difficult (and unnecessary) to attempt clearly to distinguish between fauns and satyrs, Faunus, Sylvanus, and Pan, dryads and hamadryads.

Pholoe: another nymph beloved of Sylvanus. It was actually the name of a mountain in Arcadia frequented by Pan, and so transferred to a nymph or oread inhabiting the mountain.

17. *Cyparisse*: Spenser tells that Sylvanus loved the youth Cyparissus, but one day by chance killed a hind belonging to him, whereupon Cyparissus died of grief. The story in Ovid (*Met.* X. 120) is slightly different: Cyparissus himself accidentally killed his beloved stag, and

died of grief, being turned into a cypress. He was himself beloved of Apollo, who decreed that the cypress should ever be a symbol of sorrow and grief. Spenser received his version and the connexion between Cyparissus and Sylvanus from Boccaccio (*De Gen. Deorum*, XIII. 17) or Natale Conti (*Myth.* V. 10).

18. *Hamadryades*: nymphs of the trees.

Naiades: nymphs of fresh waters, whether rivers, lakes, or springs.

19. *luckelesse lucky maid*: it looks as if Spenser here *has* overdone repetitive emphasis and word play, but in fact he is using a Greek idiom: Una is unlucky in general (because of her wanderings separated from her knight) but lucky in this, that she has been delivered from her oppressor Sansloy.

her Asse would worship fayn: an allusion to mid-Lenten ceremonies still observed in Spenser's day in which a wooden ass was drawn to church on Palm Sunday, or to 'The Feast of the Ass', celebrated by the medieval church, both in honour of the ass which carried Jesus into Jerusalem. But possibly there is a reference to Aesop's fable of the ass which thought it was worshipped because people bowed down in reverence before the idol of Isis it was carrying on its back. In Alciati (*Emblemata*, No. VII) this scene is depicted with the motto *Non tibi, sed religioni*. In Apuleius, *The Golden Asse*, translated in 1566 by William Adlington, Lucius, who is turned into an ass, takes part in a procession of the goddess Isis before being restored to human shape 'by the providence of that goddesse'. Spenser, of course, makes no suggestion that the ass makes the proud mistake of the ass in Aesop or Alciati, but that the fauns and satyrs, simple ignorant beings, acknowledging Truth itself instinctively, will also worship the true Church, its proper vehicle. Incidentally, the goddess Isis symbolized veiled Truth (Plutarch, *Moralia*, V); as Una herself is veiled and represents Truth.

20. *a noble warlike knight*: this is Sir Satyrane, born of a satyr father and a 'Lady myld', somehow combining courtly qualities, for he is 'Plaine, faithfull, true, and enimy of shame', with the simplicity and instinctive behaviour of the wilds. Like those of the lion in Canto 3 and the fauns and satyrs, his honest nature, uncorrupted by courtly sophistication, instantly recognizes the simple beauty and truth of Una, and from her he learns 'her discipline of faith and veritie' (I.6.31).

21. *Thyamis*: the name perhaps comes from Greek θυμός, passion.

Labryde: perhaps from Greek λάβρος, turbulent, greedy.

Therion: Greek θήριον, wild beast.

23. *noursled up in life and manners wilde*: like Tristram in *F. Q.* VI. 2, where Spenser, taking a hint from Malory about Tristram's training as a young man in hunting and other sports, invents a longer upbringing of this kind for him. Also like Ruggiero's upbringing by Atlante (Ariosto, *Orl. Fur.* VII. 57).

35. *A silly man*: Archimago crops up again.

a Jacobs staffe: a pilgrim's staff; either from the Latin for James, because the shrine of St. James at Compostella in Galicia was one of the chief places of pilgrimage; or because the patriarch Jacob passed 'with my staff' over the Jordan (Genesis xxxii. 10) and 'worshipped, leaning upon the top of his staff'(Hebrews xi. 21).

40. *that Pagan proud*: Sansloy.

41. *his three square shield*: a triangular shield, the prevailing type in the 12th–14th centuries. That of Edward the Black Prince may still be seen in Canterbury Cathedral.

42. *Elfe*: see note on I.1.17.

where earst his armes were lent: referring to the fact that he had fought Archimago when the latter was disguised as the Red Cross Knight (Canto 3, 33–39).

should not rew: 'should not have rued'.

45. *had breathed once*: 'once they had recovered breath'.

46. *Satyrane*: now leaves the story, and does not reappear until Book III, Canto 7.

47. *thy lovers token on thy pate*: a knight often wore his lady's token, glove or kerchief, on his helmet. Sansloy means 'take, instead of a love-token on your helmet, this blow'.

Canto 7

[The Red Cross Knight, enfeebled by having drunk from an enchanted spring, is found by Duessa, who rebukes him for leaving her. They are reconciled, the Red Cross Knight again makes court to her, and, while unguarded both actually and spiritually, is seized by the giant Orgoglio. Orgoglio takes Duessa for his leman (lover) and imprisons the Red

Cross Knight in the dungeon of his castle. Una hears of his capture and possible death, but at this point Prince Arthur appears with his squire Timias, and they all go on together to relieve the Red Cross Knight.]

3. Again Spenser opens a canto with a charming or idyllic or refreshing scene in contrast with the preceding canto.

4. *the sacred Nymph*: in Greek mythology it is a commonplace that fountains or springs have their own resident nymphs.

5. *Phoebe*: one of the names of Artemis, a feminine from Phoebus, which means bright, gleaming.

all that drunke thereof: Ovid (*Met.* XV. 317) alludes to the pool Salmacis, with its strange power of affecting the mind, and Kitchin, the previous editor of this edition, does likewise, carefully not directing his readers of one hundred years ago to the story (*Met.* IV) of how Salmacis became famous because it was the scene of an amorous and immodest seduction. The nymph Salmacis, langorous and pleasure-loving, dwelt in the pool of that name. She desired the youth Hermaphroditus, and, despite his reluctance, succeeded in her embraces, so that the two bodies became one, so (from Hermes and Aphrodite) we have the word 'hermaphrodite'. The waters of the pool are said to have an enervating and enfeebling effect, and Spenser makes use of the idea for this purpose. Christian moralists emphasize the danger of the relaxed spirit and the slack will, when the vice of 'sloth' will readily admit other and more dangerous vices.

7. For the second time the Red Cross Knight, oblivious of his duty and unaware of the danger, dallies with the false Duessa, as previously in I.2.28ff. Spenser shows, in the romantic narrative, how vulnerable a knight is when put into a relaxed, idle, easy-going mood, first to the lascivious charms of an enchantress and then to the assault of a giant. Allegorically he shows how the ordinary Christian man, *l'homme moyen sensuel*, can be lulled by falseness into an unvigilant state, and so be all the more in jeopardy from the assault of greater sins, in this case Pride. In the specifically religious allegory Spenser shows how the Christian Church, dallying with and deceived by Rome, lays aside its armour and is at the mercy of Antichrist.

8. *An hideous Geant*: Orgoglio or Pride (French *orgueil*, Italian *orgoglio*), born of Earth and Wind, that is of false matter and false spirit ('puft up

with emptie wind, and fild with sinfull crime'). Natale Conti (*Myth.* VI. 21) writes that the giants were said to have been offspring of sky and earth, because those who are made of grosser matter are rarely moderate or just, and grosser beings are prone to sensual pleasures and anger; and says that he would judge them to stand for rash men, dominated by desire and impulse, who despise all gods and would destroy religion. (See *Variorum* Spenser, Book I, p. 249.)

13. *that divelish yron Engin*: artillery. The stanza conveys vividly the consternation, fear, and confusion artillery fire brought. Ariosto (*Orl. Fur.* XI. 23) expresses horror at the 'infernal' invention.

16 and 17. *gold and purple pall*: Duessa, arrayed in purple and gold, crowned with the triple crown (as of the Papacy), and riding on the monstrous beast, like the Lernean hydra with seven heads and a tremendous tail, derives here from Revelation xii. 3 and 4, and xvii. 3 and 4. which describe the 'great red dragon, having seven heads . . . his tail drew the third part of the stars of heaven' and the woman 'arrayed in purple and scarlet colour, and decked with gold and precious stones and pearls, having a golden cup in her hand'. Spenser remembered Alciati's Emblem VI, which depicts this Scarlet Whore of the Apocalypse, giving it the title *Ficta religio*, and the woodcut accompanying the second sonnet of van der Noodt's 'Visions from Revelation' which he himself had translated for *A Theatre* in 1569.

that renowmed Snake: the Lernean hydra, which lived in a swamp at Lerna near Argos and ravaged the surrounding country, before it was vanquished by Hercules (his second Labour).

Stremona: possibly as an alternative name for Thrace, of which the river Strymon forms one boundary, though Argos was not in Thrace.

20. *Fast flying*: from Sansloy.

29. *A goodly Knight*: Prince Arthur. Briefly introduced in the Proem to Canto 1 as 'that most noble Briton Prince' who sought the Faerie Queene so long throughout the world. As Spenser tells us in the prefatory Letter to Sir Walter Raleigh, he is to appear in each Book: he represents Magnificence, the perfection of all virtues, containing them all. He usually appears in about Canto 7 or 8, performing some great feat of rescue; here of the Red Cross Knight, in Book II of the hero Guyon, in Book IV slaying Corflambo, and in Book V slaying the Souldan;

but his actual rôle in *The Faerie Queene* is limited. Naturally an English poet writing a great English epic poem would make use of Arthur; it will be remembered that both Milton and Dryden at one time projected *Arthuriads*, and Tasso had prescribed Arthur, with Charlemagne, as one of the most fit subjects for epic. Spenser put himself into a difficulty when at the opening of his poem he wrote of Arthur's long search for the Faerie Queene, and made it clear, both in the poem and in the Prefatory Letter, that by the Faerie Queene he also meant Queen Elizabeth. Doubtless when he began the poem in about 1580, and for some years afterwards, there was some probability that Elizabeth would marry, but of course she never did. Possibly at the beginning Spenser meant in Prince Arthur to honour his patron Leicester, but Leicester fell out of favour, and died in 1588; later he may have meant Essex, but he set himself great problems, and it is not surprising that Arthur's rôle was never resolved. See also the note to I.12.18.

30. *Shapt like a Ladies head*: an effigy presumably of the Faerie Queene. Guyon, in Book II, has the portrait of Gloriana on his shield. Elizabeth was the virgin of English courtier-chivalry, and her face and figure favourite devices in the associated pageantry and decoration. In Geoffrey of Monmouth's *Historia Regum Britanniae*, IX. 4, Arthur is said to bear on the inside of his shield an image of the Virgin Mary.

Hesperus: the evening and the morning star (Venus), which is exceptionally bright, the brightest and first to appear after dusk, and the brightest and last to remain before dawn.

31. *For all the crest a Dragon did enfold*: like the father of Arthur, Uther surnamed Pendragon (Celtic, *pen*, head), in Geoffrey of Monmouth. But in Tasso (*Ger. Lib.* IX. 25) the Soldan's helmet bears a dragon.

32. If, in the glowing description of Arthur at his first entry in the poem—an unusually long description of eight stanzas—the radiant effect of stanzas 29 and 30 is a little offset by the fierce description of the dragon-helm in 31, stanza 32, with its beautiful images and jubilant rhythm, reasserts that this is a glorious and virtuous being. Notice always the brightness and glory of Spenser's good characters. Marlowe cribbed the image of the almond tree for Tamburlaine's helm (*2 Tamburlaine*, IV. iii. 116; Methuen ed., 1930).

Selinis: in Sicily.

33. *His warlike shield*: is, like the shield of the magician Atlante in Ariosto (*Orl. Fur.* II. 55), covered in a silken case except when it was needed in some great danger (as, for example, when Ruggiero rescued Angelica from the orc (Book X) and overcame Pinabello's knights (in Book XXII)). In Tasso (*Ger. Lib.* XVI. 29) the hermit gave Ubaldo and Carlo a diamond shield to brandish before Rinaldo in Armida's bower, so that he should come to his senses. But probably also, as this was more than the merely magic shield of the Italian epic romances, Spenser thinks of Ephesians vi. 16: 'taking the shield of faith, wherewith ye shall be able to quench all the fiery darts of the wicked'.

Adamant: white sapphire or diamond; later used for steel.

34. *Cynthia . . . staynd with magicke arts constraint*: the moon, which witches were supposed to blur and veil by their enchantments; in *Paradise Lost* (II. 665) Milton wrote:

> . . . to dance
> With Lapland witches, while the labouring moon
> Eclipses at their charms.

Pliny (*Nat. Hist.* II. 12. 1; trs. Philemon Holland) writes of the moon: 'mortall men imagine that by Magicke sorcerie and charms, she is inchaunted'. In Ovid (*Met.* VII. 207) Medea tells how she can draw down the moon with her spells.

36. *Merlin*: the great enchanter of the Arthurian story. Both in *The Faerie Queene* and in Malory he was responsible for the bringing up of Arthur.

37. *his dearely loved Squire*: Timias.

The yron rowels into frothy fome he bit: a characteristic Spenserian detail.

40 and 41. This dialogue, full of proverbial and gnomic wisdom, economical and swift, reminds one of the early Shakespeare. Note the reserve of Una, and the clever gentle process by which Arthur gains her confidence.

43. *Phison and Euphrates . . . Gehons golden waves*: three of the rivers of Paradise from Genesis ii. 11–14. Una is the daughter of the King and Queen of Paradise, Adam and Eve.

44. *An huge great Dragon*: Satan, who dispossessed Adam and Eve from Paradise.

Tartary: Spenser means Tartarus, in the infernal regions.

46. *noble order . . . of Maidenhed*: probably an allusion to the Order of the Garter, the oval and pendant of which both have a figure of St. George killing the dragon. But in any case an order devoted to Gloriana, the Faerie Queene, and so alluding to Elizabeth the Virgin Queen.

Cleopolis is red: 'is called Cleopolis', that is the city of glory, so Gloriana's, Elizabeth's, London. (See I.10.58 and note to the stanza.)

47. *fresh unproved knight*: the Red Cross Knight was said in I.1.1 and 3 never to have borne arms before, and to yearn 'his new force to learne'.

49. *my captive langour*: 'captive' like Ital. *cattivo*, English *caitiff*, so meaning 'my wretched condition of langour'.

Spenser again briefly recapitulates some of the incidents of his complex narrative.

50. *that brought not backe the balefull body dead*: '(whoever treads these paths) his doomed body will not come back alive.'

Mine onely foe: 'my special foe', that is Una's special enemy, Duessa, or Falseness.

Canto 8

[Prince Arthur, Timias and Una come to Orgoglio's castle, and Arthur and the giant fight. Arthur eventually slays the giant, captures Duessa, and ultimately finds the Red Cross Knight terribly wasted in the dungeon. Duessa is stripped of her rich garments, exposed in all her filth and ugliness, and then flees.]

1. *heavenly grace doth him uphold*: Una guides Prince Arthur to the rescue of the Red Cross Knight from thraldom to Orgoglio.

3. *horne of bugle small*: the horn of a small 'bugle' or young ox. Magic horns abound in romance literature. In Ariosto, *Orl. Fur.* XV. 14, Logistilla, who stands for Reason, after releasing Astolpho from the myrtle-tree in which he had been imprisoned by her younger sister, the enchantress Alcina, presented him with the horn of justice, which breeds terror in all misdoers. The horn of Timias, Prince Arthur's Squire, seems to have something in common with 'the word of truth, the word of God, whose sound goeth into all the earth' (Romans x. 18): see stanza 4.

9. *mortall sins*: sins of mortals.

A superb image in this stanza. It owes its inception probably to Homer (*Il.* xiv. 414) describing the blow with which Ajax felled Hector, but the careful observation, energetic detail, powerful onomatopoeia, and the majestic progress of the lines through the stanza to the final alexandrine are Spenser's own.

11. *Cymbrian plaine*: possibly the modern Crimea (the Tauric Chersonese), once inhabited by the Cimmerii. Marlowe copied the image in *2 Tamburlaine*, IV. i. 188.

14. *her golden cup*: 'full of abominations and filthiness of her fornication' (Revelation xvii. 4).

19. *Did loose his vele*: as in Ariosto, *Orl. Fur.* XXII. 85 when Ruggiero displays the enchanted shield of Atlante, and the dazzling brightness of it prostrates Pinabello's knights.

22. This splendid simile occurs in Homer (*Il.* XIV. 414), Virgil (*Aen.* II. 625ff. and V. 448), and Tasso (*Ger. Lib.* IX. 39), but only in *Aen.* II. 625ff. is it given the detail and grandeur of Spenser's version, which is more vivid because it personalizes the tree and gives a powerful impression of its broken and prolonged fall by skilful metrical arrangement, especially in the alexandrine.

25. *crowned mitre*: the papal tiara.

27. *requite with usuree*: 'reward, with interest'.

29ff. An extraordinarily clear and vivid description.

unused rust: a Latinism, 'rusty because unused'.

31. *foster father of the Gyant dead*: the foster-father of Pride (Orgoglio) is Ignorance (Ignaro). The pride of Rome has been fostered by the ignorance of the laity. An excellent conception, and he is excellently presented as an obstructing character in the narrative, old, blind, slow, stupid, uncomprehending.

35. I am not sure what Spenser had in mind here, beyond a characteristically general picture of a foul reality behind a resplendent appearance. Lilian Winstanley (*Faerie Queene*, Book I, C.U.P., 1915), who stressed throughout her edition contemporary historical allegory, suggested that the poet alludes to the splendour of Mary Tudor's court contrasted with her persecutions, or to the splendid empire of Spain and the cruelty of the Inquisition.

36. In this stanza Spenser clearly has in mind Revelation vi. 9 and 10: '. . . I saw under the altar the souls of them that were slain for the word of God, and for the testimony which they held', and refers to those slain for their faith, probably under the Roman Catholic persecutions of Mary's reign, but also on the Continent.

37ff. Powerfully vivid description. Notice in 39 the surprise and force of the alexandrine.

42. *evill starre*: referring to the belief in the influence of the stars on men's lives, for good and for ill.

44. *Best musicke breeds delight*: all editions have delight, but presumably it should be 'despight' or 'dislike', or possibly 'no delight'; 'even the best music breeds no delight in an unwilling ear'.

46. *to strip her naked all*: as the enchantress Alcina was in Ariosto (*Orl. Fur.* VII. 73) by the magic of the ring Melissa gave to Ruggiero. Duessa has many of the details given by Ariosto; she is wrinkled, thin, bald, stunted, toothless, but Spenser's portrayal is more powerfully emotive and repulsive, and, characteristically, employs the senses of touch and smell as well as of sight.

48. *foxes taile*: to suggest craftiness.

Eagles claw: for rapacity.

Beares uneven paw: for ravening cruelty.

Canto 9

[Una hears from Arthur of his unknown parentage, and his dream of the Faerie Queene, whom he seeks for ever through the world. Una and the Red Cross Knight leave Arthur and Timias, encounter a knight, Sir Trevisan, fleeing from Despair, and they come to the cave of Despair. The Red Cross Knight enters, and is tempted to suicide by Despair, who gives him a dagger. But Una snatches the dagger away.]

1. *O goodly golden chaine*: of honour. Spenser is probably thinking (a) of Chaucer's 'fair chaine of love' (*Knightes Tale*, 2990); (b) of the golden chain in Homer (*Il.* VIII. 19) that Zeus let down from heaven to earth, which the gods were to pull to see whether they were strong enough to drag him out of heaven. It was variously interpreted as a symbol of avarice, of right ambition which is honourable, and of the cosmic force which holds the universe in order. In *F. Q.* II.7.46, it is

bad ambition. Spenser apostrophizes the highest honour, made of and linking all the virtues, and thinks of Prince Arthur in these terms, as, in the prefatory Letter, he declared the Prince to be 'magnificence in particular, which vertue . . . is the perfection of all the rest, and conteineth in it them all . . .'.

3. Arthur, as in Malory (*Works*, vol. I, 10ff.), was taken from his mother at birth at Merlin's bidding and brought up in ignorance of his lineage. In Malory he is the son of Uther Pendragon and his wife Igrayne.

4. *old Timon*: in Malory the babe is entrusted to Sir Ector, but Spenser presumably chose the name Timon instead because of its meaning of 'honour'.

Rauran mossy hore: Rauran-fawr, a hill in Merioneth, although the River Dee does not, as Spenser says, rise from it. It is said by the poet to be hoary with grey moss and lichen. Spenser carefully places Arthur's upbringing in Wales, though it is usually placed in Cornwall, because the Tudors came from Wales; thereby he does further implied honour to the Queen, and associates Prince Arthur, the 'Briton Prince', with Wales, the Tudors, and the Queen. One is a little reminded of the two young British Princes in Shakespeare's *Cymbeline*, brought up in Wales by old Belarius.

7. *that fresh bleeding wound*: of love, as is to be shown in the succeeding stanzas.

8. *into smoke, etc.*: Burton, *Anatomy of Melancholy*, III. 2.2, writes of Empedocles' being present at the cutting up of one that died of love: 'his heart was conbust, his liver smoky, his lungs dried up. As the heat consumes the water, so doth love dry up his radical moisture.'

14. Odd that a precursor of Arthur here (although the idea is common in Romance literature) should be Chaucer's Sir Thopas (*Works*, ed. Robinson, 1961, pp. 164ff.). Sir Thopas dreamed that the 'elf-queen' should be his leman, and set off to find her; but he never did, for the Host stinted Chaucer of his tale before he had got very far.

15. It was not just a dream, for Arthur found the grass pressed down where she had lain beside him.

19. *That any wound could heale incontinent*: it is not until Book IV, Canto 8 that Arthur makes use of the liquor, reviving Amoret.

A booke: Logistilla (Reason) gave Astolfo a book which would preserve him from evil in *Orl. Fur.* XV. 13.

21. *of Pegasus his kind*: of the breed of Pegasus, the famous winged horse of Greek mythology.

21–54. John Aikin, who published an edition of Spenser in 1802, wrote of these stanzas: 'It seems impossible by the medium of words to call up visual images in the mind with more force and distinctness ....' And Aubrey de Vere, in Grosart's edition of 1882, wrote, 'It proves that narrative poetry may, in the hand of a great master, fully reach the *intensity* of the drama, and carry to the same height those emotions of pity and terror through which to purify the soul was, according to Aristotle, the main function of tragedy.'

22. *an hempen rope*: we learn in stanza 29 that the rope was given to the knight Trevisan by Despair. It 'ill agrees' with his 'glistring armes' because hanging was the method of execution for knaves, too disgraceful for knights.

23. *what mister wight*: 'what manner of person'. 'Mister' derives, from 'mister' meaning 'trade', 'employment', ultimately from L. *misterium* = *ministerium* (as in Shakespeare, *Measure for Measure*, IV.ii.30, and *Othello*, IV.ii.29).

26. Another example of Spenser's little-praised skill in both speech and dialogue.

28ff. *Despaire*: the picture owes something to Skelton's *Magnificence*, in which Magnificence falls under the power of Despair and Mischief, who offer him a knife and a halter (*Complete Poems*, ed. Henderson, 1931, pp. 236–7); and to John Higgins's 'Legend of Cordelia' in the 1574 and 1575 edition of *A Mirrour for Magistrates*, in which Despayre offers her a choice of instruments for suicide, and she accepts the blade with which Queen Dido of Carthage slew herself. Despair, a form of *accidie*, slothful despondency, 'wanhope', is said by Chaucer in *The Parsones Tale* (*Works*, 1961, p. 250) to be 'despeir of the mercy of God, that comth somtyme of to muche outrageous sorwe and somtyme of to much drede . . . thurgh which despair or drede he abaundoneth al his herte to every maner synne, as saith Seint Augustin. Which dampnable sin . . . is cleped synnyng in the Hooly Goost'. Despair, by tempting to self-destruction, shuts off the hope of repentance and salvation;

if the despair does not go as deep as that, it is still exceedingly dangerous, for in the grip of despair a man may well, as Chaucer says, abandon himself to all sorts of other sins. Later in this canto we are to see the Red Cross Knight himself helpless in the power of Despair.

30. *his charmed speeches*: Despair's power to charm and lull and persuade is well shown in stanzas 38–40, 42–47, more beguiling and blandishing than the speech of any enchantress.

31. *the Castle of his health*: Spenser perhaps knew Sir Thomas Eliot's *Castle of Helthe* (1534), or remembered, from Sackville's Induction to the 1563 edition of *A Mirrour for Magistrates*, l. 130: 'When sickenes seekes his castell health to skale'. Spenser gives a protracted allegorical portrayal of 'man in the castle of his health' in his account of the House of Alma or Temperance in Book II, Canto 9.

32. *for gold nor glee*: as we should say, colloquially, 'for love or money'.

33–36. Again Spenser achieves a powerful and indeed inescapable presentation by his characteristic use of emphasis, repetition, onomatopoeia and hyperbole. Note the succession of: *low, hollow, darke, dolefull, drearie, greedie, grave, carrion, carcases, ghastly, shrieking, balefull, ghosts, waile, howle, ragged, wretches, griesie, disordred, hollow, deadly, dull, rawbone, penurie, pine, shronke, ragged, drearie, corse, wallowd, wound, rustie.*

49. *painted in a table*: in a picture. Spenser must have seen many depictions of the Last Judgement in church wall-paintings and in stained glass. Many survive in parish churches all over the country.

51. *a leafe of Aspin*: the aspen poplar. Its fairly large leaves are joined to the twigs by long stems which are broad at both ends but narrow down considerably at their middle, so that the leaves stir at the slightest breath of wind.

52. When Una discovered that the Red Cross Knight had deserted her she was reproachful, but sad, not angry. Here she is 'enraged' when he is about to kill himself and reproaches him sternly and resolutely.

54. A final imaginative touch: Despair cannot kill himself. But in the days of the Last Judgement and the Second Coming, then Despair will die, for God will re-assume the world.

Canto 10

[Una brings the Red Cross Knight to the House of Holiness, where he meets Dame Caelia and Faith, Hope, and Charity. Fidelia teaches him; Speranza gives him comfort; Amendment, Penance, and Remorse discipline him; and Charissa instructs him and shows him the path to heaven, sending Mercy to accompany him to the hermitage of Contemplation. Contemplation shows him the new Jerusalem, and tells him of his origins and his future: he is destined to be a Saint, in fact St. George, the patron saint of England. The Knight returns to the waiting Una and they take their leave.]

3. *not farre away*: this is not casually written. Spenser means that God's help is always near at hand, as the House of Holinesse is when the Red Cross Knight is weak and broken after his sorry encounter with Despair.

4. *Caelia*: 'heavenly'.

Three daughters: Faith, Hope, and Charity (Corinthians, xiii). We learn more of them in stanzas 12–16.

5. *Humiltá*: Humility is the warden of the castle in Hawes's *The Exemple of Vertu* (1512). Spenser probably knew this work, in which Youth sets out to win Cleanness, the daughter of the King of Love, resists the temptations of Sensuality and Pride, and overcomes a dragon with three heads representing the world, the flesh, and the Devil. Youth wears the armour of Christ, as does the Red Cross Knight.

Streight and narrow was the way: as, in Matthew vii. 14, 'is the way, which leadeth unto life, and few there be that find it', in contrast to the wide gate and broad way 'that leadeth to destruction . . .'.

6. *francklin*: a freeholder, a man of position and substance. But Spenser plays on the word 'free', meaning the generous freedom and energy of spirit that is, or should be, characteristic of Christian zeal. Probably he remembers Chaucer's affectionate portrayal of his Franklin and the generosity of spirit shown in all the characters of *The Franklin's Tale*.

8. *at her beades*: Spenser means to show us a holy and devout woman, not, of course, a Roman Catholic nun.

12. *Fidelia*: Faith bears a chalice with wine and water mixed (as in the Holy Communion) and with a serpent in it, and in her other hand a book. The serpent is an emblem of health and regeneration, because it renews itself every year when it sloughs its old skin, and also of eternity when 'enrold'. The book is the New Testament, signed and sealed with blood because it reports the life and death of Christ, having

'darke things . . . hard to be understood' (The Revelation of St. John the Divine); and, as St. Peter said (2 Peter iii. 16) of Paul's epistles, in them 'are some things hard to be understood . . .'.

14. *Speranza*: Hope, clad in blue, the Virgin Mary's colour, and the colour of truth, with a silver anchor, from Hebrews vi. 19: 'Which *hope* we have as an anchor of the soul, both sure and stedfast.'

16. *Charissa*: Charity is not present because she is in childbed. (Spenser was careful to refer to her in stanza 4 as being married.) Charity is usually depicted in medieval and Renaissance art as having children about her, as Faith and Hope are depicted with the symbols Spenser records.

20. *poure out her larger spright*: show her greater powers (in a number of examples from the Bible of the power of Faith).

the hastie sunne to stay: as it did with God's help when Joshua commanded it upon Gideon, 'until the people had avenged themselves upon their enemies' (Joshua x. 12).

Or backward turne his course: as, in 2 Kings xx. 10, it does as a sign from God that Hezekiah will live, and indeed live for an extra fifteen years.

hostes of men she could dismay: as in Judges vii Gideon's depleted army of 300 men routed the Midianites in their thousands.

parts the flouds in tway: as in the miraculous passage of the Israelites through the Red Sea in *Exodus* xiv. 21ff., and as the waters of Jordan were divided for Joshua (in Joshua iii. 14ff.).

And eke huge mo: ntaines: Matthew xxi. 21: 'If ye have faith, and doubt not, . . . if ye shall say unto this mountain, Be thou removed, and be thou cast into the sea; it shall be done.'

22. The Red Cross Knight is in despair with anguish at his sins, but Hope gives him comfort.

30. *in yellow robes*: yellow being the symbolic colour of fertility, because of the golden colour of ripe corn and the golden sun. In *F. Q.* VII. 7 and 30 the personifications of both August and Autumn·are described as being arrayed in gold or yellow.

36. *seven Bead-men*: 'seven men of prayer'. 'Bead' originally meant 'prayer', and acquired its later sense because of the string of perforated balls used by the religious to count their prayers. They are seven because they stand for the seven distinctions of good works: to entertain travellers; to feed the hungry; to clothe the naked; to relieve prisoners;

to comfort the sick and dying; to bury the dead; and to care for widows and orphans, as Spenser goes on to enumerate.

39. *His owne coate he would cut*: as did St. Martin of Tours for a beggar.

40. *From Turkes and Sarazins*: the ransoming of Christian captives from the Turks was a common work of charity, much needed in the 16th century, when the Turks overran much of Eastern Europe and threatened Vienna and Northern Italy.

he that harrowd hell: refers to the tradition that Christ descended into hell, fought with and overcame the powers of darkness, and returned leading with him the ransomed souls of men. 'The harrowing of hell' is a common medieval phrase for the despoiling of hell by Christ, from the old English *hergian*, 'to act as an army', 'to ravage'; cf. 'harry'. The action of Christ's 'harrowing of hell' comes originally from the probably 4th-century apocryphal *Gospel of Nicodemus*, chs. xviiiff. (see M. R. James, *The Apocryphal New Testament*, Oxford, 1924). It is dramatized in the English mystery-cycles, most fully in Chester (Early English Text Society, Extra Series 115, 1916) and York (ed. L. Toulmin Smith, Oxford, 1885). There is a prose translation of the Gospel in Old English, and a Middle-English verse rendering, but the finest non-dramatic version is in *Piers Plowman* (B Text, Passus XVIII, E.E.T.S., 1884).

42. *me graunt, I dead be not defould*: a rare personal intrusion by the poet. We may suppose that, like the concluding two lines of the poem (VII.8.2), it is heartfelt. His prayer was granted, as he was buried in Westminster Abbey in January 1599.

50. *Whereof the Keyes* . . . : Faith can unlock the gates of heaven.

52. *thou man of earth*: the Red Cross Knight is not a faerie knight, but a man. His ancestry is told in stanza 65.

53. *the highest Mount*: it is compared to that which Moses at God's behest climbed, and on which he spent forty days and nights (Exodus xxiv. 15ff.) after the miraculous crossing of the Red Sea (Exodus xiv. 21ff.). But the writer of Exodus does not refer to the bloody letters writ in stone, though St. Paul does (2 Corinthians iii. 7); and the 'flashing fire' may refer to Acts vii. 30, or to Deuteronomy iv. 11.

bloud-red billowes: of the Red Sea.

54. *that sacred hill*: the Mount of Olives.

that pleasaunt Mount: Parnassus, where dwelt the 'thrise three learned Ladies', the Muses.

55. *a goodly Citie*: the new Jerusalem of Revelation xxi. 10ff., which gave off light 'like unto a stone most precious, even like a jasper stone, clear as crystal'; it 'had a wall great and high', 'the twelve gates were twelve pearls', and 'the foundations of the wall ... were garnished with all manner of precious stones'. The romances *Huon of Burdeux*, *Libeaus Desconus*, and *Arthur of Little Britain* all have great cities or palaces on the tops of mountains that shine brilliantly as if made of crystal. (See *Variorum Spenser*, Bk. I, p. 290.)

58. *great Cleopolis*: London. See note to I.7.46.

Panthea: the crystal tower of Panthea may be Westminster Abbey, a sort of 'Pantheon' housing the tombs of Elizabeth's ancestors, or it may be the Queen's Palace of Richmond, also known as Shene (shene = bright).

60. An unusual remark in a poem that celebrates chivalry. Spenser says that once he has achieved the earthly conquest upon which and to which he is bound, the Red Cross Knight, an English mortal, must thereafter shun earthly conquest, 'For bloud can nought but sin, and wars but sorrowes yield'. It is an indication of the serious purpose ever present behind the romantic and epic adventures.

61. *Shalt be a Saint*: the Red Cross Knight, now revealed to be a mortal, and called George, will become a Saint and the patron saint of England. Spenser has nothing to do with the reputed Cappadocian or Cilician origins of Saint George.

There was an English version of the life of St. George in the 9th-century *Lives of the Saints* by Aelfric, but the later English versions, which blend with the traditional saint's life some elements of the myth of Perseus, were modelled on the *Legenda Aurea* composed between 1260 and 1270 by Jacobus de Voragine, Archbishop of Genoa, translated and printed by Caxton in 1487 as *The Golden Legend*. The story was disseminated through mummers' plays of St. George, and through such works as the collection of saints' lives, entitled *A Festival*, by John Mirk, published by Caxton in about 1482, and used as homilies on saints' days. The Italian poet Mantuan (Battista Spagnoli, 1448–1516), whose work Spenser knew well (he modelled the September and October

eclogues of *The Shepheardes Calender* on two of Mantuan's), wrote a
long poem on St. George, from which it seems Spenser drew some
details, such as the watchman reporting the struggle, the command to
open the gates of brass, the obeisance made to the victorious knight,
his proclamation as saviour of the city, the rumour that he was some great
hero sent by God, the gifts of ivory and gold presented by the king, the
reception of the princess by her parents, and the festivities with which
the story concludes. John Lydgate (*c.* 1370–1440) wrote a poem, probably
to illustrate a tapestry or mural decoration, in which he refers to St.
George as protector, patron, lodestar of knighthood and holy martyr,
and writes (stanza 3):

> This name George by Interpretacion
>   I sayde of tweyne, the first of hoolynesse,
> And the secound of knighthood and renoun,
>
> . . . .
>   The feond venqwysshing of manhoode and prowesse,
> The worlde, the fleashe, as Crystes owen knight.

In stanza 4 he is shown leaving his country 'Cristes feyth for to magne-
fye', and 'thoroughe his noblesse and his chyvallerye Trouthe to sous-
teene . . .'.

In Lydgate the damsel leads a sheep with her. The Spenser *Variorum*
edition (Vol. I, pp. 379ff.) also points to the popularity of the St. George
story in pageants and displays before the monarch.

65. There are several medieval tales and some Irish ones in which the
knight or other hero is revealed to be not a fairy at all but a changeling,
often stolen at birth. (See *Variorum* Spenser, Vol. I, p. 292.) It is, of
course, of great importance that the knight whose companion is, or
should be, Truth, and whose task is to overcome Satan, should be
human, with all a human being's errors and without any magic fairy
power: when St. George is helped by a sort of magic, it is the 'magic'
of God's grace.

66. *Georgos*: Greek γεωργός ('a man of earth'), a 'husbandman',
'ploughman'. In the prefatory Letter he is introduced as a 'clownishe
younge man'. But the story of his being found in a ploughed field is

from the account in Ovid (*Met.* XV. 553) of the discovery of Tages, later the instructor of the Etruscans in the arts of augury.

67. Though a son of earth, the Red Cross Knight, significantly, cannot look down at the earth after his sight of the new Jerusalem, so dazzled is he by its brightness.

68. *for his paines hyre*: 'as a return for the trouble he had taken'.

Of her adventure: 'of the quest or venture taken on for her', that is to overcome the dragon.

Canto 11

[Una and the Red Cross Knight come at last to the kingdom of her parents, ravaged by the Dragon, and to the castle in which they are imprisoned. The Knight fights the dragon, is sorely wounded, and at evening is hurled to the ground, but falls into 'the well of life'. The Dragon thinks it is victorious, but the Knight is restored by the water of the well, and the next day emerges fresh for the fight. Another terrible day's fighting ensues, and the Red Cross Knight eventually slips, recoiling from the dragon's fiery breath, near 'the tree of life' growing hard by the stream of life. Again he is revived, and the following morning, healed of all his wounds, he renews the fight and kills the dragon.]

1. *her captive Parents deare*: they stand for Adam and Eve, that is for mankind, dispossessed from Eden by Satan (the dragon).

5. *O thou sacred Muse*: Clio, the Muse of History, the child of Apollo and Mnemosyne (or Memory). Apollo is not only the god of light, often identified with the sun, but also the god of music and prophecy. See note to Proem, 2.

Nourse of time, and everlasting fame: Clio is nurse of time and fame because history records events.

7. *Till I of warres and bloudy Mars do sing*: Mars is the god of war. Spenser seems to imply that he will later be writing of great wars. Possibly, because of the reference to *Briton fields with Sarazin bloud bedyde*, he still thought, at this stage in the writing, of further following the Italian romantic epics by presenting the great contest between Christian and Saracen that lay behind those narratives. There are also, at I.12.18, III.3.27, and III.3.52, references to wars with Saracens, the first two implying or stating, as here, outright, war between Gloriana

and the Paynim king, one of them mentioning invasion. This intention was never developed. Perhaps he abandoned it after 1588 and the failure of the Spanish Armada, the threat of invasion by foreign Papistical powers having receded; perhaps he realized it would complicate the narrative appallingly to have a Faerie-Saracen opposition running throughout the poem as well as all the other situations and *motifs*. The Sarazins are not necessarily Pagans in *The Faerie Queene*, however, but Roman Catholics, and the Paynim king is probably meant to stand for Philip II of Spain. In Book V the 'Souldan' figures as a great antagonist of Prince Arthur and Artegall (Canto 8). See note to I.2.12.

8ff. Notice how Spenser makes use of the senses in his account of the Dragon: sight, sound, and touch in 9, touch in 12, smell in 13. The description has its grotesque side, and is perhaps too circumstantial here and there, but splendidly onomatopoeic; at points terrifying, as in the passages about the 'deepe devouring jawes' (12) and the 'trickling bloud and gobbets raw / of late devoured bodies' (13); suitably repulsive, as in the passage about its 'stinking gorge' (13); and ultimately haunting, in the description of its eyes (14). Also, it is difficult to envisage a more successful presentation of the mere *size* of a monster.

12. *the griesly mouth of hell*: in the medieval mystery-plays, in church mural decoration, and in stained glass, hell-mouth, into which damned souls were thrown or pitch-forked, is usually a dragon's, sometimes a fish's mouth.

13. *Three rankes of yron teeth*: in Ovid (*Met*. III. 34) the dragon Cadmus later slays has three rows of teeth.

14. *two broad Beacons*: probably refers to the beacon-fires lit on 29 July 1588, when the Spanish Armada was first sighted off the Cornish coast.

18ff. Many of the images and epithets here, as well as the vivid description, show a skilled knowledge of falconry; *sailes* are the wings of a hawk; *stoup* is the swoop of the bird on to its prey; *haggard* is 'wild'; *pounces* are the claws of a hawk; *to trusse* is to bundle up together as the butcher does in trussing a bird for cooking, and as the hawk does with an unwieldly victim before flying off with it.

20. *disseized of his gryping grosse*: 'having lost his strong hold'.
uncouth smart: unwonted, unaccustomed pain.

21. *his stedfast henge*: 'his hinge'; that is, out of its place or orbit.

27. *that great Champion*: Hercules, who successfully accomplished his 'twelve huge labours'.

furies and sharpe fits: 'fearful pains and agonies'.

the poysoned garment: the shirt of Nessus the centaur. Hercules killed him for attempting to violate his wife Deianira. The dying Nessus gave his bloodstained and poisoned shirt (poisoned because Nessus's blood was poisoned by the spear which Hercules had dipped in the venomous blood of one of his earlier victims, the Hydra) to Deianira, saying it would preserve the love of her husband. Deianira accordingly gave it, all unknowing, to Hercules, who died in torment as a result. As usual, Spenser follows Ovid (*Met.* IX. 153ff.).

29. *The well of life*: this is the 'pure river of water of life' of Revelation xxii. 1, which contains the 'living water' of John iv. 10 and 14. The episode no doubt comes from the romance *Sir Bevis of Hamtoun* (Early English Text Society, Extra Series, 1894), in which Bevis, fighting his dragon, falls into a well to which, because of the might of Christ Jesu, no 'worm' (dragon) can approach nearer than seven feet.

30. *Silo*: the pool of Siloam, the waters of which help to cure the blind man in John ix. 7.

Jordan: in which Naaman bathed at Elisha's prompting, and was healed of leprosy (2 Kings v. 14).

Bath: the town in Somerset, famous for its healing waters in pre-Roman as in Roman times and since.

Spau: near Liège in Belgium, celebrated for its waters, and making the name 'Spa' available for other such places.

Cephise: a river in Bœotia whose waters were strongly cleansing, and so famous (Pliny, *Hist. Nat.* II. 106) for making fleeces very white.

Hebrus: a river in Thrace, said by Horace (*1 Epist.* XVI. 13) to be very pure.

33. *Titan*: the sun.

34. *As Eagle fresh*: '. . . it is a true fact that when the eagle grows old and his wings become heavy and his eyes become darkened with a mist, he goes in search of a fountain, and, over against it, he flies up to the height of heaven, even unto the circle of the sun: and there he singes his wings and at the same time evaporates the fog of his eyes, in a ray

of the sun. Then at length, taking a header down in the fountain, he dips himself three times in it, and instantly he is renewed with a great vigour of plumage and splendour of vision.

'Do the same thing, O Man, you who are clothed in the old garment and have the eyes of your heart growing foggy. Seek for the spiritual fountain of the Lord and lift up your mind's eyes to God—who is the fount of justice—and then your youth will be renewed like the eagle's.' (*The Book of Beasts*, twelfth-century Latin Bestiary, trs. T. H. White, Cape, 1954.) The idea and the moral are common in bestiaries.

So new this new-borne knight to battell new did rise: this alludes to baptism (see stanza 36), as, in stanza 48, there seems to be an allusion to the other sacrament, the holy communion.

41. *Cerberus*: the savage three-headed dog that guarded the gates of hell.

44. *as burning Aetna*: the volcano in Sicily. It was in fact unusually active in the sixteenth century. But Spenser probably remembers Virgil's description of Aetna in eruption (*Aen.* III. 571ff.), and Tasso's likening of Satan to the volcano (*Ger. Lib.* IV. 8).

46. *the tree of life*: 'To him that overcometh will I give to eat of the tree of life, which is in the midst of the paradise of God' (Rev. ii. 7).

47. *Another like faire tre*: '. . . the tree of life also in the midst of the garden, and the tree of knowledge of good and evil' (Gen. ii. 9).

In *Huon of Burdeux* (E.E.T.S., Extra Series, 1884), Huon, fighting with a griffin, is healed of his wounds by the clear waters of a fountain: 'he had no sooner dronke thereof but incontynent he was hole of all his wounds and as fressh and lusty as when he came from the castel . . . by this fountayne there grew an appell tree charged with levys and frute', of which Huon ate and gave to his friends, for the fruit had a restorative power.

49. *deadly made*: a child of death, not life.

As dawn and early morning are always described rapturously and jubilantly by Spenser, so evening and night are shown as sad, dreary, deadly, cheerless.

51. *The joyous day*: this is, significantly, the morning of the third day of the struggle, recalling the days between the Crucifixion and the Resurrection.

faire Aurora: see note to I.2.7.

54. *So downe he fell*: with effective reiteration, Spenser says it four times in this superbly onomatopoeic and vivid stanza.

Canto 12

[The dragon killed, the inhabitants of the castle come out joyfully to gaze on the victor and the beast. Una's parents, the King and Queen of Eden, give him thanks and gifts, and lead Una and the Red Cross Knight to the castle. The Red Cross Knight says that he must return to the Faerie Queene's court, for he has another six years of service to perform before his avowed marriage to Una can take place. Una unveils. A messenger comes with a letter from 'Fidessa' warning the King that the Knight is affianced to her and has wronged her. The messenger is found to be Archimago, and is bound and cast into a dungeon. The King then performs the sacred betrothal rites for Una and the Red Cross Knight, and there is great joy and feasting. The book ends with the Red Cross Knight's return to do his further service for the Faerie Queene.]

This canto is unusual in *The Faerie Queene* in presenting a crowd of people, well-realized, from ordinary life. It is also remarkable for its tone of quiet happiness, especially marked after the violence and stir of the long fight in Canto 11.

7. *Diana*: the virgin goddess of the chase.

9. *the raskall many*: both 'raskall' (from O.F. *rascaille* = rabble) and 'many' mean 'rabble'.

10. Some good, vivid, semi-humorous detail here.

18. *her to serve six yeares*: this would make, presumably, seven altogether, which contradicts the outline given in the prefatory Letter, in which Gloriana is said to hold her annual feast twelve days, 'uppon which xii severall dayes, the occasions of the xii severall adventures hapned, which being undertaken by xii severall knights, are in these xii books severally handled and discoursed'. The fact that in Book I it is implied that there are to be seven, not twelve, separate adventures, and that some books of *The Faerie Queene* seem to reach a climax in Canto 7 (in I.7 the Red Cross Knight is captured by Orgoglio (Pride); in II.7 Sir Guyon is in the underworld with Mammon (Avarice) and near to

death; in IV.7 Amoret is captured by the giant (Lust)), has led Miss Janet Spens to propose persuasively, if not completely convincingly, that originally the poem was to be an eight-book moral epic based on the seven deadly sins (*Spenser's Faerie Queene*, London, 1934). See also the note to I.7.29. In any case the prefatory Letter is an unreliable guide to the poem as we have it.

that proud Paynim king: see note to I.11.7.

22. At last Una, Truth, is shown unveiled, now that the Devil dragon has been killed and her parents restored to their lost Eden by true Faith. Spenser writes of Una, who is eventually (stanza 19) to be married to the Red Cross Knight, in language reminiscent of Revelation xix. 7, 8: '. . . the marriage of the Lamb is come, and his wife hath made herself ready. And to her was granted that she should be arrayed in fine linen, clean and white: for the fine linen is the righteousness of saints', with reference to the mystical union, symbolized in marriage, of Christ and the Church; that is, all the members of the Christian Church, after the victory of the Lamb, Christ, over the powers of the dragon, Satan, in Revelation xvii. The 'fine linen, clean and white' makes a clear contrast with the 'purple and scarlet colour, and decked with gold and precious stones and pearls' of the woman riding on the beast, and Spenser obviously had this in mind when contrasting Una and Duessa throughout Book I.

At the lower allegorical level of contemporary relevance, the marriage of Una and the Red Cross Knight suggests the marriage of England and its reformed 'true' religion.

24. An expert delaying twist to the story, which reminds us again of the ever-presence of duplicity and falsehood.

26. *great Emperour of all the West*: the Romish power.

27. *the burning Altars, which he swore*: Duessa claims that he had sworn before the altars on which sacrifices were burning.

guiltie heavens of his bold perjury: 'the heavens charged to avenge the guilt of his perjury'.

29. Spenser sometimes arrests the narrative and gives us a series of close-up shots of great power and clarity. It is one of the features of his literary craftsmanship that assures us of the human reality of what he is writing about, and convinces us that *The Faerie Queene*, for all its

romance and imaginativeness, is firmly based on human actions, character, motives, and behaviour.

32. *royall richly dight*: 'dressed in rich and royal clothing'.

Unwares me wrought: 'brought me unsuspecting'.

37. *housling fire*: 'sacramental fire'; houseling means 'of the Eucharist
or Holy Communion', from Old English *húsel*. Spenser, however, is
not thinking of any eucharistic rites, but of the ancient Roman marriage
ceremony.

sacred lampe: a lamp burns in Catholic churches as a symbol of the
presence there of the blessed elements of the eucharist, and therefore of
the mystical presence of Christ.

38. *sprinckle all the posts with wine*: a Roman custom.

the house did sweat with great aray: 'the whole house seemed to exude
wine and perfumes'.

39. *trinall triplicities*: the angelic beings were arranged in three orders
of three by the Scholastic theologians, notably St. Thomas Aquinas
(*c.* 1225–74), deriving it through the *Celestial Hierarchy* of Dionysius
the Areopagite from St. Paul's list of the powers in the spiritual world,
'thrones, or dominions, or principalities, or powers' in Colossians i. 16.
There were three Hierarchies, each subdivided into three Orders of
Choirs. Seraphim, Cherubim, and Thrones formed the first Hierarchy;
Dominations, Virtues, and Powers the second; and Principalities, Archangels, and Angels the third. Each of the orders possessed some special
quality: the Seraphim were burning lustrous beings; the Cherubim
had special powers of sight (so they keep watch in Milton, *P. L.* IV.
778ff.); the Archangels were the 'chief messengers', as the Greek indicates, of God, and the chief intermediaries between God and Man.

GLOSSARY
by
ALAN WARD

THE Glossary contains all the words glossed at the foot of the pages of text, except for those involving points of accidence or syntax only. In general the aim has been to gloss all words likely to give difficulty to readers not widely acquainted with Elizabethan English: some other words have been included for their special interest.

There was considerable variation in spelling, even in printed books, at the time Spenser was writing, and because of his interest in the look of his lines he presents us with perhaps greater difficulty than most of his contemporaries. Some words unfamiliar at first glance would be recognized in their modern spelling: in such cases the spellings are glossed at page-foot once only, though the Glossary has a complete list of them. In addition to the most obvious spelling variations, the following have not normally been covered:

au for *a* (e.g. *daunce*)
ee for *ie, ea*, and vice-versa (*passim*)
ew for *u* (e.g. *dewly*)
g for *j* (e.g. *gealous*)
-ie for *-y* (e.g. *beautie*)
igh for *i* and vice-versa (e.g. *spight*; *nie*)
o for *a* (e.g. *lond*)
ou for *oo* (e.g. *drouping*)
w for *u* (e.g. *sownd*)
y for *i* (e.g. *fyre, fayle*)

Omission and addition of final *-e* (e.g. *hast* (for *haste*); *heare*). Certain contractions, such as *cald* for *called*.

Often the context determines the degree of difficulty, and this has been taken into account. Further, the archaic prefix *y-* and the archaic *-en* endings of verbs have not been glossed separately except where the verb occurs only in one or other of these extended forms in Book I. No attempt has been made to give a complete coverage of variant spellings in the Glossary and cross-references have been kept to a minimum. The symbols '(+ other sp.)' have, however, been added to some entries to indicate that the same word is spelled in a more familiar way or ways elsewhere in Book I. Spenser's frequent use of the comparative adjective for the superlative (imitating Latin idiom), is noted only the first time it appears and is not normally recorded in the Glossary.

Glossing must often of necessity be little more than a rough guide to meaning, particularly with poetry: and the problem is again particularly difficult with Spenser, who is often unorthodox in his use of words, frequently employing them (for example) in a very general sense, and using a broad band, as it were, of the meaning-spectrum. In some cases a double meaning seems to be involved. For this reason the Glossary, and especially the foot-of-page glosses, should be used with caution; and sometimes in the Glossary a group of meanings is offered from which the reader is advised to make his own selection of one or more. (Attention is drawn there to the more difficult cases.) Perusal of the *O.E.D.*, of Osgood's *Concordance* to Spenser's poems, and wide reading of Elizabethan poetry are strongly urged if the full quality and colour of Spenser's language is to be appreciated.

Many difficult lines and idioms are dealt with in the notes, and do not call for further attention. Here, however, may be noted certain periphrastic, and somewhat archaic, uses of the definite article and relative *that*, such as *the which*, and *which that* for *which*; *after that* for *after*, etc.

In order to make the Glossary a fuller guide to Spenser's vocabulary, a complete record of all the instances of words glossed and their meanings in Book I has been given unless otherwise stated. Where a word thus glossed has (in Book I) additional meanings that do not require glossing, the words '(+ other sense(s) or . . . uses)' are added as appropriate. Where a word is first or last recorded in Spenser by the *O.E.D.* this has been noted, and so also have major changes of meaning. In this way some idea of the amount and degree of Spenserian archaism and innovation may be gained; though of course not all words first recorded in Spenser are likely to have been created by him, nor are all words last recorded in his poetry necessarily archaic in the sense defined on p. 30. The most clearly archaic of the other words are noted as 'probably archaic', though a full list of likely archaisms would undoubtedly be much larger. Words occurring once only in Spenser's poetry are also noted.

Occasionally the *O.E.D.* has seemed to be in error: in these few instances corrections have been made without comment.

A

About, 11.11 (4), out of. (+ other senses.)

Abouts, 9.36 (3), around, about. (Last recorded here.)

Accompted, 10.60 (2), accounted, considered.

Acquite, 7.52 (6), 8.1 (4), to release.

Addresse, 2.11 (7), 8.6 (7), dressed, fitted out; 10.11 (3), directed. (+ other senses.)

Advaunce, 5.16 (5), praise. (+ other senses.)

Advise, 1.33 (6), 1.50 (5), 3.19 (4), to consider, reflect. (+ other senses.)

Advizement, 4.12 (8), 10.23 (5), counsel, advice.

Afflicted, Pr. 4 (8), low, humble.

Affray, 3.12 (7), terror. (This sense last recorded here.)

Affray, 5.8 (7), 5.30 (4), 7.34 (4), to frighten, terrify.

Affronted, 8.13 (2), confronted, opposed.

Afore, 10.49 (7), 11.8 (6), 11.37 (8), 12.1 (4), in front, ahead. (+ other sense.)

Agraste (p.t. of *aggrace*), 10.18 (7), showed favour to. (First recorded in Spenser. Apparently from *a* + *grace* (vb.), partly on the basis of It. *ag(g)ratiare*, 'to grace'.)

Albe, 5.45 (4), 10.44 (9), although.

Alight, 12.25 (5), to halt, stop. (This sense first recorded here, and rare.) (+ other senses.)

All (were), 10.47 (3), 12.23 (7), although . . . were.

Aloof, 11.5 (1), away, aside.

Als, 9.18 (5), also; 9.21 (7), as.

Amate, 1.51 (4), 9.45 (4), to daunt, subdue.

Amiddes, 1.36 (7), amidst.

Amis, 4.18 (8), amice (a priest's vestment.)

Amove, 4.45 (3), 8.21 (1), 9.18 (3), 11.16 (6), to move. (This sense last recorded here.)

Amounted, 9.54 (1), rose up. (Only once in Sp.)

Andvile, 11.42 (6), anvil.

Annoy, 6.17 (9), vexation, annoyance.

Appall, 7.35 (5), to subdue. (+ other sense.)

Appease, 1.54 (6), 3.29 (9), 5.34 (7), 11.38 (9), to subdue, make quiet, cease (sorrowing).

Apply, 10.46 (7), to attend to. (+ other sense.)

Approve, 6.26 (1), 8.3 (9), 9.37 (1), to prove, demonstrate.

Aread, Pr. 1 (7), 12.28 (4), to command; 9.6 (5), 9.23 (7), 9.28 (6), 10.64 (5), to tell, say; 8.31 (9), 8.33 (9), to explain, indicate; 10.51 (4), to show, direct.

Ared (p.t. of *aread*), 10.17 (9), ?interpreted, ?told.

Argument, Pr. 4 (8), subject.

Armorie, 1.27 (5), armour.

Arras, 4.6 (6), 8.35 (2), tapestry.

Arrested, 4.44 (7), (here) charmed (to sleep). (See note.)

Aslake, 3.36 (8), to pacify, calm down.

Assay, 2.13 (3), proved value; 7.27 (2), 8.8 (7), attack, onslaught.

Assay, 2.24 (5), 6.11 (1), 11.32 (2), 12.9 (9), to assail, attack. (+ other senses.)

Assoiled, 10.52 (8), absolved.

Astond, 2.31 (8), astonished, amazed.

Astonied, 2.15 (8), 2.16 (5), 6.9 (8), stunned, astonished, amazed.

Astownd, 7.7 (7), 8.5 (7), 9.35 (7), 11.6 (9), to astonish, amaze.

Attacht, 12.35 (5), seized, arrested.

Attaint, 7.34 (6), to sully, make dim.

Avale, 1.21 (5), to fall, decline, droop.

Avengement, 4.34 (5), 9.43 (4), vengeance.

Avise, 5.40 (2), 8.15 (5), to consider.

Avouchen, 10.64 (8), to prove, establish. (Only once in Sp.)

Ay(e), 1.16 (8), 1.48 (4), 7.51 (8), 9.10 (5), 9.33 (6), 10.30 (8), 10.54 (6), 10.62 (7), 10.63 (3), ever, always.

B

Baite, 1.32 (9), to feed, refresh. (Only once in Sp.) (+ other vb. *bait*.)

Bale, 1.16 (7), 7.28 (6), 7.39 (6), 8.14 (5), 9.16 (3), 9.29 (2), ?evil, mischief, trouble, sorrow, grief. (Often a blend of one or more of these senses seems involved.)

Balefull, 2.2 (9), 5.14 (8), 7.25 (8), 8.38 (5), 9.33 (7), 12.2 (7), pernicious, malignant, grim; 4.3 (4), 10.53 (8), unhappy, miserable, wretched; 7.50 (5), ?doomed. (Sense often difficult to determine. See note on *bale* above.)

Banes, 12.36 (7), banns (of marriage). (Only once in Sp.)

Bauldrick, 7.29 (8), baldric, belt.

Bayes, 7.3 (1), bathes. (Found only here; perhaps suggested in part by *bathe*. See also *embay* below.)

Beades, 1.30 (7), 3.14 (5), 10.3 (8), 10.8 (3), prayers. (+ other sense.)

Beame, 11.20 (5), shaft (of a spear). (+ other senses.)

Beare up (with), 12.1 (3), put the helm up towards, sail towards.

(Become); where is she become?, 10.16 (2), what has become of her?

Bed, 9.41 (5), bids, commands.

Bedeawd, 12.16 (9), bedewed.

Bedyde, 11.7 (3), dyed.

Beheast, 4.18 (3), 6. Arg., 6.26 (9), behest, command, bidding. (+ other sp.)

Behight, 10.50 (7), entrusted; 10.64 (6), to pronounce, name. (Probably archaic.)

Behot (a ppl. of *behight*), 10.38 (4), promised.

Bequeathed, 10.63 (7), entrusted.

Beseeme, 8.32 (2), 10.14 (2), 10.15 (8), 10.59 (4), to be fitting, suitable, seemly.

(Beseene); well beseene, 12.5 (3), appropriate; 12.8 (8), appropriate-looking.

Bestedd, 1.24 (1), situated, circumstanced.

Bet (p.t., ppl. of *beat*), 3.19 (1), beat; 6.5 (2), 7.28 (7), beaten.

Bethrall, 8.28 (6), to make captive. (Found only here; formed from *be* + *thrall*.)

Bever, 7.31 (6), beaver, movable part of helmet covering the face.

Bewaile, 6.1 (3), to cause, bring about. (This sense found only here.)

Bewray, 4.39 (3), 5.30 (7),. 7.38 (8), 9.16 (2), to accuse, reveal, betray.

Bidding . . . be(a)des, 1.30 (7), 10.3 (8), saying (his, her) prayers.

Bilive, 5.32 (3), 9.4 (1), quickly, forthwith.

Bit, 3.14 (4), 8.41 (3), (morsel of) food.

Blame, 2.18 (9), injury. (+ other senses; this sense last recorded here.)

Blent, 6.42 (4), ?connected (i.e. blended closely with), ?tainted.

Blesse, 2.18 (9), 7.12 (3), 9.28 (3), to protect, deliver; 5.6 (4), 8.22 (3), brandish. (This latter sense first recorded here.) (+ other senses.)

Blesse, 10. Arg., bliss. (+ other sp.)

Blunt, 10.47 (3), dim (of eyesight).

Bond, 1.3 (1), 12.28 (1), bound.

Boot, 4.49 (5), 5.23 (6), 8.7 (9), 11.41 (9), to avail; 3.20 (1), 3.40 (7), him booteth, her booteth: it avails him, her.

Bootlesse, 2.2 (4), 5.33 (5), 6.19 (8), 7.11 (9), unavailing(ly).

Bost, 3.24 (5), boast.

Boughtes, 1.15 (3), 11.11 (3), bends, folds.

Bounch, 2.11 (6), 8.30 (6), 8.37 (5), bunch, cluster. (+ other sp.)

Bound, 10.67 (4), to lead (of a way or path). (This sense first recorded here.) (+ other senses.)

Bowrs, 8.41 (6), muscles. (This sense first recorded here.)

Boystrous, 8.10 (1), rough and massive (of a club). (+ other sense.)

Brand, 3.42 (7), sword.

Bras, 10.40 (3), money; or possibly a copper or bronze coin. (If 'money', this would be the first record of this sense.) (+ other sense.)

Brast, 5.31 (8), 8.4 (9), 9.21 (7), burst, shattered.

Breares, 10.35 (3), briars.

Brent, 9.10 (6), 11.28 (1), burnt.

Broad, Pr. 1 (8), 4.16 (6), abroad. (+ other *broad*.)

Brond, 4.33 (3), 9.53 (7), brand, burning piece of wood. (+ other sp.)

Buffe, 2.17 (1), 11.24 (7), blow.

Bugle, 8.3 (5), wild ox.

Buxome, 12.37 (6), yielding.

C

Call, 8.46 (5), netted cap, head-covering of net. (Only once in Sp.)

Can (+verb), 1.8 (5), 1.50 (8), 2.29 (1), 4.46 (1), 11.23 (7), 11.39 (3), began (to), or in some cases (e.g. 2.29 (1)) simply indicates the p.t. of the verb. (See also *gan*, of which *can* was an originally Northern and North-midland equivalent.)

Canon bit, 7.37 (6), smooth, round bit (for horses). (This expression first recorded here.)

Canto, heading of first section of Book I (subsequent sections have *Cant.*) (First recorded here: from It. *canto* in the same use.)

Carefull, 1.44 (4), 5.52 (1), 6.6 (1), 6.33 (8), 7.22 (5), 7.28 (5), 7.39 (4), 8.15 (5), 9.15 (6), 10.29 (6), full of care, sorrow. (+ other senses.)

Carelesse, 1.41 (8), 1.53 (4), 2.45 (4), 3.17 (6), free from care, sorrow. (+ other sense.)

Carke, 1.44 (4), sorrow, grief.

Carle, 9.54 (2), churl, base fellow.

Carre, 2.1 (7), chariot, carriage.

Cast, 2.37 (3), 2.38 (3), 5.12 (6), 6.3 (6), 7.1 (4), 9.15 (6), 10.2 (8), 10.68 (2), 11.28 (7), 11.40 (6), to intend, resolve, plan. (+ other senses.)

Caytive (adj.), 5.45 (9), 7.19 (3), 8.32 (8), 9.11 (9), captive. (+ other sense.)

Centonell, 9.41 (8), sentinel.

Certes, 7.52 (3), 9.32 (1), indeed, certainly.

Chalenged, 4.20 (3), claimed. (+ other sense.)

Charet, 5.20 (6), 5.29 (9), 5.32 (2), 5.37 (2), 5.38 (5), 11.51 (7), chariot, carriage.

Chaufe, 3.33 (6), 7.37 (8), 12.35 (6), to chafe; 3.42 (6), 11.15 (6), to heat; 7.21 (5), to rub.

Chaunticlere, 2.1 (6), name for a cock. (Only once in Sp.)

Chaw, 4.30 (2), 4.30 (5), to chew, munch.

Chaw, 4.30 (4), jaw. (+ *jaw.*)

Chearen, 10.2 (8), to be made cheerful, be restored to health and spirits.

Cheere, 1.2 (8), 2.27 (5), 2.42 (1), 2.45 (6), 12.21 (4), countenance, facial expression, mien.

Chose, 5.14 (3), 10.10 (4), to choose. (+ other sp.)

Clift, 8.22 (6), 9.33 (3), 11.54 (5), cliff.

Clomb, 10.49 (9), climbed. (Probably archaic or dialectal.)

Coche, 4.16 (2), 4.17 (1), coach.

Compare, 4.28 (5), to acquire. (This sense last recorded in Sp.) (+ other senses.)

Conceiveth fire, 7.13 (5), ignites, catches fire.

Consort, 12.4 (7), accord.

Corse, 1.24 (9), 2.24 (6), 3.20 (5), 5.36 (9), 5.53 (2), 9.36 (5), 10.42 (2), corpse; 3.5 (6), 3.42 (3), 4.22 (8), 5.31 (2), 7.15 (6), 8.40 (8), 10.26 (2), 11.9 (3), 11.48 (8), (living) body.

Couch, 2.15 (3), 3.34 (4), 11.16 (1), (of spear) to lower for attack; 7.31 (6), 11.9 (2), to set, place.

Could, 10.39 (4), cold. (+ other sp.)

Counterfesaunce, 8.49 (6), deceit. (First recorded here: from Fr. *contrefaisance*.)

Covet, 10.59 (5), 12.20 (1), to desire.

Covetise, 4.29 (3), 4.31 (7), 5.46 (4), covetousness.

Creast, 8.6 (4), 12.2 (3), crest.

Croslet, 6.36 (6), small cross. (Only once in Sp.)

Cruddy, 5.29 (6), curdled.

Crudled, 7.6 (7), 9.52 (2), curdled, frozen. (*curdle, crudle,* first recorded here: a frequentative form of *curd,* 'to curdle'.)

Cure, 5.44 (6), charge, care. (+ other sense.)

Curious, 7.30 (7), 12.38 (7), ingenious, skilfully wrought, elaborate.

D

Daint, 10.2 (7), dainty. (First recorded here: probably a shortened form of *dainty*.)

Dainty, 2.27 (9), fastidiousness. (This sense first recorded here.) (+ other sense.)

Damnifyde, 11.52 (7), damaged.

Dant, 9.49 (3), to daunt, overwhelm.

Darrayne, 4.40 (2), 7.11 (5), to prepare for battle, to offer or engage in battle.

Date, 9.42 (5), 9.45 (7), assigned term of life.

Deare, 7.48 (7), hurt, injury.

Deaw, 1.36 (4), 1.39 (8), 12.6 (8), dew. (Also *deawy*.)

Deaw-burning, 11.35 (6), glittering with dew. (Apparently first recorded here, and once only in Sp.)

Debonaire, 2.23 (5), gracious, courteous.

Decay, 2.41 (8), 6.48 (7), 10.10 (9), ruin, destruction, death. (+ other uses.)

Deceived (of), 8.41 (4), denied, cheated of.

Deface, 3.29 (5), 5.24 (5), to put out of countenance, daunt, destroy. (+ other sense.)

Defeasance, 12.12 (4), defeat. (Only once in Sp.)

Deformed, 9.30 (5), 9.48 (6), hateful, terrible. (+ other uses.)

Defray, 5.42 (8), to appease.

Deluded, 2.2 (6), frustrated. (+ other uses.)

Deriv'd (to), 3.2 (9), transferred to, conveyed to.

Despight, 1.50 (3), 2.6 (4), 4.35 (4), 4.41 (5), 5.14 (5), 7.49 (6), 8.45 (7), 9.11 (9), 11.17 (6), 11.25 (7), 11.44 (1), anger, defiance, spite, malice.

Deteast, 4.21 (9), to detest.

Devise, 10.12 (1), 12.14 (3), 12.17 (9), 12.18 (2), to talk, converse. (+ other senses.)

Devoyd, 9.15 (1), void, empty. (This use without *of* first recorded here.) (+ other uses.)

Dight, 4.6 (6), 4.14 (8), 7.8 (1), 9.13 (3), 11.9 (6), 11.52 (3), 12.6 (6), 12.23 (9), 12.24 (1), 12.32 (4), to prepare, arrange, dress, adorn, decorate; 8.48 (4), (here) covered.

Disaventures, 9.45 (4), misfortunes.

Disaventurous, 7.48 (7), 9.11 (8), unfortunate, disastrous. (First recorded here: from *disa(d)venture*, on the model of *a(d)venturous*.)

Discrete, 7.40 (7), suitable, wise.

Disdaine, 1.14 (9), loathsomeness (first record of this sense); 1.19 (6), 2.8 (4), 2.39 (5), 8.13 (2), indignation, anger. (The modern sense,

'scorn', is also recorded and perhaps colours some of these uses.)

Disdaine, 1.1 (7), 11.23 (9), to dislike, be indignant (at). (There are examples of 'to scorn' also, some of which seem coloured by these other senses: likewise there is probably a touch of 'disdain' about 1.1 (7), and 11.23 (9).)

Disdainefull, 1.53 (7), 3.19 (6), 3.43 (6), 4.48 (4), angry. (+ 'scornful'. What was observed under the noun *disdaine* may also apply here.)

Disgrace, 2.38 (8), (here) to disfigure. (+ other senses.)

Disgrace, 3.29 (4), mischief, harm. (+ other senses.)

Dispiteous, 2.15 (2), cruel.

Display, 1.14 (7), 1.16 (3), 4.4 (4), 4.44 (1), 11.10 (1), 11.18 (1), 11.20 (7), to extend, stretch out, unfold (perhaps with some sense of 'display' also.) (+ other senses.)

Disple, 10.27 (2), to discipline (here, scourge). (Only once in Sp.)

Disport, 2.14 (1), entertainment, diversion.

Dispredden, 4.17 (9), to spread. (First recorded here: from *dis* + *spread* (vb.).)

Dissolute, 7.51 (3), weak.

Distaynd, 11.23 (8), stained.

Distraine, 7.38 (4), to oppress, afflict.

Dites, 8.18 (4), raises. (An apparently unique occurrence in this sense: *O.E.D.* describes this use as 'erroneous'.)

Diverse, 1.44 (2), ? diverting. (If so, a unique usage.) (+ other senses.)

Divide, 5.17 (7), a technical term of music: to perform divisions, i.e. rapid runs. (See note.) (This sense first recorded here.) (+ other senses.)

Do, 5.13 (2), to take. (+ other senses.)

Do . . . (to) die, 7.14 (7), 8.36 (4), 8.45 (7), 9.54 (8), 11.47 (9), to cause . . . to die, to put to death.

Doen, 10.59 (7), to do; 3.14 (8), 3.39 (8), 4.43 (9), 5.3 (9), 8.36 (4), 10.8 (4), 11.47 (9), 12.19 (6), done.

Donne, 10.33 (4), to do. (+ *donne*, 'done'.)

Doted, 8.34 (2), foolish, stupid.

Doubt, 6.1 (5), 11.33 (8), fear. (+ other senses.)

Dragonets, 12.10 (6), young dragons. (Only once in Sp.)

Dreary, 5.24 (1), 5.30 (7), 7.2 (1), 7.22 (1), 8.38 (1), 9.33 (4), 9.36 (5), doleful, gloomy, grim, terrible; 6.45 (5), gory, bloody. (This sense last recorded here.)

Dred, Pr. 4 (9), 6.2 (3), object of reverence.

Dreed, See *dred*.

Drere, 8.40 (9), gloom.

Dreriment, 2.44 (4), 11.32 (8), sorrow; 8.9 (4), terror. (First recorded in Sp.: from *dreary* + *ment*; cf. *merriment*.)

Drest, 9.54 (7), 11.15 (7), prepared. (+ other senses of *dress*.)

Drift, 2.9 (4), intention, aim. (+ other sense.)

Droome, 9.41 (9), drum. (Only once in Sp.)

Dry dropsie, 4.23 (7), ? dropsy causing thirst. (*Dropsy* only once in Sp.)

Dugs, 1.15 (6), 8.47 (6), breasts.

Dye, 2.36 (7), hazard, chance, luck.

E

Each where, 10.54 (7), everywhere.

Earne, 1.3 (6), 6.25 (9), 9.18 (5), to yearn. (First recorded in Sp.: app. a variant of *yearn*.)

Earst, 5.9 (5), 5.12 (3), 6.40 (7), 6.42 (7), 7.48 (4), 8.18 (3), 8.42 (4), 9.15 (3), 9.29 (6), 10.27 (9), 11.27 (8), 11.27 (9), 12.33 (7), previously.

Edifyde, 1.34 (5), built.

Eeke, 5.42 (8), to increase.

Efforce, 6.4 (9), to gain by force.

Effraide, 1.16 (1), scared, frightened. (This vb. last recorded here.) (Only once in Sp.)

Eft, 9.25 (3), again.

Eftsoones, 1.11 (8), 2.3 (1), 2.19 (2), 2.39 (6), 3.34 (3), 3.42 (6), 7.6 (4), 10.24 (4), 10.36 (1), 11.4 (4), 11.15 (5), 11.47 (7), 12.35 (4), soon after, forthwith.

Eke, Pr 4 (1), 1.48 (7), 3.21 (2), 3.35 (5), 4.23 (2), 4.29 (6), 4.32 (6), 4.48 (6), 4.50 (6), 6.36 (9), etc. (23 examples), also.

Eld, 8.47 (2), 10.8 (9), old age.

Elfe, 1.17 (1), 4.51 (4), 5.2 (6), 5.11 (1), 5.13 (8), 6.42 (1), 7.7 (7), one of the knights of Sp.'s 'faerie' land. (No similar use prior to Sp.)

Elfin, 1.46 (2), 2.43 (1), 4.13 (1), 4.39 (7), 4.42 (8), 4.49 (9), 5.22 (8), 6.1 (8), 10.44 (1), 10.65 (8), elf-like, pertaining to an elf (in Sp.'s special sense: see *Elfe* (above). (First recorded here; derived (obscurely) from *elf*.)

Elfin, 10.60 (2), elf. This sense first recorded here.)

Embard, 2.31 (3), 7.44 (8), confined, enclosed.

Embay, 9.13 (5), 10.27 (5), to bathe. (First recorded here: ? from *en* + *bay*, 'to bathe'. But this *bay* is app. itself a Sp. coinage: see *bayes* above.)

Embosse, 3.24 (4), 9.29 (2), 11.20 (3), to enclose, envelop, sink (in). (First recorded here: perhaps from *en* + *boss*, 'cask'.)

Embowd, 9.19 (2), ? encircled.

Emboyled, 11.28 (1), (here) ?panting, ?agitated. (First recorded here: from *en* + *boil* (vb.).)

Embrew, See *imbrew*.

Empa(i)re, 7.41 (9), 9.2 (1), 10.63 (5), to impair, weaken.

Empassioned, 3.2 (1), deeply moved. (App. first recorded here: O.E.D. derives from It. *impassionare*.)

Empeach, 8.34 (9), to hinder.

Emperst, 11.53 (8), pierced.

Emprize, 9.1 (4), 12.18 (4), undertaking, enterprise, adventure.

-En, archaic ending of the infinitive of vbs., the pres. pl. of vbs., and the plural of some nouns. *-en* possibly archaic also in *withouten* (6.27 (9)).

Enchace, 12.23 (5), to adorn, embellish (with engraved figures, or figures resembling engraving).

Enfouldred, 11.40 (2), ? black as a thunder-cloud. (App. recorded only here: probably from *en* + OF *fouldre*, 'thunderbolt'.)

Engorged, 11.40 (5), swallowed.

Engrave, 10.42 (2), to bury, entomb.

Enhaunst, 1.17 (8), 5.47 (6), raised, lifted up.

Enlargen, 8.37 (9), to set free.

Emmove, 2.21 (6), 7.38 (9), to move, affect with emotion.

Enmoved, 9.48 (1), moved with anxiety, disturbed. (cf. *emmove*.)

Enraung'd, 12.7 (8), at large, ranging. (First recorded in Sp.: from *en* + *range* (noun or vb.).

App. found only in Sp.) (+ other senses.)

Ensample, 4.1 (9), 5.52 (2), 6.1 (9), 8.16 (3), 8.44 (7), 9.12 (1), example.

Enterprizd, 7.45 (2), endeavoured.

Entirely, 11.32 (4), earnestly.

Entraile, 1.16 (4), fold, coil. (First recorded here: from *entrail* (vb.).) (+ other *entrail*(s).)

Envy, 9.1 (6), to grudge. (+ other senses.)

Equall, 8.27 (7), 9.47 (2), impartial. (+ other senses.)

Errant, 2.34 (9), 4.38 (4), 10.10 (1), 12.27 (4), wandering.

Erst, See *earst*.

Esloyne, 4.20 (1), to remove, detach. (Only here in Sp.)

Essoyne, 4.20 (3), exemption. (Only here in Sp.)

Eugh, 1.9 (4), yew.

Ewghen, 11.19 (2), made of yew.

Excheat, 5.25 (9), gain, exchange.

Expire, 7.9 (7), (here) to give birth. (Appears to be a unique use of the word: not recorded in O.E.D.); 11.45 (5), to breathe out. (First record of this sense; though *breathe one's last* current.) (+ other senses.)

Extirpe, 10.25 (6), to extirpate, totally destroy. (Only here in Sp.)

Eyas hauke, 11.34 (6), young hawk.

Eyne, eyen, eien, Pr 4 (5), 2.27 (6), 4.9 (6), 4.21 (4), 8.21 (9), 9.15 (4), 9.35 (6), 10.47 (3), 10.67 (6), 11.14 (7), eyes.

F

Fact, 4.34 (7), 9.37 (7), evil deed.

Fain(e), fayn(e), 1.6 (9), 4.10 (7), 6.12 (9), 6.19 (9), 7.21 (2), 9.25 (3),

9.34 (8), 10.62 (5), 11.37 (7), glad, gladly.

Faine, 7.1 (5), 7.38 (7), 12.35 (8), to feign.

Falsed, 2.30 (3), deceived.

Falsed (hast), 9.46 (7), (hast) been false to.

Far renowmed, 5.5 (1), 5.43 (6), far-famed, renowned afar.

Fatall, 9.7 (1), ordained by fate. (+ other senses; though they are also coloured by this one.)

Fattie, 1.21 (3), rich, fertilizing. (First record of this sense; and only here in Sp.)

Faytor, 4.47 (4), 12.35 (5), deceiver, villain. (Probably archaic.)

Fearefull, 1.13 (9), 2.24 (1), 2.28 (7), 3.19 (2), 3.20 (6), 3.22 (1), 6.28 (1), 6.38 (6), 9.30 (4), alarmed, frightened.

Feld, 8.47 (7), ? fallen. (+ the sense 'felled'.)

Fell, 2.10 (6), 2.15 (4), 6.10 (3), 6.25 (1), 6.26 (5), 6.43 (1), 8.32 (7), 8.39 (6), 11.2 (5), 11.24 (2), 11.31 (8), fierce.

Felly, 5.34 (6), fiercely.

(Felt); themselves not felt, 7.6 (6), did not feel themselves (to be changed). (+ other senses.)

Fere, 10.4 (8), companion, husband.

Fervent, 7.4 (7), hot. (+ other senses.)

File, 1.35 (7), to polish, smoothe (the tongue).

Fit, 11.7 (1), strain (of music). (+ other senses.)

Flaggy, 11.10 (1), drooping.

Flit, 4.5 (5), to give way. (+ other senses.)

Foltring, 7.4 (7), 9.24 (9), stammering.

Fond, 9.39 (7), foolish.

Fone, 2.23 (8), foes.

Food, 8.9 (3), feud. (A common 16th C. spelling.)

Fool happie, 6.1 (6), fortunate. (Seems to be first recorded here.) (Only once in Sp.)

Fordonne, 5.41 (8), 10.33 (7), 10.47 (8), 10.60 (4), exhausted, ruined utterly. (Exact senses difficult to determine.)

Foreby, 6.39 (8), 7.2 (7), 10.36 (2), close by, near.

Forecast, 4.34 (8), 4.45 (2), to think beforehand, plan.

Forelifting, 11.15 (2), lifting up in front. (Seems first recorded here: only once in Sp.)

Forespent, 9.43 (7), utterly wasted. (Only once in Sp.)

Forlore, 10.21 (5), worthless. (+ other sense.)

Forlorne, 7.19 (4), (left) abandoned. (+ other uses, some of which are possibly to be included here.)

Forrayed, 12.3 (9), ravaged, harrassed.

Forthright, 4.6 (1), at once.

Forwandring, 6.34 (3), wandering astray.

Forwasted, 1.5 (8), 11.1 (3), laid waste, utterly ravaged.

Forewearied, 1.32 (5), 9.13 (1 10.17 (4), 11.45 (8), tired out, exhausted.

Forworne, 6.35 (1), worn out. (Only once in Sp.)

Fraight, 12.35 (2), fraught, laden.

Frame, 8.30 (3), to support, steady. (+ other senses.)

Francklin, 10.6 (4), freeholder. (Only once in Sp.)

Fraught, 7.13 (3), filled. (+ other senses.)

Fraunces fire (St.), 4.35 (8), erisypelas. (See note.) (Only once in Sp.)

Fray, 1.38 (5), 1.52 (9), 3.19 (3), 12.11 (7), to frighten.

Freakes, 3.1 (4), 4.50 (1), 12.16 (8), whims, caprices.

Free, 2.11 (8), 3.33 (3), 9.12 (7), 9.27 (4), 10.6 (4), noble. (+ other senses.)

Frounce, 4.14 (7), to wave, wrinkle (of hair). (Only once in Sp.)

Fry, 12.7 (1), swarms, troops (of children).

G

Gage, 4.39 (5), 11.41 (6), pledge, security, token.

Gall, 1.19 (6), 2.6 (4), 7.3 (9), bile, bitter substance, asperity, rancour.

Gan (p.t. of *gin*, which see below. See also *can*.):
- (1) **Gan,** 6.38 (1), began.
- (2) **Gan to** (+ vb.), 1.17 (5), 1.42 (5), etc. (37 examples), began to . . .
- (3) **Gan** + vb. (without *to*), 1.50 (5), 1.55 (6), etc. (76 examples), began to, or equivalent to the p.t. of the vb. (It is often difficult to know which use is involved.)

Gate, 1.13 (4), way. (This sense last recorded here.) (+ other *gate*.)

Gent, 9.6 (1), 9.27 (6), noble, gracious.

Gentle, Pr. 1 (5), Pr. 3 (8), 1.1 (1), 1.55 (2), 3.34 (1), 7.6 (1), 7.37 (1), 7.40 (1), 8.39 (4), 9.3 (9), 9.17 (1), 9.24 (7), 9.37 (3), 10.7 (1), 12.16 (7), 12.33 (8), noble, chivalrous; 4.13 (3), well-born. (+ other sense, 'gentle': but there is considerable

sense-mixture in most examples of this word in Sp.)

German, 5.10 (8), 5.13 (2), brother.

Gest, 10.15 (9), exploit, deed of arms.

Ghesse, 6.13 (1), 6.40 (4), 8.34 (4), 12.34 (8), to guess.

Gin (see also *can, gan*):
- (1) **Gin to** (+ vb.), 1.21 (1), 1.21 (5), 1.23 (2), 6.9 (7), 6.17 (1), 7.21 (9), to begin to . . .
- (2) **Gin** + vb. (without *to*), 11.21 (7), ? to begin to, or equivalent to the p.t. of the vb.

Gin, 5.35 (7), instrument (of torture).

Girlond, 1.48 (9), 2.30 (7), 2.37 (5), 4.7 (2), 4.22 (3), 5.5 (9), 6.13 (9), 7.4 (5), 7.45 (6), 10.54 (5), 12.6 (6), 12.8 (6), garland.

Giusts, 1.1 (9), jousts, encounters on horseback.

Glee, 5.16 (7), 9.14 (1), 10.6 (5), 10.15 (7), joy, pleasure; 9.32 (7), beauty, bright colour.

Glitterand, 4.16 (9), 7.29 (4), glittering.

Gnarre, 5.34 (6), to snarl, growl. (Only once in Sp.)

Go, 4.23 (2), 4.29 (8), to walk. (+ other senses.)

Gobbets, 1.20 (3), 11.13 (3), small lumps (of flesh).

Graile, 7.6 (2), gravel. (First recorded here: ? a contraction of *gravel*.)

(Graine); in graine, 7.1 (4), in a fast colour, thoroughly (dyed). (+ other *grain*.)

Grate, 8.37 (6), grating. (Only once in Sp.)

Grate, 1.19 (6), to fret, be affected painfully or unhappily.

Gree, 5.16 (4), good will, pleasure.

Greedily, 4.40 (1), eagerly, fiercely. (+ other senses.)

Greedy, 1.14 (1), 5.6 (6), 6.5 (3), 8.29 (3), 8.48 (7), eager. (+ other senses.)

Grenning, 6.11 (7), grinning.

Griefe, 11.38 (8), 11.44 (1), pain. (+ other uses.)

Griesie, 9.35 (4), ?grizzled. (If so, the first instance of this usage and the only one in Sp.) But the word may be coloured by, or even be, *grysie*, 'hideous', recorded elsewhere in Sp.

Griesly, 1.37 (4), 4.11 (1), 5.20 (1), 5.30 (5), 9.21 (4), 11.12 (8), grim, terrible.

Grieve, 8.17 (4), 9.7 (9), 11.28 (1), to hurt, injure. (+ other uses.)

Griple, 4.31 (7), grasping, niggardly.

Groning, 5.23 (4), sorrowful. (+ other senses.)

(Ground); on ground, 9.7 (9), 12.32 (3), in the world, anywhere.

Grudging (adj.), 2.19 (7), complaining.

Gryfon, 5.8 (2), griffin (a fabulous animal).

Guerdon, 3.40 (3), 7.15 (2), 10.59 (8), reward.

H

Habiliments, 3.17 (7), 6.30 (7), 12.5 (3), clothing, attire.

Hable, 11.19 (6), 12.5 (7), able, skilful.

Hagard, 11.19 (5), wild, untamed. (Only once in Sp.)

Hanging (adj.), 2.16 (6), doubtful, in the balance. (Only once in Sp.)

Hardiment, 1.14 (1), 9.12 (6), courage, boldness.

Hardy-hed, 4.38, (7), boldness

audacity. (First recorded in Sp. from *hardy* + *-head*.)

Harrowd, 10.40 (8), robbed, despoiled.

Hartlesse, 9.24 (3), disheartened.

Haught, 6.29 (5), haughty, proud.

Haughtie, 11.7 (7), (here) high-pitched. (But n.b. other (familiar) meanings of the word, also found in Book I.)

Heape, 4.5 (1), building, collection of buildings. (Apparently a unique usage, not recorded by the *O.E.D.*)

(Heare); so evill heare, 5.23 (7), fare so evilly, are so unfortunate. (This use of *hear* is imitated from Gk. (εὖ) ἀκούειν, L. (*male*) *audire*, 'be (ill) spoken of', but app. with altered sense. Only once in Sp.)

Heben, Pr. 3 (5), 7.37 (2), ebony.

Heft, 11.39 (6), heaved. (+ *heaved.*)

Henge, 11.21 (8), hinge. (This word once only in Sp.)

Hew, 1.46 (9), 2.40 (6), 2.45 (5), 3.11 (9), 4.33 (7), 5.5 (8), 5.20 (5), 6.38 (5), 7.35 (9), 8.38 (6), 8.42 (9), 9.16 (2), 9.20 (8), 9.24 (3), aspect, appearance, hue.

Hight (1), 2.44 (1), 7.46 (4), 9.14 (9), 9.27 (3), 9.32 (5), 10.5 (8), 10.7 (6), 10.12 (6), 10.14 (1), 10.55 (8), 12.32 (2), 12.32 (3), (is), (was), called. (Probably archaic.)

Hight (2), 4.6 (3), entrusted. (One of a number of senses peculiar to Sp., and app. derived by him from *Hight* (1). See *O.E.D.*)

(Hight); on hight, 5.16 (8), 8.7 (3), 12.6 (9), on high. (This phrase app. last recorded in Sp.)

Holme, 1.9 (9), holm-oak.

(Hond); out of hond, 12.3 (7), immediately, at once.

Hore, 3.10 (6), 10.3 (5), hoary, gray.

Horrid, 6.25 (3), terrible; 7.31 (1), rough, bristling. (First recorded here.)

Horror, 6.11 (6), roughness. (+ other senses.)

Hot, 11.29 (8), was called. (App. last recorded here; archaic (originally ppl.) form from the same vb. as *hight* above.)

Housling, 12.37 (4), sacramental. (Only once in Sp.)

Hove, 2.31 (8), to stand on end (of hair).

Humblesse, 2.21 (4), 3.26 (9), 12.8 (3), 12.25 (6), humility.

Humour, 1.36 (2), 9.13 (5), moisture. (+ other *humour*.)

Hurtlen, 4.16 (3), jostle. (+ other uses.)

Husher, 4.13 (3), usher. (Only once in Sp.)

Hire, 5.10 (7), 9.46 (3), 10.68 (5), wages, payment, reward.

I

Idle, 1.46 (1), 5.8 (4), 5.51 (7), 7.19 (6), 8.8 (2), 9.10 (1), 9.31 (1), 11.17 (3), 12.9 (8), 12.30 (1), 12.35 (8), vain, empty, useless, pointless. The sense of 'lazy' is perhaps also present in some of these examples.

Ill (adj.), 5.31 (9), evil, wicked.

Ill favored, 1.15 (7), evil-looking; 8.46 (8), ugly. (But perhaps a blend of both meanings in both cases.)

Imbrew, 6.38 (7), 7.17 (9), 7.47 (3), 11.36 (7), to soak, be soaked, drenched.

Impatience, 8.17 (4), want of endurance.

Impatient, 8.11 (2), 11.25 (6), 12.30 (2), intolerant (of), suffering with difficulty.

Impe, Pr. 3 (1), 1.26 (2), 6.24 (1), 9.6 (1), 10.60 (1), 11.5 (7), child, offspring.

Imperceable, 11.17 (7), un-pierceable. (Only once in Sp.)

Implyes, 4.31 (5), 6.6 (7), 11.23 (5), enfolds, entangles.

Improvided, 12.34 (3), unforseen, unlooked-for. (Only here in Sp.)

In, 1.33 (7), lodging.

Incontinent, 6.8 (5), 9.19 (5), straightaway, immediately.

Inly, 1.4 (6), 9.24 (8), 10.8 (8), inwardly.

Inspire, 7.9 (4), to quicken, make fertile. (A particularly imaginative use: no other sense at the time quite like this.)

Intended, 11.38 (2), stretched out. (This sense first recorded here: one of a group of senses introduced in the later 16th C. and after, directly from Latin.) (+ other senses.)

Intendiment, 12.31 (3), careful consideration. (This sense first recorded here.)

Invent, 6.15 (2), to find, discover.

Irkesome, 1.55 (5), 2.6 (5), tired. (This sense last recorded here.); 3.4 (1), distressing, painful, loathesome.

J

Jolly, 1.1 (8), 2.11 (7), 5.37 (1), 12.42 (1), handsome, excellent.

Journall, 11.31 (4), diurnal, daily. (This sense first recorded here: first use of the word as an adj.)

Joy, 2.3 (9), 6.1 (6), 6.17 (8), 10.15 (4), to be cheerful, rejoice, delight (in).

Joyaunce, 4.37 (8), 11.15 (4),

delight, gladness. (First recorded in Sp.: from *joy* (vb.) + *ance*.)

K

(Keepe); takes keepe, 1.40 (9), takes heed.

Keeping, 11.2 (4), watch, guard. (+ other sense.)

Kend, 12.1 (4), known, (here) seen.

Kest, 11.31 (5), cast (ppl.).

Kilt (ppl.), 5.26 (5), 10.57 (5), killed. (+ *kild*.)

Kindly, 3.28 (7), 8.11 (6), 9.9 (3), 10.18 (1), 10.47 (4), natural.

Kirtle, 4.31 (1), tunic, gown.

Knees, 9.34 (3), rocky projections. (This sense first recorded here (the only example in Sp.), and app. rare.) (+ other sense.)

L

Lam, 10.57 (6), lamb.

Languor, 1.52 (7), sorrow; 7.49 (2), sorrowful plight. (N.B. the present-day sense of this word was not yet current.)

Launch, 3.42 (8), 4.46 (5), 7.25 (7), 9.29 (3), to pierce.

Lay-stall, 5.53 (2), refuse-tip. (Only once in Sp.)

Lazars, 4.3 (6), lepers. (Only once in Sp.)

Leach, 5.17 (2), 5.44 (1), 5.44 (6), 10.23 (7), physician.

Leake, 5.35 (9), leaky.

Leasing, 6.48 (1), lie, falsehood.

Least, 1.12 (2), 2.31 (5), 3.20 (9), etc., lest.

Leman, 1.6 (7), 7.14 (9), sweetheart, lover; 1.48 (6), loose woman.

Lenger, 1.26 (8), 3.39 (9), 5.19 (3), 5.52 (3), 7.2 (4), 7.22 (3), 9.2 (4), 9.30 (2), 9.43 (1), longer. (This form last recorded in Sp.; Sp. also

has *longer* (twice in Bk. I).)

Let, 8.13 (5), hindrance.

Let, 7.20 (4), to hinder. (+ *let*, 'to allow'.)

Lever (comparative of *liefe*), 9.32 (9), rather. (i.e. *lever had I die*, 'I would rather die'.)

Libbard, 6.25 (8), leopard.

Liefe, 3.28 (9), 9.17 (9), beloved (one), darling.

Light, 1.55 (2), wanton. (+ other senses.)

Lignage, 6.20 (3), 9. Arg., 9.3 (3), 9.5 (6), family, descent, lineage.

Lilled, 5.34 (4), lolled (the tongue). (Only once in Sp.)

Lin, 1.24 (5), 5.35 (4), to cease.

List, 2.22 (4), 10.20 (1), to choose, desire; 7.35 (5), 7.35 (8), 9.2 (4), 11.10 (6), in the same sense, but used impersonally with the oblique case of the pronoun.

Lively (adj.), 1.45 (4), lifelike; 2.24 (1), 7.20 (8), living.

(Loft); upon the loft, 1.41 (3), in the air. (This sense last recorded here.)

Longs, 4.48 (6), belongs. (+ other sense.)

Lout, 1.30 (1), 10.44 (6), to bow.

Lustlesse, 4.20 (7), listless, feeble.

Lynage (another form of *lignage*), 1.5 (3), lineage, descent.

M

Maine, 7.11 (2), 8.7 (7), 11.43 (4), might, strength. (Last recorded in Sp. except in the phrase *might and main*.)

Make, 7.7 (8), 7.15 (5), companion, mate.

Mall, 7.51 (4), club, large wooden hammer.

Many (noun), 12.9 (1), crowd, multitude.

Mart, Pr. 3 (7), Mars. (The form *Mars* also appears.)

Mart, 3. Arg., ?business, ?pursuits. (Only once in Sp.)

Massie, 7.33 (6), massive.

Mated, 9.12 (2), overcome, defeated.

Mayne, See *maine.*

Maynly, 7.12 (1), powerfully, mightily, violently.

Meane, Pr. 1 (7), lowly.

Meed, 1.9 (1), 2.37 (5), 3.36 (3), 4.39 (8), 7.14 (9), 7.23 (9), 10.68 (4), reward.

Meere, 3.28 (5), pure, complete.

Mell, 1.30 (9), to meddle.

Member, 2.31 (9), 5.38 (7), 8.6 (9), limb.

Menage, 7.37 (5), to manage, handle (a horse).

Ment, 2.5 (4), joined.

Mery, 10.61 (9), pleasant, agreeable. (+ other senses.)

Mew, 5.20 (4), den, place of confinement.

Minisht, 11.43 (8), diminished. (Only once in Sp.)

Mirkesome, 5.28 (3), murky, dark. (First recorded here: from *murk + -some.* Only once in Sp.)

Misdeeme, 2.3 (8), 4.2 (2), 7.49 (4), 11.55 (4), to misjudge, mistake.

Misdiet, 4.23 (8), wrong feeding.

Mishappen, 3.20 (9), to happen amiss. (Only once in Sp.)

Misseeming, 7.50 (8), false show. (First recorded here: from *mis + seeming.*)

Misseeming, 8.42 (9), 9.23 (9), unseemly.

(Mister); what mister (wight), 9.23 (2), what kind of (person). (This idiom archaic.)

Misweening, 4.1 (6), mistaking.

(Last record of this noun: the vb. *misween* was in some use, however, and is first recorded in Sp.)

Mo(e), 4.35 (6), 5.50 (9), 9.44 (9), more. (Originally the comparative of the adv., and distinct from *more* (also found in Book I) the comparative of the adj.)

Mossy hore, 9.4 (6), hoary with moss. (Only once in Sp.)

Mote, 2.29 (6), 2.37 (8), 2.43 (6), etc., might, could. (Acc. to *O.E.D.* this word did not survive in colloquial use after *c.* 1550.)

Mother pearle, 7.30 (9), mother-of-pearl. (Only once in Sp.)

Mought, 1.42 (3), could, was able to.

Mould, 2.39 (9), 4.5 (3), 7.22 (4), 7.26 (5), 7.33 (6), 10.42 (6), shape, form.

Muchell, 4.46 (4), 6.20 (5), much, great. (Probably archaic.)

N

Name, 12.13 (8), reputation. (+ other senses.)

Nathelesse, 9.54 (8), 11.52 (9), nevertheless.

Nathemore, 8.13 (6), 9.25 (6), none the more, not the more. (Last recorded in Sp.)

Nephewes, 5.22 (7), 5.23 (9), 5.26 (5), 5.41 (9), grandchildren, descendants.

New fanglenesse, 4.25 (4), novelty, innovation.

Nicer, 8.40 (3), too fastidious.

Ni'll, 9.15 (9), will not.

Noblesse, 8.26 (7), nobleness.

Nosethrill, 11.22 (9), nostril.

Note, 12.17 (4), know not (?arch.).

N'ould, 6.17 (8), would not. (This form first recorded in Sp.: probably, like *ygo* (for *ago*) and others, an imitation or 'pseudo'-archaism.)

Nouriture, 9.5 (4), training, education.

Noursled (up), 6.23 (8), reared, brought up, educated. (This vb. seems first recorded here: a variant of *nousle* (in the same sense) blended with *nurse* (vb.).)

Noyance, 1.23 (7), annoyance.

Noyce, 6.8 (3), noise. (+ *noise*, etc.)

Noyd, 10.24 (3), 11.45 (2), hurt, harmed. (Prob. archaic.)

Noyous, 5.45 (1), 8.40 (2), 11.50 (9), noxious, harmful, irksome.

O

Ofspring, 6.30 (4), (here) origin, source whence one springs.

Origane, 2.40 (7), wild marjoram. (Only once in Sp.)

Ought, 4.39 (7), possessed. (+ other *ought*.)

Outrage, 11.40 (1), (here) ?furious clamour.

Outrageous, 2.18 (7), 6.9 (4), 8.13 (8), 11.25 (2), 11.53 (3), mighty, violent, furious.

Outwell, 1.21 (3), to pour forth. (First recorded here.)

Overcraw, 9.50 (5), to exult over. (This form first recorded here, though *overcrow* is found from 1562.)

Owches, 2.13 (5), 10.31 (6), ornaments, jewels.

P

Paire, 7.41 (8), to impair, weaken. (Only once in Sp.)

Paled, 5.5 (3), enclosed with a pale (i.e. fence). (Only once in Sp.)

Palfrey, 1.4 (7), 2.13 (7), 3.8 (8), 3.40 (9), saddle-horse; i.e. an ordinary riding horse as distinct from a war-horse.

Pall, 4.16 (4), 7.16 (3), 8.46 (2), cloak, robe, mantle (esp. of a rich material).

Pap, 9.3 (7), nipple, breast.

Parbreake, 1.20 (9), vomiting. (Only once in Sp., and seems to be a rare word.)

Pardale, 6.26 (4), leopard. (Only once in Sp.)

Passionate, 12.16 (2), to express with feeling. (Once only in Sp.)

Paynim (noun and adj.), 3.35 (1), 3.40 (6), 4.41 (1), 4.44 (9), 5.10 (1), 5.29 (2), 6.5 (9), 6.38 (9), 6.39 (5), 6.47 (9), 7.20 (3), 7.26 (4), 11.7 (4), 12.18 (8), pagan, heathen.

Peece, 10.59 (3), work of art, structure. (This sense app. first recorded here.)

Pennes, 11.10 (4), quills. (Only once in Sp.)

Perdie, 6.42 (6), a mild oath. (From OF *par dé*, lit. 'by God'.)

Pere, 8.7 (6), champion. (+ other senses.)

Persant, 10.47 (5), piercing.

Pight, 2.42 (7), 8.37 (6), 9.33 (3), 11.25 (5), 11.43 (9), 12.25 (7), placed, set, fixed.

Pine, 4.21 (7), 8.40 (8), 10.48 (9), to waste away (through privation, hunger). (+ other sense.)

Pine, 9.35 (8), starvation, famine.

Pittifull, 12.16 (1), full of pity; 12.16 (3), to be pitied.

Playnd, 1.47 (8), complained, lamented.

Platane, 1.9 (8), plane-tree. (Only once in Sp.)

Pledges, 10.4 (9), (here) children. (This sense first recorded here.) (+ other senses.)

(Point); armed to point, 1.16 (6), 2.12 (6), fully armed.

Points, 9.41 (8), appoints. (+ other *point* (vb.).)

Pollicie, 4.12 (7), statecraft (with suggestion of intrigue and cunning, as commonly with this word at the time.)

Portesse, 4.19 (1), breviary. (Only once in Sp.)

Posterne, 5.52 (7), small back gate or door.

Pouldred, 7.12 (4), pulverized, reduced to powder.

Pounces, 11.19 (7), claws of a hawk (or other bird of prey).

Pourtrahed, 8.33 (7), portrayed.

Poynant, 7.19 (7), sharp.

Poyse, 11.54 (7), weight; hence, heavy fall.

Practicke, 12.34 (5), cunning.

Prancke, 4.14 (8), to show off, display.

Praunce, 7.11 (3), to swagger, strut arrogantly.

Pray, 9.20 (3), to prey on. (App. first recorded here in this sense, and a rare usage.) (+ other vb. *pray*.)

Preace, 12.19 (4), to press.

Prease, 3.3 (3), press, throng.

Presage, 10.61 (1), to point out. (This sense first recorded here.)

Presume, 4.9 (2), (here) to venture in. (+ other sense.)

Pretence, 12.24 (7), show, (here) concern.

Prick, 1.1 (1), 2.8 (4), 3.33 (2), to spur a horse, ride on horseback; 9.12 (5), to urge forth. (+ other senses.)

Price, 5.26 (4), 9.37 (9), to pay the price of, pay for. (This sense last recorded here.)

Priefe, 8.43 (6), 9.17 (8), (a) testing; 10.24 (5), efficacy.

Prime, 2.40 (4), 6.13 (5), springtime. (+ other uses.)

(Privitie); in privitie, 9.5 (5), in private.

Prove, 1.50 (6), 4.13 (9), 4.26 (4), 5.24 (8), 8.21 (3), 11.17 (9), 12.11 (9), to test, try out. (There may be other instances, since it is sometimes difficult to know whether this or the sense 'prove' (also current) is intended.)

Prowes, 9.17 (8), of bravery, valour.

Prowest, 4.41 (7), 5.14 (2), bravest. (*O.E.D.* notes that the adj. *prow* was app. obsolete from the 16th C., but the superlative *prowest* 'was much affected by Spenser', whence its appearance in later poets.)

Puissance, 1.3 (7), 2.17 (4), 3.7 (2), 3.35 (6), 3.42 (2), 8.16 (3), 8.32 (7), 10.20 (9), 11.24 (3), 11.43 (5), strength, prowess, valour.

Puissant, 6.45 (3), 10.17 (8), 10.66 (9), 11.16 (6), 11.17 (9), powerful.

Purchase, 3.16 (9), robbery.

Purfled, 2.13 (3), fringed, bordered, embroidered (on the edge).

Purpose(s), 2.30 (2), 7.38 (7), 12.13 (9), conversation, discourse. (+ other senses.)

Purveyance, 12.13 (5), provision.

Pyne, See *pine*.

Q

Quayd, 8.14 (8), subdued. (Found only here: *O.E.D.* suggests ?an alteration of *quail* (vb.).)

Quight, See *quit, quite*.

Quit, 5.11 (4), 6.6 (9), 6.10 (8), 8.10 (4), 10.63 (9), to free, release.

Quite, 1.30 (2), to respond (to);

2.17 (3), 8.26 (9), 8.27 (9), 10.15 (8), 10.37 (7), 10.67 (1), to repay, reward.

R

Rablement, 6.8 (7), 12.9 (2), rabble.

Raft (p.t. of *reave*), 1.24 (8), took away (i.e. cut off).

Rage, 8.11 (6), (strong) feeling. (+ other senses.)

Raile, 6.43 (7), to flow, gush. (+ other sense.)

Raine, 7.24 (5), rule, mastery.

Rampe, 3.5 (2), 5.28 (9), 8.12 (3), 11.33 (7), to bound, prance; 3.41 (5), to raise the fore-paws.

Rapt, 4.9 (8), carried away.

Raskall, 7.35 (5), 12.9 (1), base, worthless.

Raught, 6.29 (2), 7.18 (2), reached; 9.51 (2), handed (to).

Ravine, 5.8 (5), 7.44 (4), 11.12 (9), prey, plunder.

Read, 1.13 (8), 10.17 (5), to advise. (+ other senses.)

Reave, 3.36 (2), 11.41 (6), to rob, take away, wrench.

Rebellowed, 8.11 (4), re-echoed loudly. (First recorded here.)

Rebut, 2.15 (9), to recoil; 11.53 (5), to make recoil.

Recoyle, 10.17 (5), to retreat, return. (+ other senses.)

Recure, 5.44 (9), 9.2 (2), 10.24 (7), 10.52 (9), 11.30 (4), to recover, cure, restore to health and vigour.

Red, 7.46 (7), named, called; 8.33 (4), understood; 11.46 (4), declared. (+ other senses.)

Redoubted, 4.40 (2), terrible, fierce. (+ other uses.)

Redound, 6.30 (9), to proceed, issue.

Redounding, 3.8 (1), overflowing.

Redresse, 5.36 (9), to restore, cure.

Reed, 1.21 (9), to see, perceive. (This sense first recorded here, and found only in Sp.) (Other senses of this word also found in Book I.)

Reele, 5.35 (3), to (cause to) roll. (+ other vb. *reel*.)

Reft (p.t. and ppl. of *reave*), 3.41 (6), 6.39 (6), 9.26 (9), 9.31 (8), 10.65 (6), 12.39 (8), robbed, taken away, deprived (of).

Reherce, reherse, 4.50 (9), 9.48 (4), to relate, tell.

Remorse, 3.5 (8), 5.53 (4), pity. (+ other uses.)

Rencountring, 4.39 (9), engaging in battle. (+ other sense.)

Renowmed, 7.17 (1), 10.3 (2), 11.2 (8), 12.15 (6), renowned, famous.

Renverst, 4.41 (9), reversed, upside-down. (First recorded here.)

Repaire, 1.39 (3), 6.30 (3), to make (one's) way; 4.37 (7), to approach. (+ other senses.)

Respire, 9.8 (9), 11.28 (7), to rest. (This sense first recorded here.) (The sense 'to breathe' also recorded in Book I.)

Repining, 2.17 (6), fierce, furious; 3.36 (5), restless, discontented.

Repriefe, 9.29 (4), reproof.

Retrate, 1.13 (5), 8.12 (7), to retreat.

Reverse, 9.48 (5), to bring back. (This sense last recorded here.)

Revoke, 1.12 (7), 6.28 (3), to call back.

Riddes, 1.36 (5), sends away.

Riotise, 4.20 (5), 5.46 (5), riotous conduct. (First recorded here: from *riot* (noun) + *-ise*.)

Rode, 12.42 (2), sheltered, near-shore anchorage. (Only once in Sp.)

Roome, 2.1 (9), 9.41 (8), place. (+ other senses.)

Rove, Pr. 3 (3), to shoot at.

Rude, 3.11 (3), 3.13 (2), 6.8 (7), 6.9 (9), 12.9 (2), 12.23 (4), 12.35 (3), simple, unsophisticated, rough, crude; 11.38 (2), roughly.

Rudely, 1.25 (2), 1.42 (4), 2.15 (7), 3.35 (8), 3.41 (3), 8.25 (3), 11.9 (6), 11.16 (3), 11.16 (8), roughly, heavily, crudely.

Ruefulnesse, 4.25 (7), dolefulness, dejection. (Only once in Sp.)

Ruffin, 4.34 (1), ruffianly, disordered. (Only once in Sp.)

Rusty, 5.32 (2), rust-coloured. (+ 'rusty'.)

Ruth, 1.50 (8), 5.9 (7), 6.12 (7), 8.39 (4), pity, compassion; 2. Arg., pitiable situation.

S

Sacred, 8.35 (9), accursed. (+ other senses.)

Sad, 1.2 (8), 1.29 (5), 7.11 (5), 10.7 (3), 12.5 (3), 12.15 (4), 12.15 (7), 12.21 (4), grave, sober, serious; 1.4 (6), 1.19 (1), etc. (47 examples), sad, melancholy; 1.36 (2), heavy; 3.10 (9), firm, steady. (The exact sense is often difficult to determine; sometimes a combination of one or more senses may be involved.)

Sallow, 1.9 (5), (kind of) willow.

Salvage, 3.5 (3), 3.42 (2), 6. Arg., 6.11 (3), 6.19 (3), 6.21 (8), 6.23 (4), wild, savage, fierce.

Sam, 10.57 (8), together. (Probably archaic.)

Say, 4.31 (1), fine-textured cloth, resembling serge.

Scald, 8.47 (3), a scabby disease (esp. of the scalp). (Once only in Sp.)

Scape, 4.3 (3), 8.28 (5), 9.28 (4), 12.35 (9), to escape.

Scarlot, 2.13 (2), 12.13 (8), a rich cloth (often bright red). (+ 'scarlet'.)

Scath, 4.35 (3), 12.34 (3), hurt, harm.

Scowre, 2.20 (5), to run fast.

Scrip, 6.35 (9), small bag (esp. one carried by a pilgrim, shepherd, or beggar). (Only once in Sp.)

Scryne, Pr. 2 (3), chest, box for valuables.

Seeled, 7.23 (9), made blind.

Seely, 6.10 (4), innocent, harmless.

Semblaunt, 2.12 (1), semblance, appearance.

Sent, 1.43 (9), perception, senses. (This sense rare, last recorded here.)

Shamefast, 2.27 (6), 10.15 (5), modest, bashful, shy.

Share, 2.18 (8), 3.2 (9), piece, portion.

Shaumes, 12.13 (2), musical instruments similar to the clarinet.

Shend, 1.53 (8), to disgrace, (here) reproach. (Probably archaic.)

Shonne, 10.33 (5), 10.60 (7), to shun. (+ other sp.)

Shrowd, 1.6 (8), 1.6 (9), 1.8 (3), 4.48 (3), 5.13 (9), to shelter. (+ other sense.)

Silly, 1.30 (6), 2.21 (3), 4.47 (7), 6.35 (1), innocent, simple, defenceless.

Sith, sith that, 5.43 (1), 7.22 (5), 8.28 (1), 10.64 (9), since (causal), seeing that . . .

Sithens, 4.51 (1), 9.8 (6), since (causal), seeing that . . .

Sits (with), 8.33 (5), befits; 1.30 (9), (*sits not with*) is not suitable,

fitting. (This usage probably archaic.)

Skyen, 4.9 (8), skies. (+ other sp.)

Slights, 7.30 (7), designs, patterns. (This sense found only here.)

Snaggy, 7.10 (7), knotty. (Only once in Sp.)

Snubbes, 8.7 (4), stubs, boughs cut short. (This sense first recorded here; only once in Sp.)

Solemnize, 10.4 (7), solemnization, solemn rite. (Found only here: from the vb.)

Sooth, 3.29 (1), truth.

Souce, 5.8 (7), to strike heavy blows.

Soust, 3.31 (3), plunged into water, drenched. (This vb. only once in Sp.)

(Sort); in sort as, 1.46 (5), 12.20 (2), in the way that, even as, since.

Southsayer, 5.8 (8), soothsayer, foreteller of the future. (Only once in Sp.)

Sownd, 12.5 (7), ?to wield (i.e. ?make resound). (+ other senses.)

Sowne, 1.41 (4), sound. (+ *sound*.)

Spersed, -t, 1.39 (1), 4.48 (1), dispersed.

Spill, 3.43 (4), to destroy.

Spoile, 2.24 (1), 3.17 (7), 7.44 (5), 8.45 (9), 9.31 (2), to rob, despoil, ravage.

Spright, 1.38 (2), 1.45 (2), 1.55 (5), 1.55 (9), etc. (19 examples), spirit (in various senses). (+ other sp.)

Stadle, 6.14 (8), staff.

Staid, 7.41 (7), constant, fixed, firm.

Starke, 1.44 (5), rigid, unfeeling. (+ other sense.)

Stay, 6.35 (7), 10.5 (7), to support, rest. (+ other senses.)

Stayd, 10.40 (4), (here) imprisoned. (+ other senses.)

Ste(a)rne, 1.3 (9), 3.33 (7), 6.25 (8), 11.6 (9), grim, fierce. (Difficult to distinguish in some cases from sense 'severe, stern' which also appears in Book I.)

Sted(d), 9.41 (4), 11.46 (7), place, locality. (+ other sp. and uses.)

Stew, 11.44 (5), cauldron. (Only once in Sp.)

Stole, 1.4 (5), 1.45 (9), 1.49 (6), 3.4 (6), 12.22 (2), (long) robe.

Stond, 6.48 (6), stand, standing-place. (Also at 9.41 (5) spelled *stand*. The *-o-* sp. of the noun was probably archaic.)

Stound, 7.25 (8), 8.25 (5), 8.38 (4), 11.36 (8), time, particularly time of sorrow or difficulty; 8.12 (2), peril.

Stound, 7.12 (9), stunned.

Stowre, 2.7 (9), 3.30 (5), 4.46 (9), 5.51 (9), 7.12 (5), 7.48 (3), 8.5 (8), 10.40 (8), time of stress or anxiety. (This sense first recorded in Sp.)

Streight, 10.25 (9), strait, strict, restricted. (+ *streight*, 'straight'.)

Streighter (comparative of *streight*), straiter, 11.23 (5), narrower, tighter.

Stye, 11.25 (8), to mount, rise (up). (Probably archaic.)

Subject, 11.19 (1), situated beneath, lying beneath. (+ other sense.)

Suffised, 2.43 (8), satisfied, appeased. (+ vb. *suffise, suffice*.)

Suit, 10.60 (7), pursuit.

Sullein, 9.35 (3), gloomy.

Swaid, 11.42 (7), swung. (This sense first recorded here.)

Swaine, 2.4 (6), 4.37 (9), 6.21 (6), 8.13 (6), young man, youth.

Swarved, 10.14 (9), swerved, turned.

Glossary

Glossary   *341*

Swelt, 7.6 (9), burned.

Swinged, 11.26 (6), singed, scorched. (This vb. first recorded here: ? an alteration of *singe*, perhaps influenced by *sweal*, 'to burn' (*O.E.D.*).) (Only once in Sp.)

Swownd, 5.19 (5), 7.24 (3), swoon. (+ other sp.)

Swowne, 1.41 (5), 2.45 (4), 7.15 (7), 9.52 (3), swoon. (+ other sp.)

Swowning, 5.12 (2), swooning, fainting.

T

Table, 9.49 (6), picture.

Tala(u)nts, 8.48 (7), 11.41 (3), 12.11 (2), 12.11 (5), talons.

Teade, 12.37 (6), torch.

Teene, 9.34 (7), 12.18 (8), grief, hurt, harm.

Tempt, 1.50 (6), to test. (+ other uses.)

Termes, 5.37 (9), 9.29 (4), 12.30 (4), words, language. (+ other senses.)

Then, 1.4 (2), 1.24 (6), 2.26 (7), etc. (very common), than.

Thewes, 9.3 (9), 10.4 (4), good qualities, virtues.

Tho, 1.18 (5), 1.50 (8), 5.11 (7), 5.12 (5), 5.39 (6), 5.41 (5), 8.42 (5), 11.42 (1), then.

Thorough, 1.32 (3), 4.28 (7), 10.1 (7), through. (+ *through*.)

Thrill, 3.42 (7), 6.6 (2), 6.37 (1), 7.25 (2), 8.6 (9), 8.39 (2), 10.19 (9), to pierce.

Thrillant, 11.20 (2), piercing. (First recorded here, and rare: from the vb. *thrill*+-*ant*.)

Thristed, 6.38 (8), thirsted. (This vb. only once in Sp.)

Throughly, 5.45 (5), 9.50 (1), thoroughly, completely.

Throw, 10.41 (8), throe, pang.

Thyes, 11.23 (2), thighs, flanks. (+ other sp.)

Tinsell, 2.13 (8), glittering, made to sparkle or glitter by the use of gold or silver thread, plating, etc.

Tire (1), 4.35 (9), ?train, ?mob. (Exact sense uncertain, but clearly a new one: *O.E.D.* has this as 'rank, grade', under *Tier* (sb.).)

Tire (2), 8.46 (5), 10.31 (5), 10.39 (2), headdress.

Told, 4.27 (5), counted. (+ other senses.)

Tong, Pr. 2 (9), 3.6 (2), 5.34 (4), 7.24 (7), 7.30 (9), 10.55 (5), tongue. (+ other sp.)

Tort, 12.4 (4), wrong, wrongdoing.

Tosse, 1.42 (8), 1.55 (6), 7.27 (9), 7.48 (9), to trouble, agitate. (+ other senses.)

Toy, 1.47 (9), amorous play; 6.28 (8), sport, amusement.

Trace, 8.31 (5), to go, walk.

Tract, 1.11 (5), 3.10 (5), track (i.e. route, path, mark (such as a footprint, etc.)).

Traine (1), 1.18 (6), 1.18 (9), 4.10 (5), 8.17 (3), 11.37 (5), tail.

Traine (2), 3.24 (7), 6.3 (6), 6.41 (2), 7.1 (2), 7.26 (2), 8.4 (5), 9.31 (9), 12.36 (4), snare, wile. (+ *train*, 'retinue'.)

Transmew, 7.35 (6), to transmute, change.

Treachour, 4.41 (5), 9.32 (2), deceiver, traitor.

Treatie, 6.3 (6), entreaty, persuasion.

Treen, 2.39 (9), 7.26 (5), of trees. (This use rare.)

Trenchand, 1.17 (3), 11.24 (1), sharp-cutting, trenchant.

Trinall, 12.39 (5), threefold, triple. (This sense first recorded in Sp.)

Trusse, 11.19 (8), to clutch firmly, seize in its talons (of bird of prey).

(Tway); in tway, 7.27 (4), 10.20 (5), in twain, in two. (This form of the phrase last recorded in Sp.)

Twyfold, 5.28 (4), twofold. (Only once in Sp.)

Tyne, 9.15 (7), toil. (First recorded here: a by-form or altered form of *teen*, 'grief, harm', etc. According to the *O.E.D.* this word is only found 'in and after Spenser'.)

Tyranesse, 5.46 (6), female tyrant. (First recorded here: from *tyran(t)* +-*ess*.)

Tyrans, 6.26 (9), 10.9 (5), tyrant's.

U

Unacquainted, 5.21 (4), 10.29 (9), unfamiliar.

Unbid, 9.54 (5), unprayed-for. (This sense first recorded here; only once in Sp.)

Uncouth, 1.15 (8), 1.50 (1), 6.9 (6), 8.31 (1), unusual, strange. (+ other possible cases. It is difficult to know whether this sense or the more restricted present-day sense is involved.)

Undight, 3.4 (5), unfastened.

Uneasie, 5.36 (6), uncomfortable. (Only once in Sp.)

Uneath, 9.38 (9), 10.31 (7), with difficulty, not easily; 11.4 (3), ?underneath, ?almost (or the same as the other instances?).

Unhable, 4.23 (2), 8.40 (7), unable. (+ *unable*.)

Unkind, 12.30 (4), unnatural. (+ other possible cases. It is sometimes difficult to know whether this or the present-day sense is involved.)

Unkindly, 1.26 (2), unnatural, (here) lacking natural affection.

Unlich, 5.28 (5), unlike. (+ *unlike*: the -*ch* form only once in Sp. and probably archaic.)

Untill, 11.4 (9), unto, towards. (+ *unto*, and other senses.)

Unwary, 12.25 (2), unexpected. (This word first recorded in Sp.: from *un*+*wary*. This sense found only here.)

Unweeting, 2.40 (2), 2.45 (2), 4.47 (3), 5.18 (3), 7.6 (1), 7.49 (3), 10.9 (9), 10.65 (6), 10.66 (3), 11.29 (2), not knowing, unwitting.

Up bare, 10.44 (4), upbore, supported. (n.b. also the infinitive *upbeare* at 10.35 (8).)

Up-blowne, 4.21 (3), swollen, blown up. (First recorded here.)

Uprore, 1.5 (7), rebellion, outbreak of disorder.

Upstaring, 9.22 (3), (of hair) bristling, standing on end. (First recorded here: from *up*+*stare* (in the same sense).)

Upstart(ed), 1.16 (1), 2.5 (1), 7.7 (8), 11.34 (1), leapt up.

Use to rew, 9.9 (8), are used to lamenting; **use to fly,** 11.42 (6) are wont to fly. (+ *used* (*to*) . . .)

V

Vantage, 4.49 (4), to profit. (Only once in Sp.)

Vele, 1.4 (4), 6.4 (7), 8.19 (2), veil.

Venery, 6.22 (5), prey, wild animals hunted as game. (Only once in Sp.)

Vere the maine shete, 12.1 (3), let out the main sheet.

Vilde, 3. Arg., 6.3 (5), 9.46 (8), vile. (+ *vile*.)

Vildly, 1.20 (4), 3.43 (7), vilely.

Visour, 7.1 (3), mask, disguise.

Vitall, 4.49 (6), 5.19 (5), 8.41 (8), relating to life.

Voyage, 9.18 (4), 10.63 (4), 12.15 (9), journey (not necessarily by sea). (Also used of a sea-journey elsewhere in Book I.)

Vulgar, 5.8 (9), the common people. (This sense app. first recorded here.)

W

Wade, 1.12 (9), to go. (+ other *wade*.)

Wage, 4.39 (7), reward.

Ward, 8.3 (4), to guard. (+ other senses.)

Ware, 7.1 (1), 8.44 (6), wary, aware.

Warrayd, 5.48 (2), harrassed with war.

Wastfull, 1.32 (1), 3.3 (4), 8.50 (3), (of landscape) wild, waste. (+ other sense.)

Wayne, 4.9 (2), 4.19 (7), 5.41 (2), waggon, chariot.

Wayting, 3.26 (2), watching. (+ other *wait*.)

Weare, 1.31 (7), to spend, pass (time). (+ other senses.)

Weed(s), Pr. 1 (2), 1.29 (2), 2.21 (5), 6.35 (1), 7.19 (4), 9.28 (8), clothing, garment(s), attire.

Weene, 1.10 (3), 1.10 (6), 1.25 (5), 1.48 (3), 3.21 (9), 3.26 (9), 3.41 (5), 4.47 (1), 6.5 (4), 7.40 (2), etc. (17 examples), to think, intend, know. (Exact sense often difficult to determine.)

Weet, 3.6 (3), 3.11 (2), 5.3 (3), 6.8 (4), 6.14 (7), 6.34 (5), 8.5 (8), 8.37 (8), 9.23 (2), 12.3 (3), to know, know of. (The *O.E.D.* observes that this word was apparently obsolete in ordinary speech from the middle of the 16th C., but was in frequent use as a literary archaism.)

(Weete); to weete, 3.17 (1), indeed, (literally) to wit.

Welfavourd, 5.28 (2), handsome, good-looking.

Welke, 1.23 (2), to fade, grow dim.

Welkin way, 4.9 (7), way through the sky. (This phrase first recorded here.)

Well, 2.43 (7), well-being. (Only once in this sense in Sp.)

Were not, 7.12 (3), had it not been for . . .

Wex, 2.4 (7), 4.30 (9), 7.34 (8), 9.2 (3), 9.9 (9) (twice), 9.16 (1), 10.31 (4), 11.1 (1), to grow, become. (+ *wax*.)

Whally, 4.24 (3), ?glaring, ?greenish. (First recorded here and rare: ? from *whall*, *wall* (which are formed from *wall-eyed*, 'having eyes very white, or streaked').)

Whereas, 3.12 (3), 4.38 (4), 5.29 (2), 5.33 (4), 6.40 (5), 7.2 (6), 10.25 (8), where.

Whether, 2.37 (4), which of two. (+ other senses.)

Whilome, Pr. 1 (1), 4.15 (5), 5.23 (3), 7.36 (4), 11.29 (6), 12.41 (6), formerly, previously; 9.7 (4), continuously. (This last sense presumably rare: not recorded by *O.E.D.*)

Whot, 10.26 (8), hot. (+ other sp.)

Whyleare, 9.28 (4), a while ago.

Wight, 1.6 (8), 1.31 (7), 1.32 (2), 2.4 (7), 2.30 (4), 2.39 (1), 2.42 (9), 3.2 (6), 3.10 (3), 4.10 (9), etc. (43 examples), creature (human or supernatural).

Will or nill, 3.43 (7), willy-nilly. (This phrase only once in Sp.)

Windy, 7.13 (3), ?airy, light. (Would be first record of this sense.)

Wist, 2.40 (3), 3.26 (8), 5.27 (3), 10.28 (9), 11.41 (3), 12.39 (6), knew.

Wit, Pr. 2 (9), 1.45 (6), 2.30 (5), 4.5 (2), 4.32 (6), 5.40 (1), 6.6 (8), 6.19 (5), 6.31 (2), 6.32 (5), mind, intelligence, ability, cleverness.

Without, 9.3 (2), outside, beyond. (+ *withouten*, 'without'.)

Wonne, 6.39 (7), to dwell. (+ *wonne*, 'won' etc.)

Wonne, 6.39 (2), fought, conquered. (+ other senses.)

Wont, 1.16 (8), 1.34 (6), 1.40 (6), 1.41 (7), 1.52 (9), 2.7 (8), 2.28 (8), 2.40 (5), 3.13 (9), 3.17 (2), etc. (22 examples), to be accustomed to, used to.

Wood, 4.34 (3), 5.20 (9), mad, furious.

Worship, 1.3 (4), honour, renown. (+ other senses.)

Wot(e), 1.13 (2), 1.32 (5), 2.18 (3), 8.44 (3), 9.31 (3), 9.43 (1), 10.17 (2), 10.65 (1), 11.36 (1), 12.31 (3), to know, think.

Woxe (p.t. of *wax, wex*), 11.52 (8), grew.

Woxen (ppl. of *wax, wex*), 4.34 (3), 5.12 (3), 10.2 (3), 10.29 (8), grown, become.

Wreakes, 8.43 (4), 12.16 (6), acts of vengeance.

Wreck, 11.21 (2), destruction.

Wrestes, 5.6 (3), wrists.

Wrizled, 8.47 (8), wrinkled, shrivelled. (First recorded here: ? a variant of *writhled*, 'wrinkled'. Only once in Sp.)

Y

Y-, Archaic prefix, frequently attached to parts of the vb., esp. the ppl. Hence *Y cladd* (1.1 (2)), *ydrad*, 'dreaded' (1.2 (9)), etc. It is also found before some other parts of speech, e.g. *ylike*, 'alike' (4.27 (9)).

Yblent, 2.5 (7), blinded. (This vb. probably archaic.)

Ydrad, 1.2 (9), dreaded, feared.

Yede, 11.5 (1), to go, move. (First found in Sackville: app. a misunderstanding of the archaic p.t. *yede*, 'went', as an infinitive.)

Yfere, 9.1 (1), together.

Ygo(e), 2.18 (3), 8.30 (5), ago. (First recorded in Sp.: an altered form (to look archaic) of *ago*.)

Yit, 2.30 (4), 9.3 (4), 10.63 (6), yet. (+ other sp.)

Ymp, See *impe*.

Yod (p.t. of *yede*), 10.53 (5), went. (Probably archaic or dialectal.)

Youthly, 2.35 (1), 5.7 (4), 9.4 (2), 9.9 (1), 11.34 (5), youthful.

Ypight, See *pight*.